50 EASY WAYS TO TAKE BETTER PICTURES

BY WILLIAM J. HAMPTON

AMPHOTO
American Photographic Book Publishing
An imprint of Watson-Guptill Publications
1515 Broadway, New York, N.Y. 10036

For my Dad,
WILLIAM J. HAMPTON, SR.
who has always known how to say complex things plainly, and who, at 95, has not yet forgotten.
With love and admiration.

All photographs taken by the author unless otherwise credited.

First published in 1982 by American Photographic Book Publishing: an imprint of Watson-Guptill Publications, a division of Billboard Publications, Inc., 1515 Broadway, New York, N.Y. 10036

Library of Congress Cataloging in Publication Data

Hampton, William J.
50 Easy Ways to Take Better Pictures

Includes index.
1. Photography. I. Title.
TR146.H18 770'.28 81-22778
ISBN 0-8174-5519-1 AACR2

Manufactured in the United States of America
1 2 3 4 5 6 7 8 9/87 86 85 84 83 82

CONTENTS

INTRODUCTION

This is a "how-to" book for the pure amateur.

It is written for the camera owner who looks upon photography as something you do from time to time, usually to record vacations, family activities and special occasions for the family album, and who would appreciate a little plain-spoken advice about how to get better pictures with the equipment he has.

The book is therefore about the *practice* of photography and not about equipment or technology. It assumes that its reader wants to know what to expect in certain common situations, that he wants some ideas that will help him improve, and that he doesn't want to hear too much talk about things like "aperture versus shutter preferred-exposure-control systems" or "film-reciprocity failure."

For the genuine amateur photographer is like the true professional in one important respect. He understands that cameras and accessories are only a means to an end, and he knows in his bones that the best pictures are arrived at by the simplest and most uncluttered route. It is the advanced amateur and the semiprofessional who are most likely to let themselves become sidetracked by hardware.

I have tried to keep my language as free as possible from the vocabulary special to photography, and to avoid becoming preoccupied with discussions of equipment or abstruse photographic principles. In planning the book, I have begun by identifying the most frequently met problems and then working backwards from there, offering suggestions for dealing with each problem, always assuming minimal equipment and a very modest technical knowledge.

Except for those credited otherwise in the picture captions, all of the photographs in this volume are by its author. All were chosen because they illustrate problems discussed in the book, or solutions to them. And it may be relevant to the purpose of the book to note that, except for three or four of the pictures, none were taken more than five or six miles from my home.

I am much indebted to a number of people for making their special knowledge available to me in preparing this book. They include: Gordon Audas, for information contained in the section on supplementing insurance records; playwright and director Gerald Blanchard, for advice on photography at the theater; Phil Brown, for his detailed knowledge of the newest in photographic equipment and for the loan of some of it; model train hobbyist and photographer Douglas Leffler, for information used in the section on scale models and miniatures; and musician Lee Piper for answering questions about today's pop music scene.

And to my wife, Nora, with love, for her help, her patience, and all those delayed dinners.

—William J. Hampton

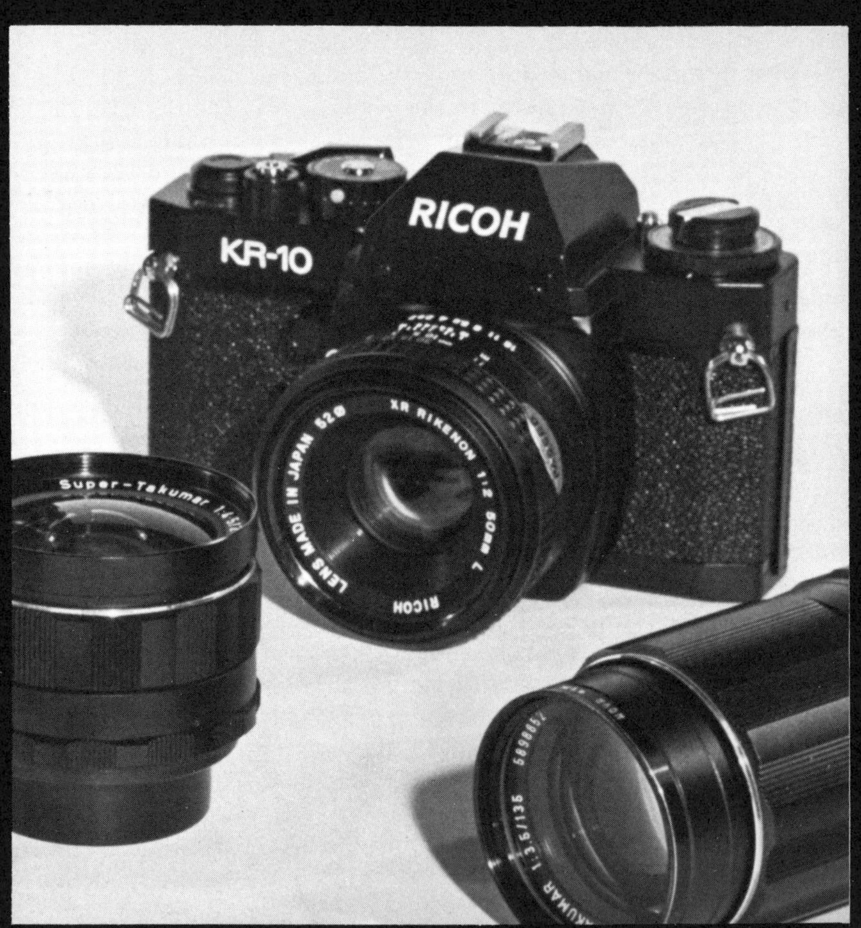
RICOH
KR-10
XR RIKENON 1:2 50mm L
LENS MADE IN JAPAN 52Ø
RICOH
Super-Takumar
1:3.5/135

Chapter 1

CHOOSING YOUR CAMERA

In the simplest sense, all cameras are nothing more than light-proof boxes designed to hold roll or sheet film, with lenses and shutters added to focus the light on the film and to control the amount of light striking it. Various refinements have been developed, especially in the last twenty years, to help the camera or, more accurately, the photographer—do these things. And it is the proliferation of these gadgets that has made the selection of a camera a confusing experience for the amateur who wants nothing more than a dependable machine to serve his particular purposes.

You can spend as little as twenty dollars for a new camera or as much as one thousand. But there is clearly no point in buying a costly camera if a less expensive one will do what you want it to do. Knowing what you want from your camera should be the starting point in your selection.

It might be helpful, therefore, to look at the kinds of cameras most used by amateurs and to point out their virtues and limitations. Somewhere among them should be one that will best meet your needs. We'll start with the simplest, easiest-to-use cameras.

FIXED-FOCUS CAMERAS

The easiest to use are the rudimentary fixed-focus cameras. They're the legitimate descendants of the old box cameras, but today they come in a variety of sizes and shapes, and with a wide range of sophisticated options. They accept roll film in several sizes, but they're fundamentally alike: you load the camera and you operate the film-advance lever to prepare for the next exposure. On the simplest models there are no other adjustments for you to make. You merely look through the viewfinder, frame your picture, and snap.

On such point-and-shoot cameras, shutter speeds are fixed at about 1/60 or 1/50 sec.—fast enough for posed pictures or scenic views. They'll stop fairly slow action, like normal walking, but you're likely to get blurred movement if you shoot someone running.

All of this makes for an extremely uncomplicated camera, but one with certain limitations. When the lighting is marginal, for example, you can't compensate for it by either opening up the lens or slowing down the shutter speed to admit more light. You must confine your photography mostly to the outdoors, and to bright or fairly bright sunshine, and you can't focus on objects closer than three or four feet away.

For these reasons, however, fixed-focus cameras are good cameras for beginners. Without the distractions of fussing with shutter speeds and focusing you can go straight to the business of shooting, composing, and framing pictures—which is what photography is all about.

To overcome some of these technical limitations most manufacturers produce fixed-focus cameras in a series of models graduated upwards to include more options. You can get them with flash attachments, for example, which will enable you to get indoor pictures with relatively poor lighting. You can also get them with built-in normal and telephoto lenses. Some come with attachments that enable you to get closer than four feet, and many are available with meters that measure light and tell you whether you'll need to use flash.

Most of these cameras are loaded with drop-in film cartridges, often in the 110-film size, which produces a negative about the size of your thumbnail. Some, however, use larger film, and this can be an advantage when you expect to enlarge your pictures to say, 5″x7″ or 8″x10″.

Each of these refinements helps to expand the potential of the camera. But each one complicates its operation a bit and inevitably adds something to the cost. For the majority of amateur photographers who want nothing much more than to document family and social activities, a camera chosen from the range of fixed-focus models available will serve very nicely. They're the easiest to operate, they cost less than the fancier cameras, and they're less expensive to operate.

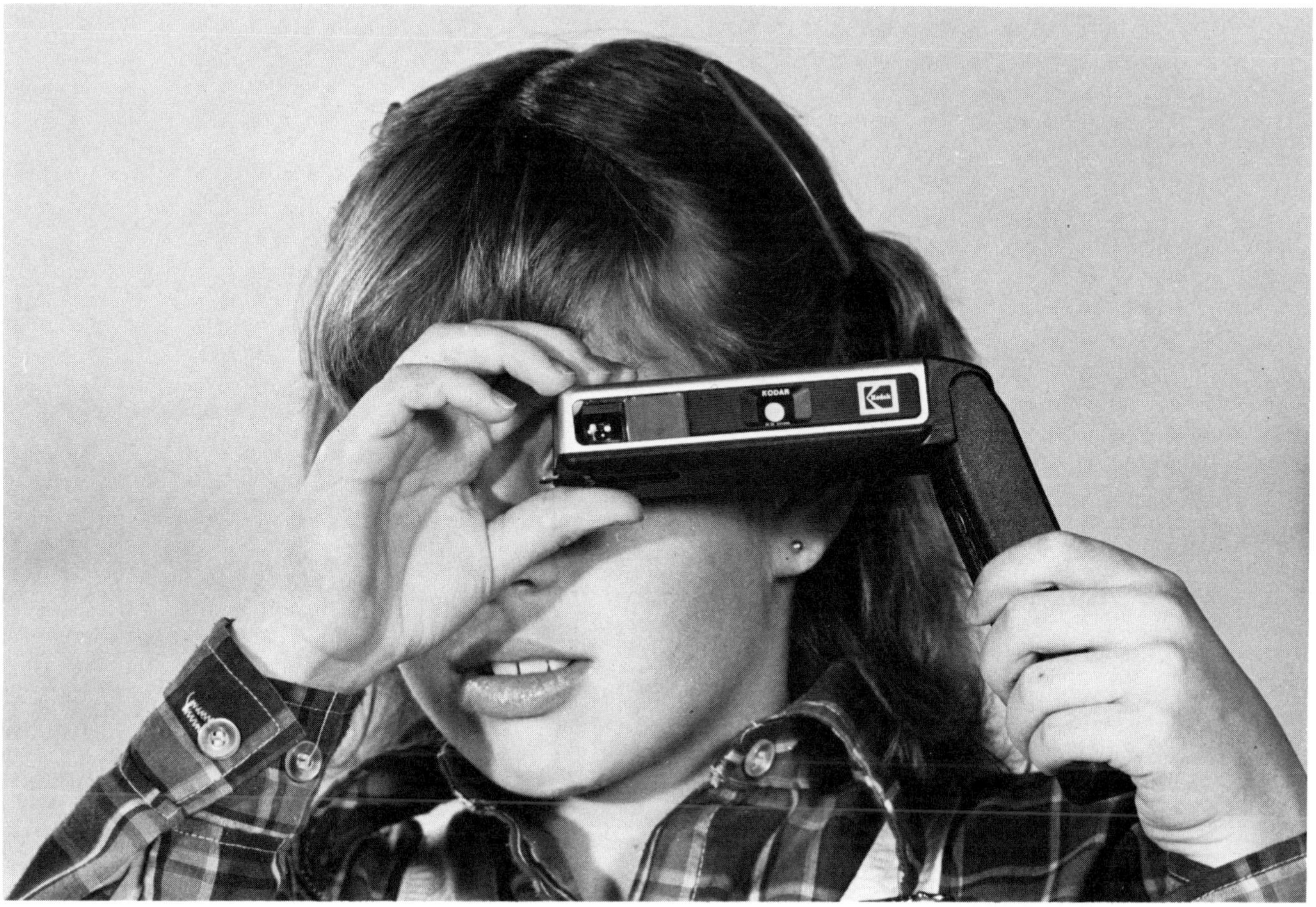

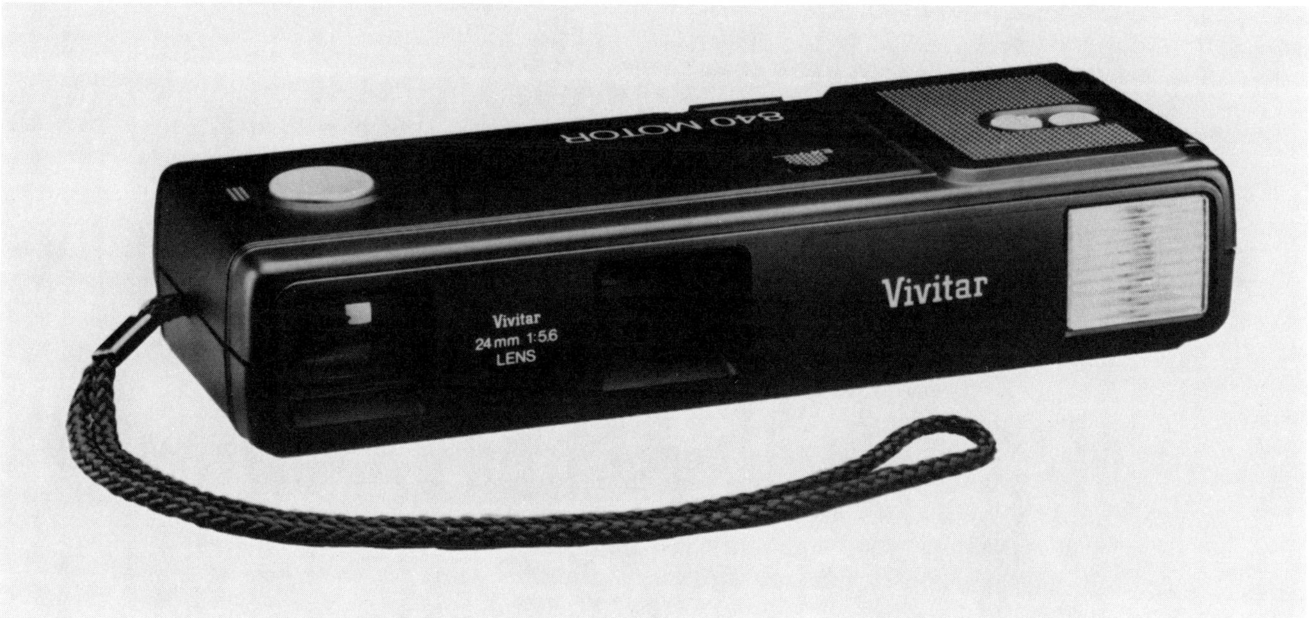

Top: Fixed-focus cameras are the easiest to use and come in a variety of shapes and sizes. This type of camera is often called a "point-and-shoot" camera. *Bottom:* Many fixed-focus cameras are now available with a wide range of sophisticated options, such as a built-in flash. (Photograph courtesy of Vivitar Corp.)

35mm VIEWFINDER AND RANGEFINDER CAMERAS

More versatile and therefore more complex than the fixed-focus cameras are the 35mm viewfinder and rangefinder cameras. The important difference is this: 35mm cameras allow you to vary shutter speed, change lens openings, and focus more precisely.

They have another noteworthy advantage: they all use the extremely popular 35mm-film size, and there are more kinds of films available in the 35mm format than in any other.

You can get fast, medium, and slow film in 35mm color or black-and-white for negatives or slides. And there are many special-purpose films available in 35mm that you can't get for fixed-focus cameras: infrared in color or black-and-white, high-contrast copy, reversal, and ultra-fast films, for example.

There are also several add-on accessories available to the 35mm camera user that, as a rule, are not available for the smaller fixed-focus cameras. These include filters, some image-altering lens attachments, and off-the-camera flash extensions.

These cameras, like the fixed-focus camera, provide you with a viewing system separate from the picture-taking lens. It is this system through which you frame your picture, and which gives you an approximate idea of the picture you'll get. It is approximate because of the discrepancy between what the "viewing" lens and the "taking" lens see when the subject is up close. The two viewpoints can't converge at near distances, and this inability is called parallax. It has to be compensated for when shooting closeups. If it isn't, someone in the picture is likely to lose the top of his head.

On the simplest of the 35mm viewfinder cameras you select a shutter speed, then estimate the distance from the camera to the subject and set that distance on the focusing scale marked on the barrel of the lens. The rangefinder camera, however, makes the job easier because its viewing system is coupled to the "taking" lens. Your eyepiece shows you two images, one from the viewer and one from the lens. You need only hold the camera to your eye and rotate the lens collar until both images overlap to form a single one. When they do, the subject is in focus.

The best rangefinders provide some sort of system for handling the parallax problem and, if you expect to do much close-up photography, you will do well to select a camera that does this precisely.

As in the fixed-focus cameras, 35mm rangefinders come with an impressive array of electronic options. All of them start with adjustable lens openings, focusing, and a range of shutter speeds, but the most automated ones will focus automatically, supply flash when it's needed, wind the film forward or rewind it, and match up shutter speed and lens apertures.

The quality of lenses on 35mm viewfinder and rangefinder cameras is usually better than those on the smaller fixed-focus cameras, and the 35mm format produces a negative or a slide larger than those produced by most fixed-focus cameras. This means that you can have enlargements made to 8″x10″ or 11″ x 14″ with less loss of detail than you might get from a smaller negative or transparency.

In summary: these cameras are for photographers who want more creative control over their picture-taking, along with a higher degree of picture quality. The great majority of amateurs will probably never need more from their cameras than the 35mm viewfinders and rangefinders can give them.

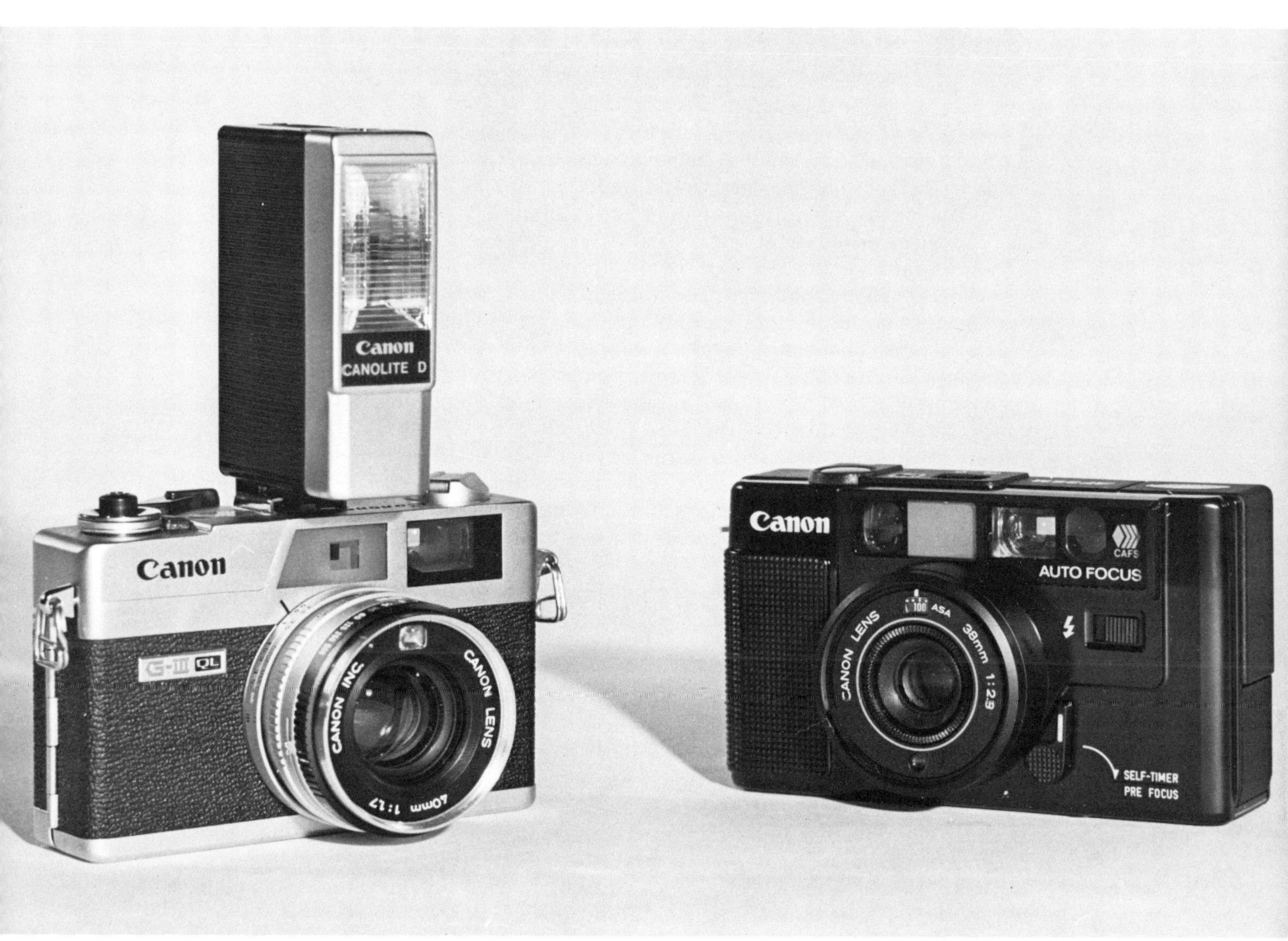

A 35mm camera allows you to vary the shutter speed, change lens openings, and focus more precisely. Also, this type of camera uses the extremely popular 35mm-film size.

35mm SINGLE-LENS-REFLEX CAMERAS

It occurred to camera designers a long time ago that, if someone could devise a small roll-film camera that didn't need a separate optical system for framing and focusing, the parallax problem would be licked.

Could a camera be built that would let the photographer see through the "taking" lens and thus know *exactly* what he was getting on film?

It turned out that it could. And the result has come to be the most popular camera among advanced amateurs, the single-lens reflex, or SLR. "Single lens" because you don't need a second lens for viewing, and "reflex" because light coming from your subject is collected by the lens, bounced off a mirror in the camera's body, and reflected into the camera's eyepiece. When you press the button to make your exposure, the mirror moves out of the way, permitting light to travel straight through the camera to strike the film.

In almost all SLRs the mirror returns automatically to its original position immediately after the exposure is made, and you're ready for your next shot. In a few, the mirror is returned to its position manually by the photographer when he moves the film-advance lever forward to advance the film and cock the shutter.

The outstanding advantage of the SLR over fixed-focus, viewfinder, or rangefinder cameras is the elimination of parallax. What you see is exactly what you get and, for photographers doing critical close-up work, it's practically mandatory.

Focusing is more precise with an SLR, too. Cameras with separate viewing systems show you an everything-in-focus scene in your viewfinder. The rangefinder cameras give you two overlapping images to line up, but they can't show you what will or won't be out of focus in the picture. An SLR can do that.

Another important advantage of any SLR is interchangeability of lenses, something that only the most sophisticated and expensive of 35mm rangefinders can offer. You can remove the normal lens from any SLR and replace it with wide-angles or telephotos, and you can do it while the film is in the camera. Each time your viewing system shows you what you're getting through that particular lens. You can fit an SLR to a telescope or a microscope, or you can add close-up attachments, image-altering lenses, or filters, and the eyepiece will show exactly what effect these add-ons have on the picture.

Because they're built the way they are, SLRs have available an enormous range of accessories which make the cameras adaptable to almost any photographic purpose. For serious amateurs who expect to expand into more sophisticated areas of photography, they demand serious consideration.

An SLR has its drawbacks, to be sure. They're much noisier than fixed-focus, viewfinder, or rangefinder cameras. The noise comes from the moving mirror, and it can be a distinct handicap if you're trying to take pictures without attracting attention: in wild-life photography, for example, or during formal ceremonies, like weddings or commencements.

They're heavier, too, because of all their built-in optical and mechanical refinements. And because they're more complicated, there are more things that can go wrong with them.

The viewing systems on SLRs sometimes don't give the bright, clear image you get with other cameras because of the circuitous route the light has to travel to get from your subject to your eye. Some of it is inevitably lost, and it makes focusing under marginal lighting conditions more of a problem than it is when a separate optical system is used.

There are dozens of manufacturers producing SLRs, and you therefore have a great deal to choose from when you're thinking about buying one. A high percentage of the cameras are from good to excellent in quality and you can expect to spend from one-hundred-seventy-five dollars to, say, four-hundred dollars or five-hundred dollars for one, depending upon the optional accessories you choose.

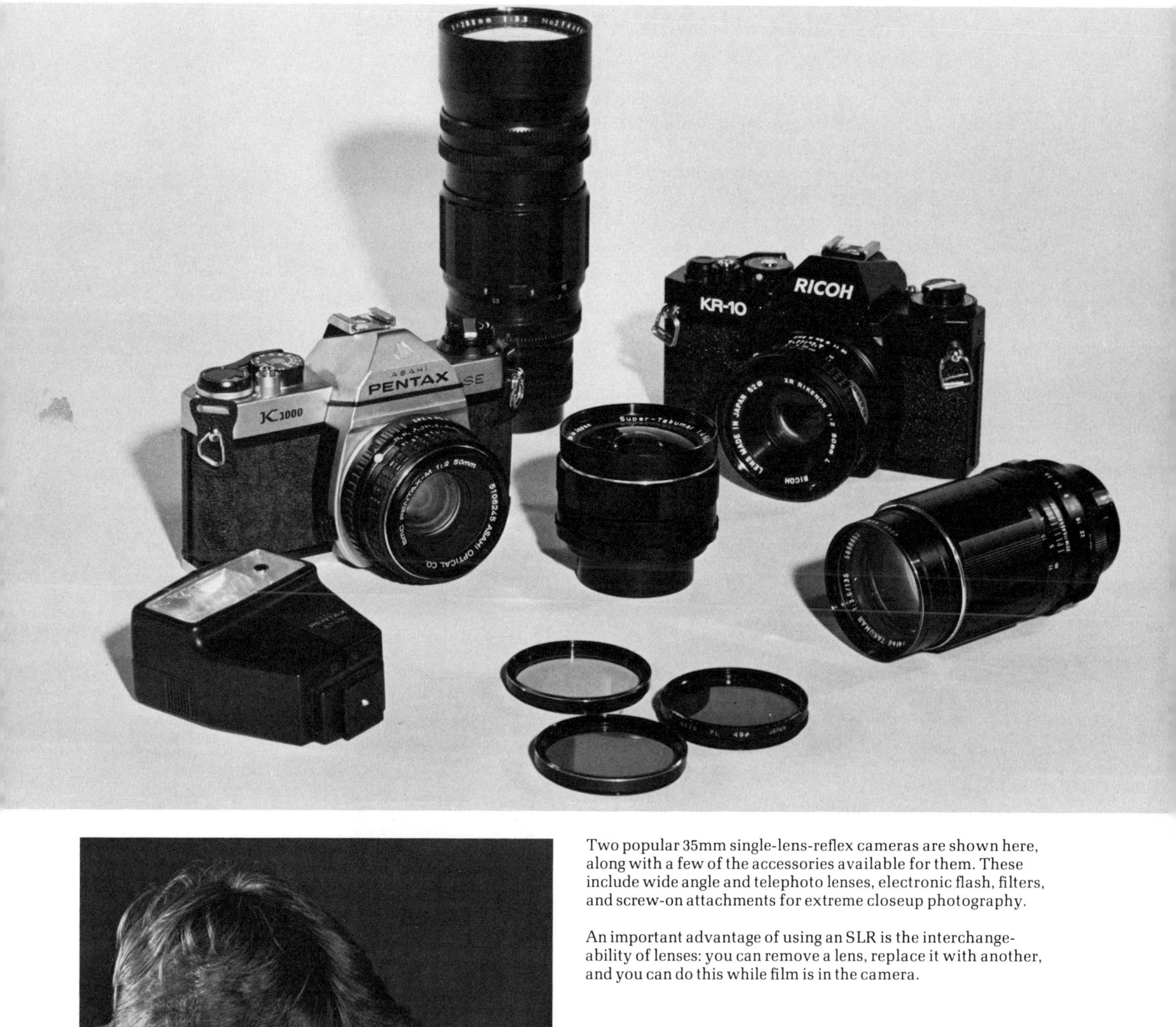

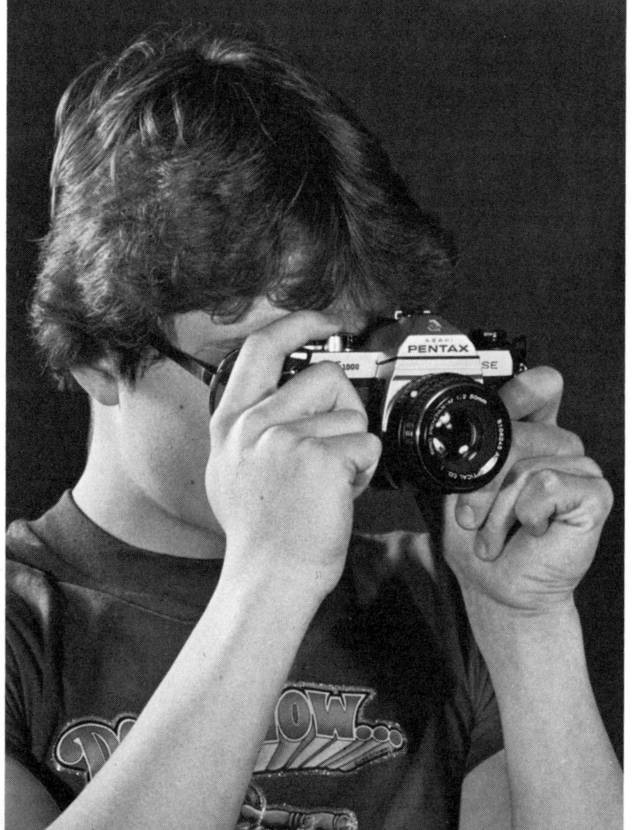

Two popular 35mm single-lens-reflex cameras are shown here, along with a few of the accessories available for them. These include wide angle and telephoto lenses, electronic flash, filters, and screw-on attachments for extreme closeup photography.

An important advantage of using an SLR is the interchangeability of lenses: you can remove a lens, replace it with another, and you can do this while film is in the camera.

INSTANT-PICTURE CAMERAS

Instant-picture cameras appeared in 1948 with the introduction of the first Polaroids, and they were immediately popular. The cameras used a special film which contained its own processing chemicals; in effect, the camera had become its own darkroom, producing a black-and-white paper negative and a positive print within minutes.

In the intervening years these cameras became increasingly sophisticated. The early models were simple fixed-focus cameras, but today they're available with both rangefinder and reflex-focusing systems; they produce pictures in several sizes in black-and-white or color, depending on the particular model; and some are capable of automatic focusing.

As they've improved, they've attracted the attention of serious amateurs as well as professionals, who like the instant feature of the cameras, their adaptability to a variety of scientific and industrial uses, and the almost grainless quality of the images they produce.

But it is the instant results these cameras give that make them so popular with amateur photographers, despite the fact that the cost-per-print is considerably higher than for one obtained by older, more traditional methods.

Since an instant-picture camera develops its own picture and there is no enlarging step involved, it must be designed to accept film large enough to produce a satisfactory-sized print. This has resulted in cameras of unusual size and shape.

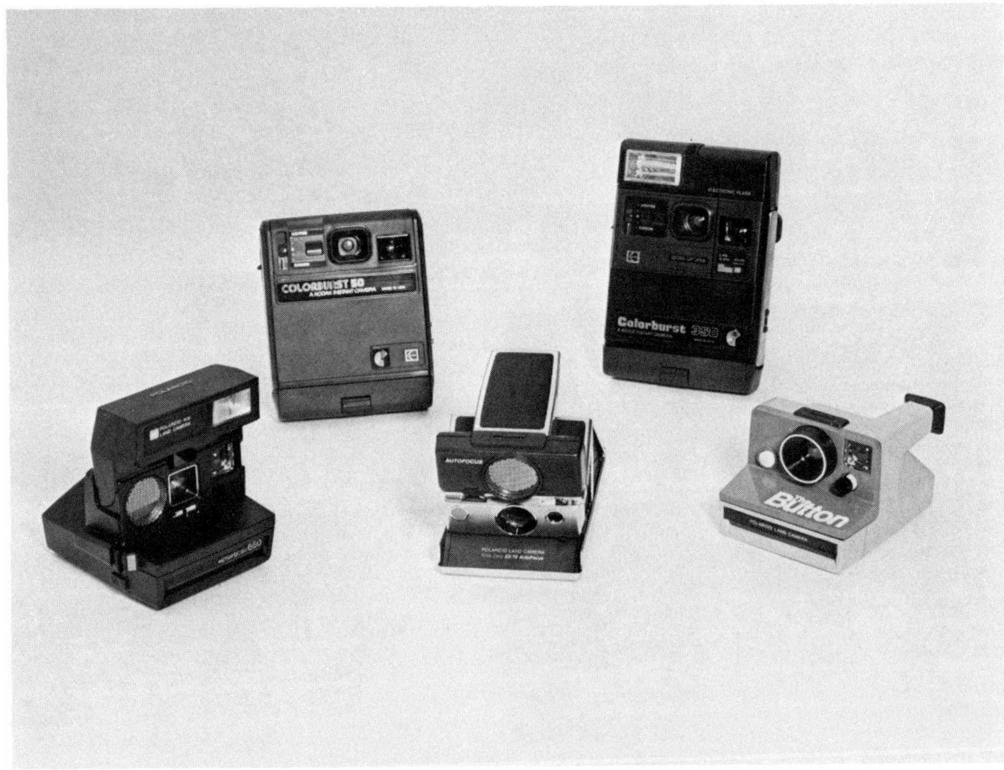

The variety of options available to instant-picture photographers is suggested by this assortment of cameras, which range in price from about twenty dollars to about two hundred. The Polaroid Button, far right, is a simple fixed focus camera which can be fitted with flash. Polaroid's Time-Zero SX-70 AutoFocus, center, offers through the lens viewing, variable lens apertures, and automatic focusing. The Kodak Colorburst 350, right rear, permits closeups to two feet and is capable of extended exposures of more than 1/15 sec. The Kodak Colorburst 50, left rear, is a fixed focus camera to which flipflash or electronic flash attachments can be added. On the far left is the Polaroid Autofocus 660, with automatic focusing and electronically-regulated flash.

TWIN-LENS REFLEXES

There was a time when you used to see much more of the waist-level twin-lens reflexes (TLRs) than you do today. Amateur photographers have turned more to the 35mm format in recent years, but the TLR remains a favorite with many advanced amateurs who prefer a larger negative.

Like the 35mm viewfinder cameras, the TLR has a viewing system separate from, but coupled to, the picture-taking lens. Focusing and composing are done by looking down into a flat, ground-glass screen, instead of peering through a peephole at eye level. But this umbilical view of the subject can be modified by raising or lowering the camera. Such cameras can also be fitted with viewfinders which enable them to be used at eye level when photographing, for example, sporting events.

Most TLRs currently being manufactured produce a 2¼″ x 2¼″ negative or slide—much larger than the 35mm format, which is a little smaller than 1⅜″ x 1″. This is an important advantage if you intend to make enlargements beyond 8″ x 10″.

TLRs tend to be solid, quiet cameras with little to go wrong in them. Because they use a separate lens for viewing, they're subject to parallax error at near distances, but all of them have methods to compensate for this. Many have built-in light meters to help in setting the lens opening and shutter speed, but there are none on the market at this time with all of the automatic options found on the more expensive 35mm cameras, like automatic focusing and built-in flash attachments.

In brief, TLRs are for photographers who want a larger image than 35mm will give them, who want to be able to compose their pictures carefully, and who don't mind doing a little of the work themselves.

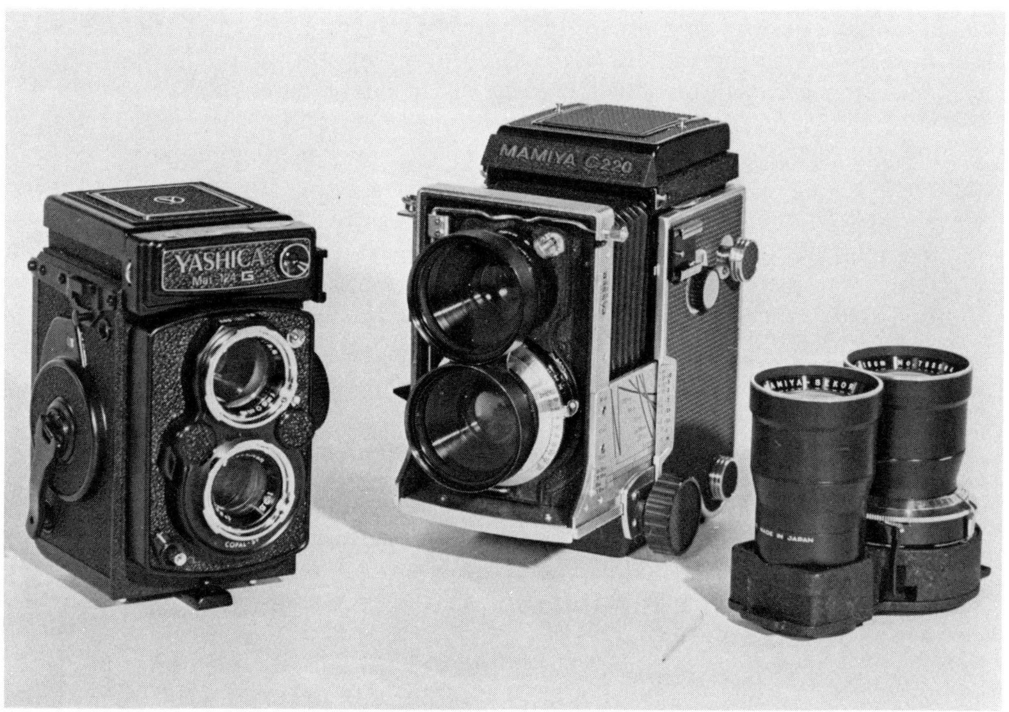

Most TLRs are equipped with non-removable lenses, as is the Yashica, left, which contains a built-in light meter. An exception is the more expensive Mamiyaflex, right, which has no meter but which permits interchanging lenses. It is shown here fitted with a 65mm wide angle lens. Beside it is a 180mm telephoto lens.

WHAT TO DO WHEN YOUR PICTURES AREN'T SHARP

Whatever the camera you wind up with, there is something you ought to remember about cameras in general. The more money you spend for a camera, the more right you have to expect dependability, versatility, and high-quality photographs from it.

Take the lens, for example. A one-hundred-fifty-dollar lens is bound to be freer of optical flaws than a cheap one. It will be capable of much better resolution, which is the ability to define clearly and sharply the component parts of the subject it is photographing, and to separate subtle differences in lighting. Optical resolution is the basic test of any lens.

It's when you decide to have the picture enlarged to 8″ x 10″ or 11″ x 14″ that these differences become important. You'll be able to do the job if the picture was recorded with a high-quality lens. If it was made with an inexpensive lens, the enlargement will quickly become fuzzy and ill-defined. This may not be at all important if you only want a camera and lens that will get the picture easily and quickly, and if you intend to do nothing more with it than to have the picture enlarged to, say, 3½″ x 5″.

When your pictures begin to look fuzzier than they used to, it's not always the fault of the lens. Check first to make sure you're not doing something you shouldn't do.

Probably the single most frequent cause of unsharp pictures is camera movement at the instant of taking the picture.

The fact is that when you're hand-holding a camera and shooting pictures at slow shutter speeds—say 1/60 sec. or slower—it's almost impossible to avoid a slight movement. And shutters on the simplest cameras are set at about 1/50 sec. Further, the lighter the camera the easier it is to let a little wiggle creep into the exposure. If you're getting consistently unsharp pictures, try this: expose a roll of film, using a tripod or some other firm support, and compare the results with the pictures you were getting before. The odds are that your tripod-supported shots will be perceptibly sharper.

If they're not, the next step is to double-check your focusing technique. Remember that with simpler cameras the lens, like the shutter, is already preset. You don't really focus it; you merely make sure that your subject is no closer than the minimum distance specified in the owner's manual. It's usually three or four feet.

If your camera requires you to align two overlapping images for exact focus, or if it gives you a ground-glass surface on which to focus, check to see that you're actually doing what the manual directs, and that you're not simply being careless.

Finally, take a good look at the surface of your lens. It can become dirty, and the result could be a hazy, indistinct quality in your pictures. A careless fingerprint on the surface will produce the same effect.

You can clean the front surface of a lens—very gently, very carefully. Don't try to clean any rear elements. In older lenses these surfaces were not hardened by the manufacturer, and thus they are susceptible to scratches. Besides, inner surfaces are not likely to have gotten dirt on them.

First, blow sharply on the glass to remove any grit or loose dirt. Then use a drop or two of lens-cleaning fluid and a soft, lint-free cloth to loosen and remove grease or dirt. Lens-cleaning tissues are available at camera stores. Don't use those silicone-treated lens cloths intended for cleaning eyeglasses. Apply the liquid cleaner very sparingly—don't flood the lens with it. Then, with a circular motion, wipe the lens dry of the cleaner. Simply wipe diligently but gently until the glass is free of dirt and streaks.

If, after you've run through these procedures, you find that you're still getting fuzzy pictures, maybe you're justified in having the camera and lens checked by an experienced technician. But not until.

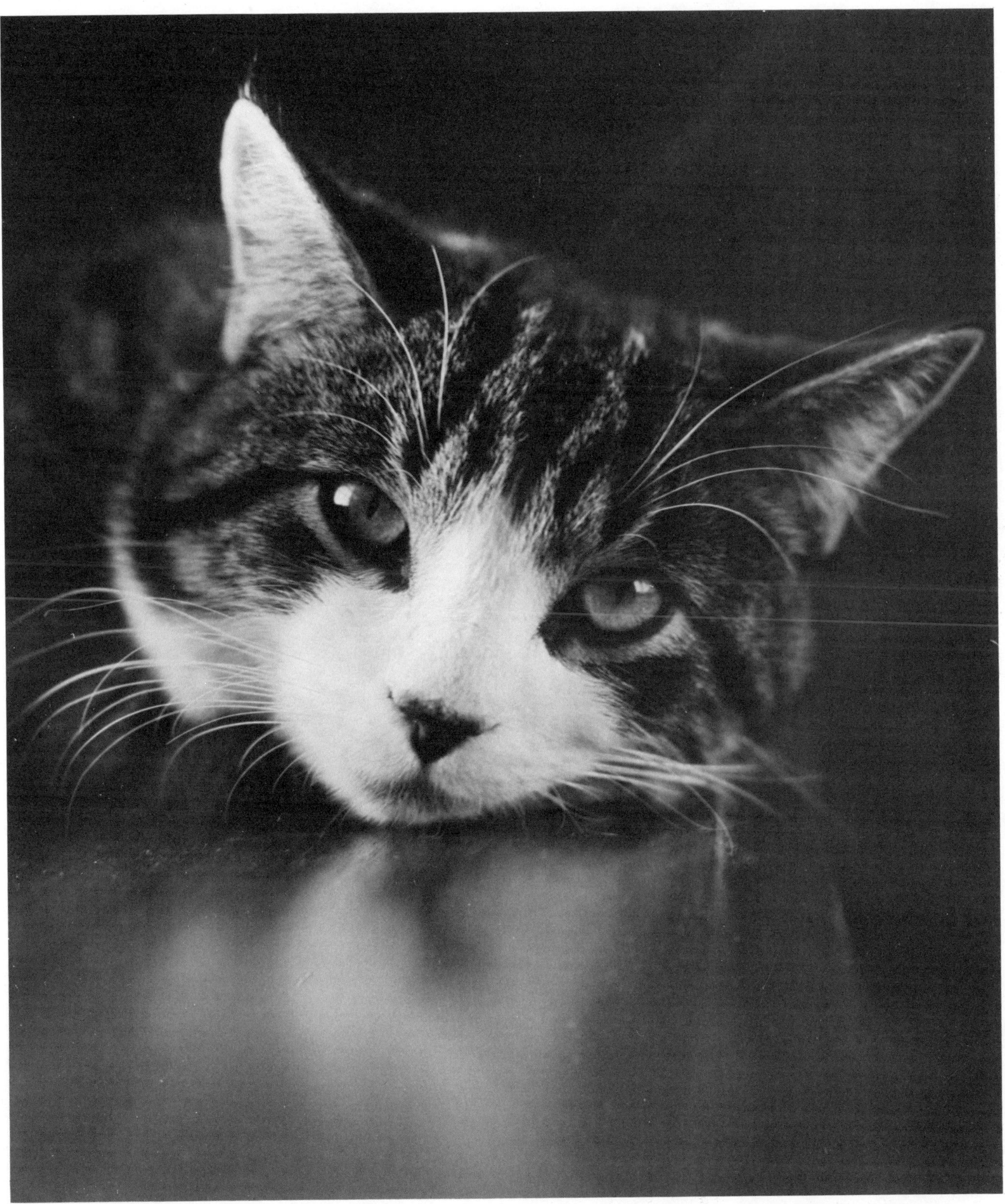

The impression of sharpness in an image is only partly a matter of lens quality and precision of focusing. It is often also a matter of contrast within the picture. This photograph juxtaposes some very strong white tones against some very dark backgrounds, which supports the impression of crispness. Conversely, an all gray cat, photographed with equal precision under more diffuse lighting, might lack such a wide range of tonal variations and be perceived as flat and unsharp.

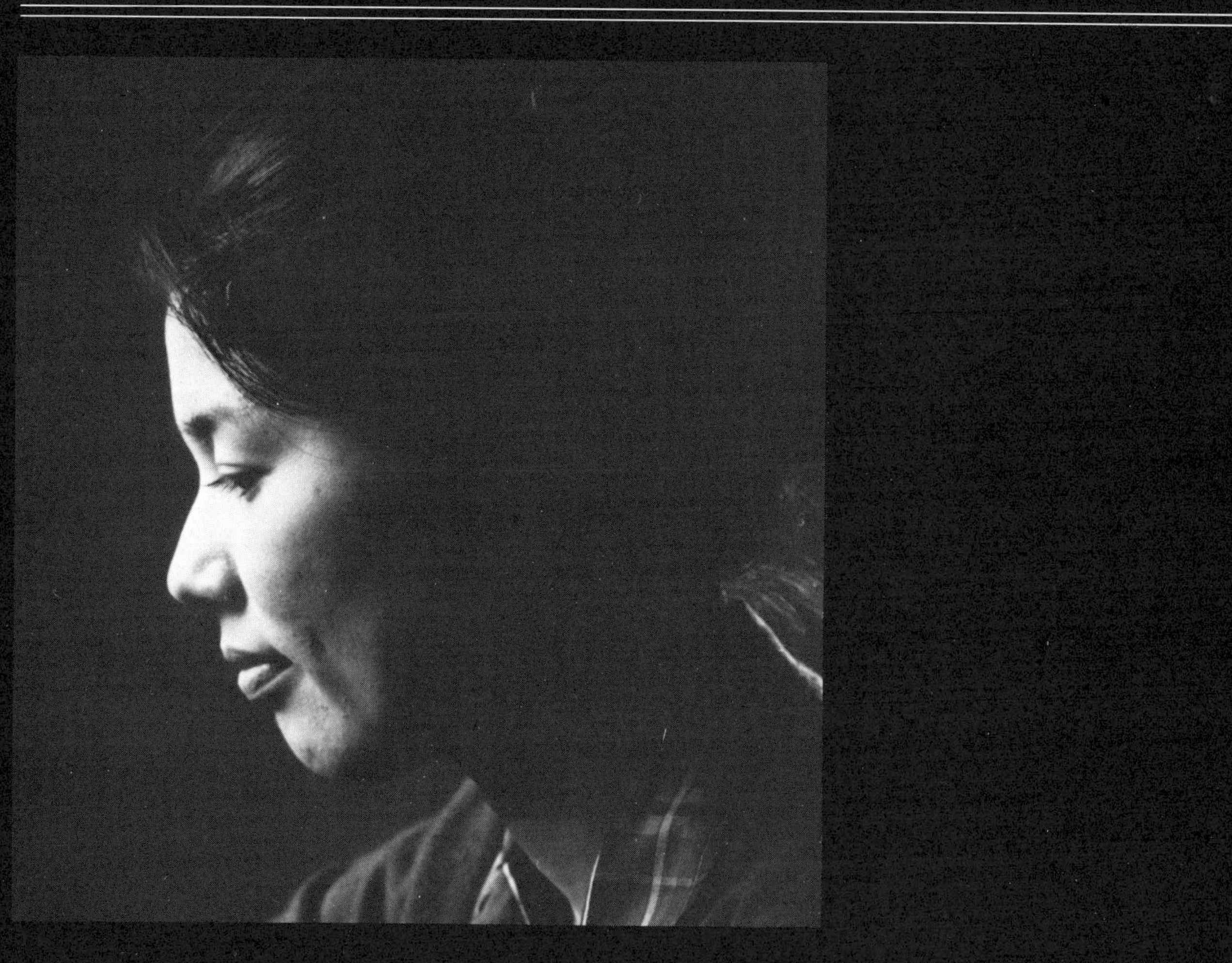

Chapter 2

USING YOUR CAMERA CREATIVELY

Your dictionary will tell you that "composing" is the business of putting something together by combining different elements; of arranging the parts to form a unified, harmonious, attractive whole. And that is the subject of the chapter that follows.

"Harmonious" is probably the most important word in such a definition. When the parts of a photograph are working together successfully to produce a planned, cumulative effect they are, indeed, in harmony. When they aren't—when there is no selectivity, no planning—the result is not likely to be a photograph but an undistinguished, dime-a-dozen snapshot.

On the following pages we will undertake to look at some of the qualities that go into a good photograph. They include using lines, mass, shapes, and dark or light areas to direct the viewer's eye into the picture. Also examined are some techniques for simplifying your pictures, for minimizing distracting backgrounds, and for further modifying the scene before you by the use of simple lens attachments.

This chapter on "Composition" is, in other words, about how you can control your picture instead of letting it control you.

COMPOSITION: THE DIFFERENCE BETWEEN SNAPSHOTS AND PHOTOGRAPHS

I'm sorry I missed the eighteenth century. Everyone seems to have been so sure of things. They called that era the Age of Reason, and they were convinced there was a logical system behind everything.

Natural rules governed science, politics, and human behavior; all one had to do was find those rules and follow them. It was the same in art: if a painting affected you deeply, it was because the artist had followed certain discoverable rules. The whole thing was a matter for rational analysis.

The English painter William Hogarth thought it all had something to do with curved lines, and he wrote a book to prove it.

Today we live in a less confident century. The rules have failed to work too many times, and we've had the social and economic disasters to prove it. Even so, we've clung to some of the eighteenth century's ideas about art simply because they seem to work. There does indeed seem to be some kind of deliberate logic going on in any good picture. You *can* make certain generalizations about color and composition, and follow them, and they will produce an effect more desirable than the mere random recording of what's in front of you.

Much of what works in painting appears to be true of photography. A good photograph is no more accidental than is a good painting. The best photographers have always been careful about planning their pictures, and it is the deliberate manipulation of all the available elements in a picture that distinguishes the competent photographer from the snapshooter.

The amateur photographer interested in improving the quality of his work must, therefore, learn to become objective about what he's doing. You can begin by becoming more picture-conscious. Not just about your own pictures, but about *anyone's* picture. When you see one you like, ask yourself why you like it. What has the photographer done to give the photograph impact?

This involves looking beyond the subject of the picture: the attractive model, the familiar face, the trees and hills of a landscape. Analyze the shapes and lines, the colors, and the lights and darks that together make up the photograph. You'll find that they are all working together to produce a total impression.

For one thing, you'll see that there's nothing in the picture that doesn't belong there or that doesn't contribute something. Photography is in this respect a subtractive process. You must spend as much time deciding what shouldn't be in your picture as what should.

A snapshot simply records, for better or for worse, whatever happens to be in front of a camera lens. A photograph eliminates the irrelevancies, selects the optimum angle of view, and limits the viewer to seeing only what the photographer wants him to see. There is a sense of control present in a good photograph that is missing in a snapshot.

A good photograph treats light not as a necessary inconvenience, but as a valuable tool in communicating mood and in moving the viewer's eye through the picture. And sometimes the *absence* of light can be as important as its presence.

A third thing: careful examination of a well-made photograph will reveal that attention has been paid to a sort of subtle internal geometry—to lines and shapes within the picture, to the balancing of lights and darks, and to the exact placement of key elements for maximum effect.

Together these are the things that make up what a photographer means when he talks about "composition." The word suggests bringing order out of disorder—a very eighteenth century idea. There's a little more to it than curved lines, but the subject is worth examining a little more closely.

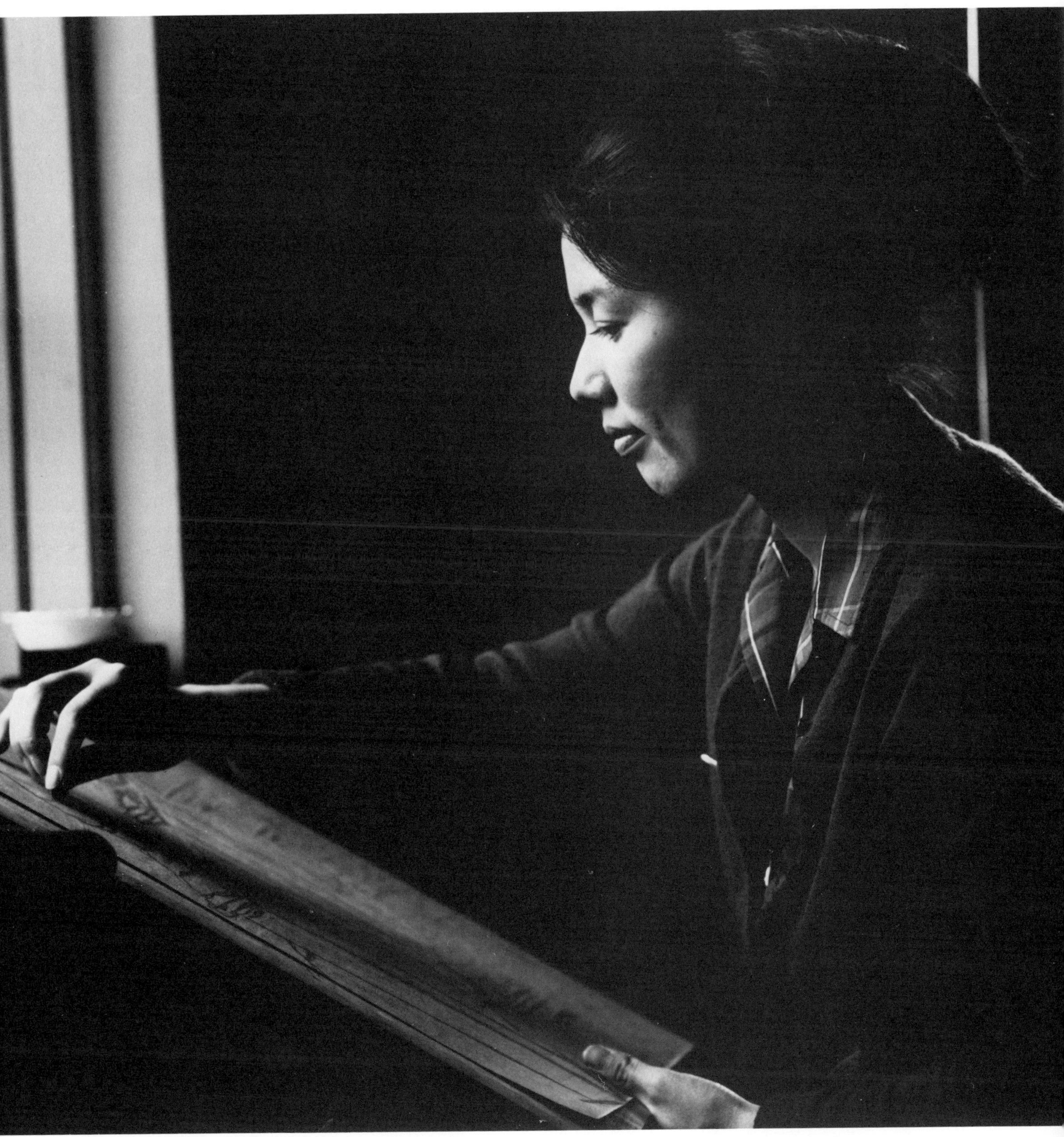

There are three main points in this portrait: the subject's face and the two hands. Together they form the key points of a triangle connected by the forearm, the drawing board, and the thin edge of light along the shoulder. The effect is to trap the viewer's eye and lead it to the face. None of these elements can be omitted without lessening the composition. Try covering the bottom hand, for example and you will see that something is lost.

COMPOSITION: LINES AND SHAPES

Once you have taught yourself to be conscious of what is happening in a good photograph, you will begin to find ways of improving the visual content of your own pictures.

You will discover, for example, that there are more ways available to you for controlling the end result than you might have thought. You can usually be more selective about your camera angle—which simply means that you can move around, trying various points of view, until you find one that is potentially more effective than the others.

You will almost always find that it's possible to move in closer to your subject, and that this will eliminate a lot of clutter that contributes nothing to the point of the picture. The same thing is true about backgrounds; they should be kept as unobtrusive as possible, so that there is nothing occurring in them that might distract the eye from the main subject.

Having exercised more selectivity about the general view, you can now begin to look at the elements remaining and to ask yourself what you can do with them to add balance, drama, and interest to the photograph.

This almost always turns out to be a matter of manipulating the lines and shapes in front of the lens. There are a few useful generalizations that can be made about this:

A "BALANCED" PICTURE IS NOT OFTEN A SYMMETRICAL PICTURE. There is something dreary about a photograph in which the main subject is rigidly centered and viewed head-on, with all of its lesser elements distributed precisely on either side, as though one side of the picture were a mirror image of the other.

Such pictures are visually unexciting because that is not how things occur in nature, and we expect photographs, unless they are deliberately experimental, to be "natural." It is paradoxical that, in any art, a natural look is achieved by contrivance.

GENERALLY, THINGS VIEWED AT AN ANGLE ARE VISUALLY MORE INTERESTING. Photographing your subject from one side or another introduces depth in the form of diminishing lines. If your composition needs three-dimensionality, this will help.

KEEP EVERYTHING INSIDE YOUR PICTURE. There is something upsetting about lines that lead out of a picture and never return . . . especially important lines. In portraiture, for example, an arm that disappears out of the frame is visually disturbing. And it's even worse when it reappears, leaving a segment missing.

DON'T LET BORDER-TO-BORDER VERTICALS AND HORIZONTALS SLICE YOUR PICTURE IN HALF. A tree or a pole coming into a composition at the top and out at the bottom can split your picture in two.

WHEN LANDSCAPES, BUILDINGS OR OTHER NON-HUMAN OBJECTS ARE THE POINT OF THE PICTURE, SUBORDINATE OTHER ELEMENTS TO IT. If people are included to add proportion or human interest, for example, keep them at a distance and to one side. Don't let them occupy center stage. Have them watch the scene, or each other, but not the camera.

USE LINES TO DRAW YOUR VIEWER'S EYE INTO THE PICTURE. The lines formed by shadows, roads, walls, branches, etc., can be used to catch the viewer's eye and lead it to the main subject. Sometimes this can be very obvious, as in a picture where, say, two roads converge with the main subject at the intersection. Or sometimes it can be very subtle, with the eye drawn along a complex path of shapes and lines.

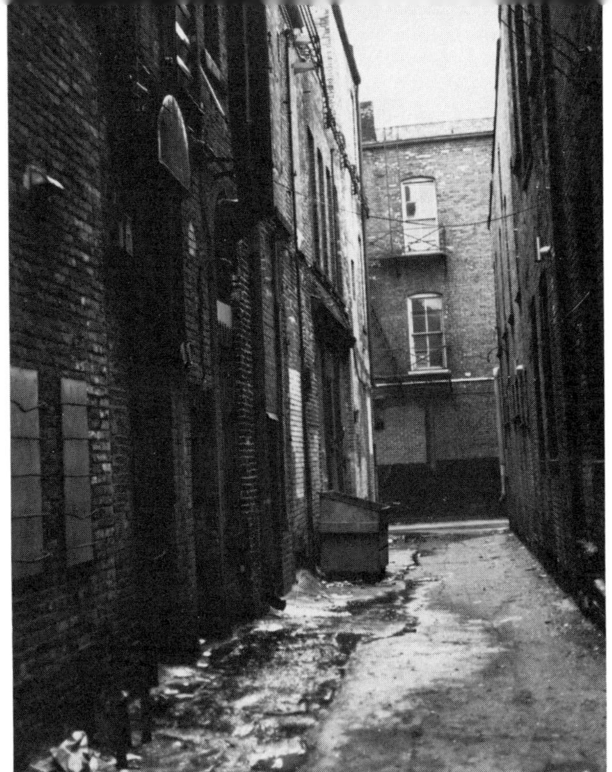

Right: Here is an obvious example of using converging lines to suggest depth. This photograph leaves the eye with nowhere to go except deeper into the picture.

Below: A subtler use of the converging of lines to produce depth: the row of trees, the shadowed path and the patch of light along the treetops make three lines which converge at right. It also gives the viewer's eye something more to do *en route* than does the accompanying picture of an alley.

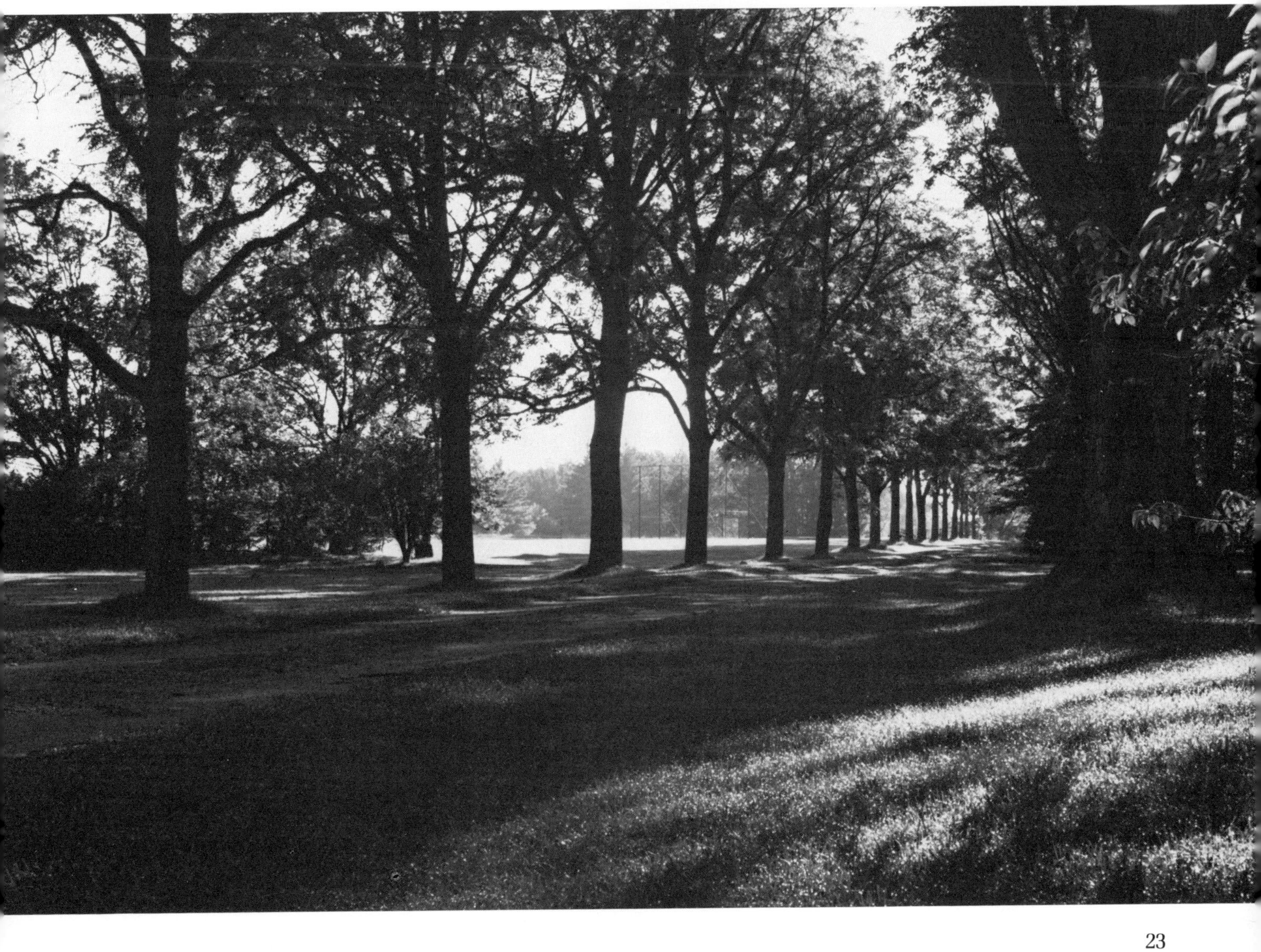

COMPOSITION: USING LIGHTS AND DARKS

Light, and the presence or absence of it, is something the amateur photographer must sooner or later become very much aware of.

It goes beyond merely asking, "Is there enough of it for an exposure?" A light meter can tell you that. But it cannot tell you anything at all about how to use that light to produce interesting, well-composed photographs.

For that, you need an awareness of the possibilities, along with an inclination to experiment.

The treatment of light and shade to produce a sense of depth in a picture is called "chiaroscuro" by painters. It means, literally, "light and dark." The adroit handling of shadows can do more than produce a feeling of three-dimensionality in a photograph. It can also add atmosphere and mood. If you've ever seen a well-photographed horror movie, you will understand that.

There are some generally accepted principles about combining lights and darks in a photograph, and here are some of them:

FRAME DISTANT SUBJECTS BY USING NEARBY DARKER OBJECTS AS BRACKETS. You can call attention to distant subjects and, at the same time, introduce a sense of depth by using shadows, branches, foliage, fence posts, or almost any darker objects as a sort of border. They give the viewer a sense of looking past them into the middle or far distance, as through a window.

At the same time you can use the frame to block out unwanted foreground objects. A tree trunk, for example, can be used to hide a building you don't want to appear in the finished composition, and leaves can be used to obscure telephone lines.

USE LIGHT AREAS TO HIGHLIGHT PRINCIPAL POINTS IN THE PICTURE. Generally, the eye is attracted to lighter portions of a picture, especially when they are surrounded by darker areas. You can build very dramatic compositions around this fact by using the shadowed areas to direct the eye to key points.

But it doesn't work very well the other way: a small, dark figure against a uniformly bright background is hard to find.

BE SUBTLE IN YOUR DISTRIBUTION OF LIGHTS AND DARKS. Don't allow large patches of light or dark to become too important, so that they become an end in themselves and distract the viewer from your central subject. Instead, keep them subordinate—make them contribute, rather than dominate.

IN OUTDOOR PHOTOGRAPHY, PAY ATTENTION TO THE TIME OF DAY. Good landscape photographers watch carefully to see where shadows are falling during the day, and they schedule their picture-taking accordingly. Don't depend on chance—plan for your best effects.

And beware of high noon, especially in outdoor portraiture. The overhead sun will make your subject squint, and it will produce dark shadows under the nose and in the eye sockets. Seek open shade, instead, where the light is softer and uniform . . . or wait for an overcast day.

A final word on this business about "rules" in photographic composition. Like all rules, they work most of the time, and certainly they'll help you improve the quality of your pictures. But they should also be regarded with a certain amount of distrust, for fear you become too reliant on them and lose your urge to experiment.

The thing to do is to combine them with imagination: bend them, stretch them, and occasionally break them.

But *try* them.

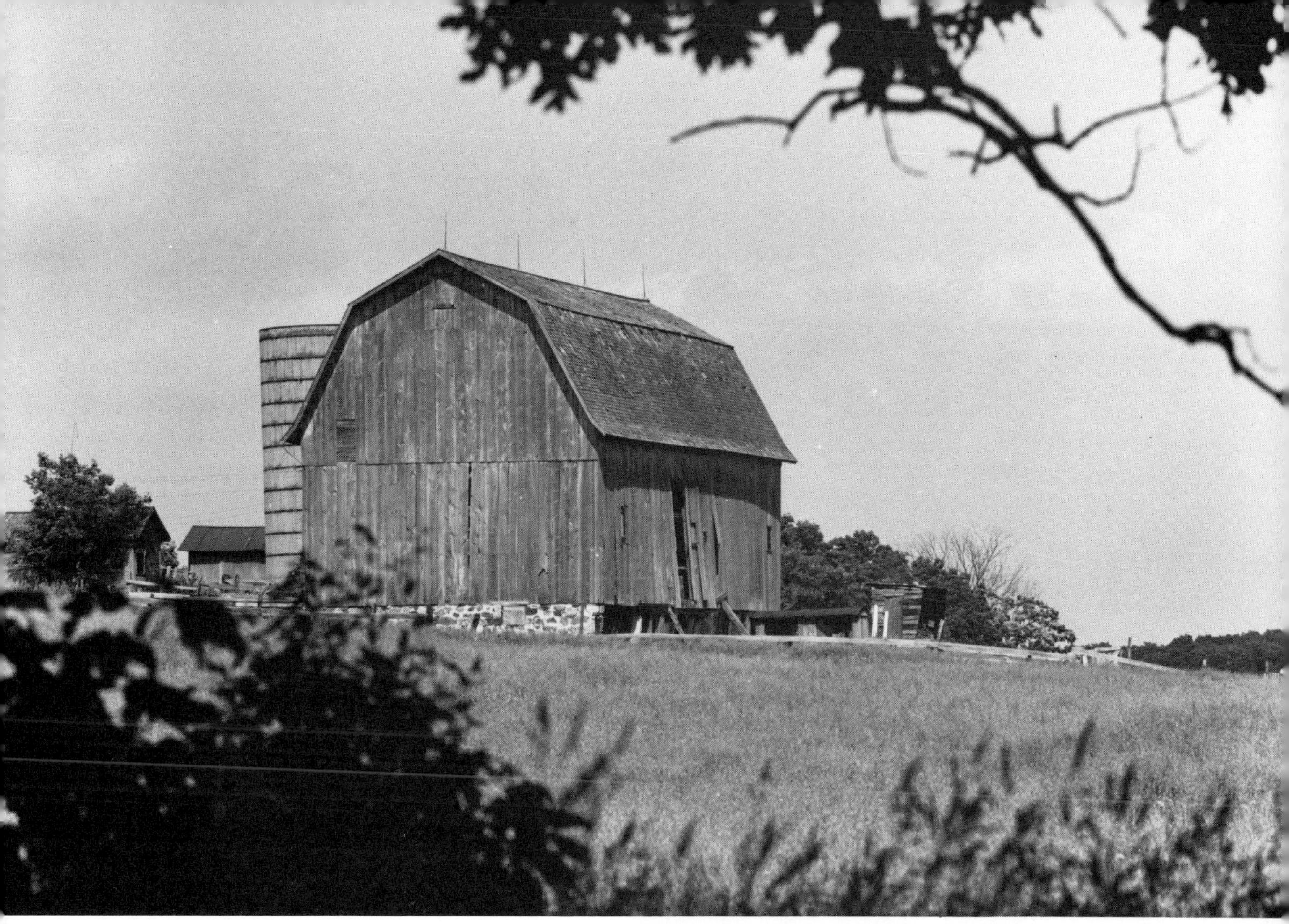

Above: A rather routine landscape is given a little more visual interest by using nearby foliage to form a frame. A sense of depth and scale is introduced by a near plane (the foliage), a middle plane (the barn), and the diminishing line formed by the trees beyond the barn.

Right: The eye is drawn instantly to the solitary subject of this picture by strong receding lines and by the patch of light surrounded by shadow. There is enough information in the shadowed areas to suggest a location, but not enough to sidetrack the viewer.

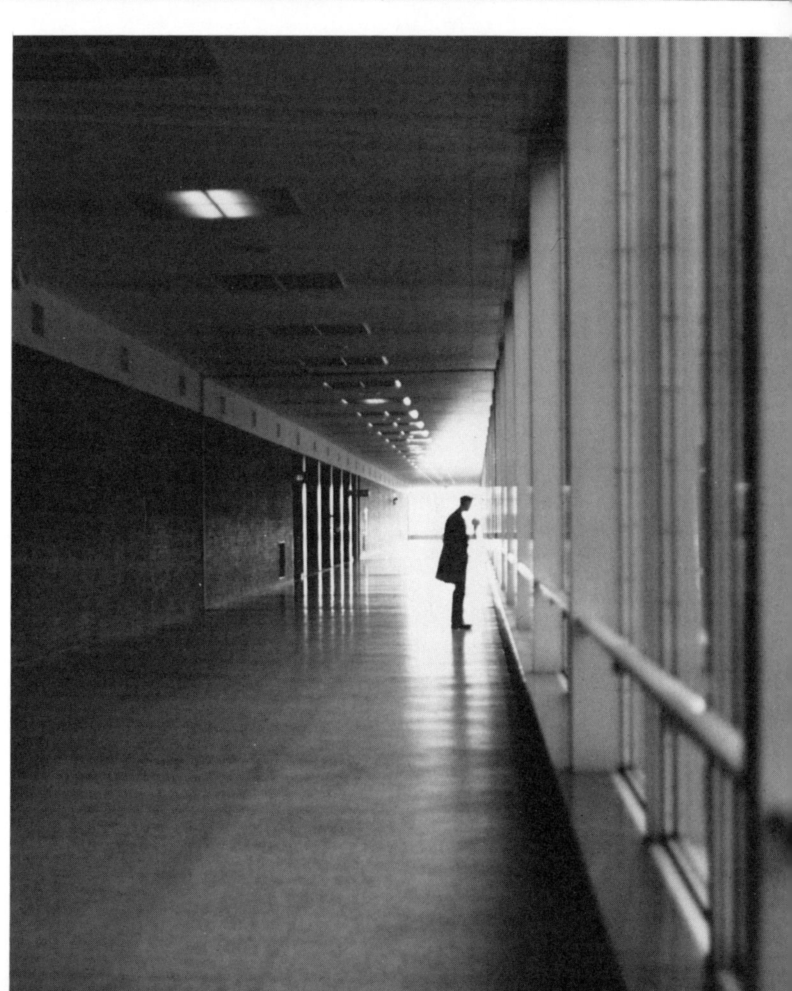

COMPOSITION: SIMPLIFYING PICTURES

There is a hopeful but not very accurate notion among many amateur photographers that the more sophisticated the camera, the better the picture will be. If by a "better" picture you mean only one that it is correctly exposed and accurately focused, that notion is true as far as it goes.

You can buy cameras today that will focus and expose automatically. If that's all you want, it should leave you with nothing but "better" pictures.

But obviously there's more to a good photograph than that. In the end, it's always the content of the picture and the manner in which it is presented that distinguishes a good photograph from a mere snapshot. Accurate exposure and focus should be taken for granted. What counts most is the photographer's vision of his subject.

Often a strong image will override poor exposure or shaky focus to produce a memorable photograph. But it is never the other way around: a badly conceived picture presented with all the technical virtuosity in the world remains a poor picture. To put it another way, a photographer with a good idea and a simple camera will get more effective results than one with the latest in automated equipment and no imagination.

It's no more complicated than that. The concept, the composition, and the rigid exclusion from your picture of everything that does not help it do what you want to do—these are far more important than what your camera costs.

It's astonishing how much you can omit from your picture, once you have a clear idea of what you want it to say. Removing the clutter from it will simplify it, and simplifying it will strengthen it. Sometimes it's only a matter of moving in closer to your subject to eliminate an irrelevant foreground and to permit the subject to dominate the image.

It will help, too, if you become almost obsessively concerned about what's going on in the background of your pictures. There's a natural tendency, when you're composing a photograph, to see in it what interests you, and to overlook the rest. But the camera overlooks nothing. It has no capacity at all for making judgments about the importance of what it sees.

You have to do that. You have to teach yourself to see what the camera is going to see, and to manipulate the components of the picture patiently until you have what you want.

If backgrounds are fighting for attention with your main subject, there are several things you can do. Often, merely changing your camera angle from one side to another will improve things. Or you can crouch down and angle up at the subject, which will give you neutral sky or ceiling for background.

If your camera permits you to change lens openings, you will often find that selecting a larger aperture will produce a shallower field of focus, with the result that objects in the background are reduced to a pleasant, unobtrusive blur. But remember: when you open up your lens, you're admitting more light, so you must restore the balance by increasing shutter speed.

If your camera is a fixed-focus type, everything from about five or six feet to infinity will be in sharp focus. In that case, your best bet is to move the subject, if it can be moved, to a more acceptable location. If it can't be moved, you must examine it from a variety of angles to see if it can't be framed against a more acceptable background.

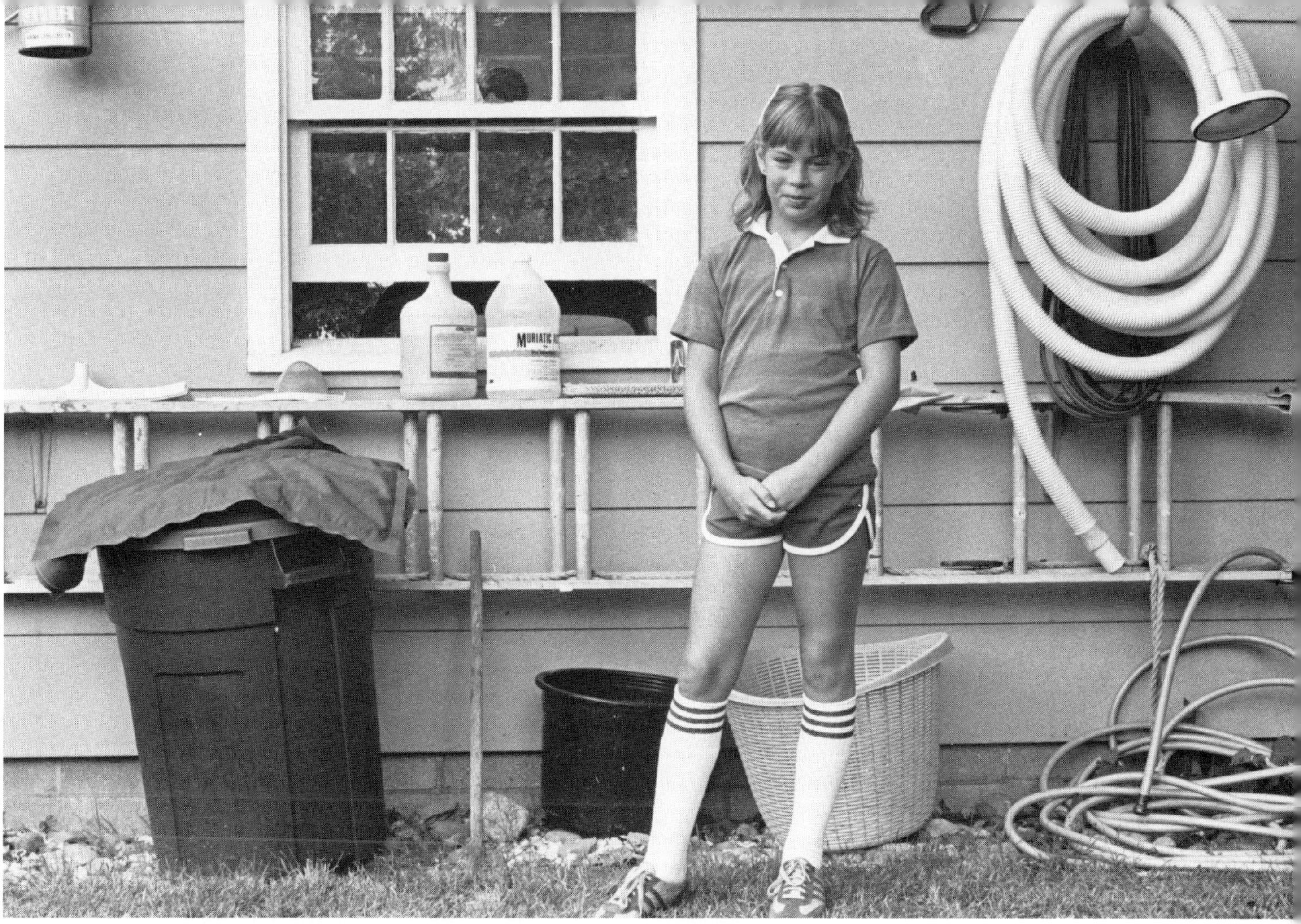

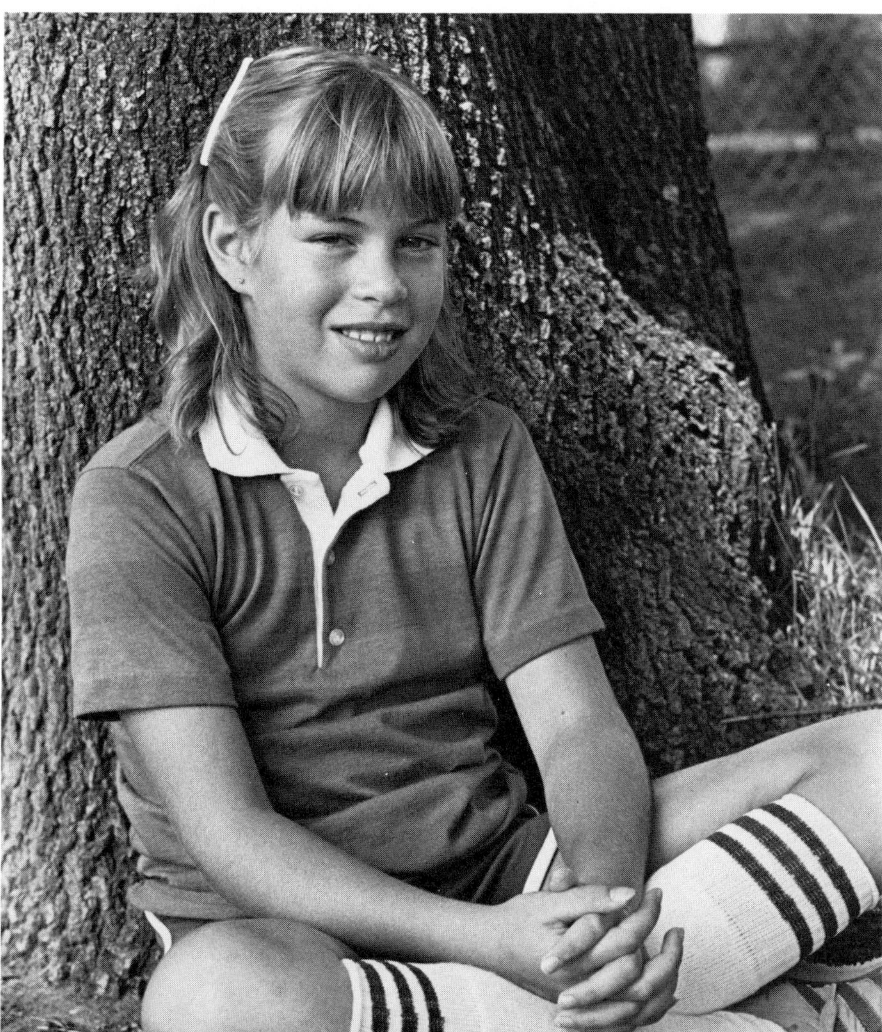

Above: Photographed against a background full of odds and ends, you see that Angie Alexander is lost in all the clutter.

Left: Taken a minute later, the portrait of Angie shows how easily a picture can be improved by simplifying it.

COMPOSITION: AVOIDING REFLECTIVE BACKGROUNDS

Most cameras designed for amateurs come equipped with a built-in electronic flash attachment. There are a help to the photographer when there's not enough natural light available to get the picture, but they can create special background problems of their own.

For example, if there's a reflective surface behind your subject: a mirror, a window, or even a highly varnished door or wall, it can pick up the light from the flash and bounce it back into the lens. The result is often an unexpected blob of light right in the middle of your picture.

And it's almost impossible to see what's happening through your viewfinder as you make the exposure. The duration of the flash is somewhere between 1/1000 sec. and 1/10,000 sec.—much too fast for you to see if you're getting unwanted highlights, and where they're occurring, and how large they are.

The only protection is to anticipate the problem and to prevent it from happening.

If your flash attachment is permanently fixed to your camera, your best bet is to study the background through the viewfinder as you frame the picture. If there's anything there that can catch the light and throw it back into your lens, don't take the chance that it will. Change your angle, move the reflective object out of the background or, if you must, move your subject to a more acceptable location.

If your flash can be detached from the camera and operated on an extension, you can move the light instead of the subject or the offending object.

Relocating the flash to a position above, below, or to either side of the camera may change the path of the light so that it doesn't reflect directly back into lens. Or you can bounce the light off the ceiling or a nearby wall. This will produce a softer, more even distribution of light, and it will eliminate those hard-edged shadows that often build up behind the subject when head-on flash is used.

Remember, though, that if you use the bounce-light method you're greatly increasing the distance the light must travel to reach the subject, and that a great deal of it is consequently lost *en route*. You will need to open up your lens to a wider aperture to compensate for the loss of light.

Just how much you'll have to open up depends upon the distance the light must travel from flash to ceiling to subject. In an average bright room with a light ceiling, an increase of two or three lens stops should be enough. More might be required if the ceiling is a high one and if the room has dark walls.

Remember also that if the wall or ceiling you're using as a reflector is painted, say, a dark green, the light can pick up the coloring and give your picture a greenish tone. Light colors and soft pastels, on the other hand, don't seem to interfere with print tones.

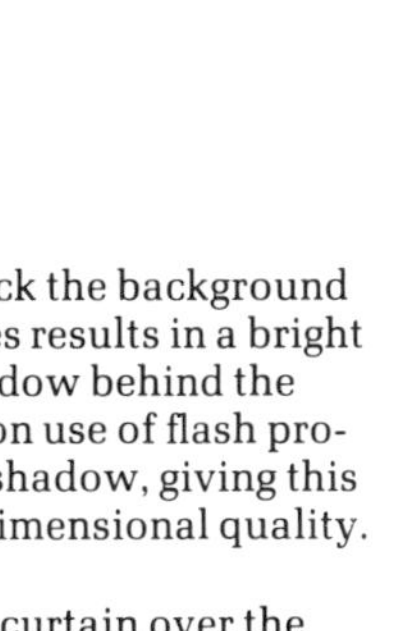

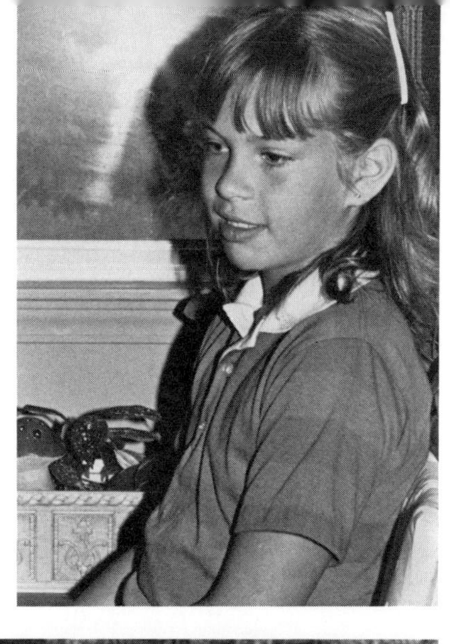

Right: Failure to check the background for reflective surfaces results in a bright highlight from a window behind the subject. Also, head-on use of flash produces a hard-edged shadow, giving this portrait a flat, two-dimensional quality.

Below: Drawing the curtain over the window eliminates the reflection, and moving the flash a little to the left of the camera removes the shadow.

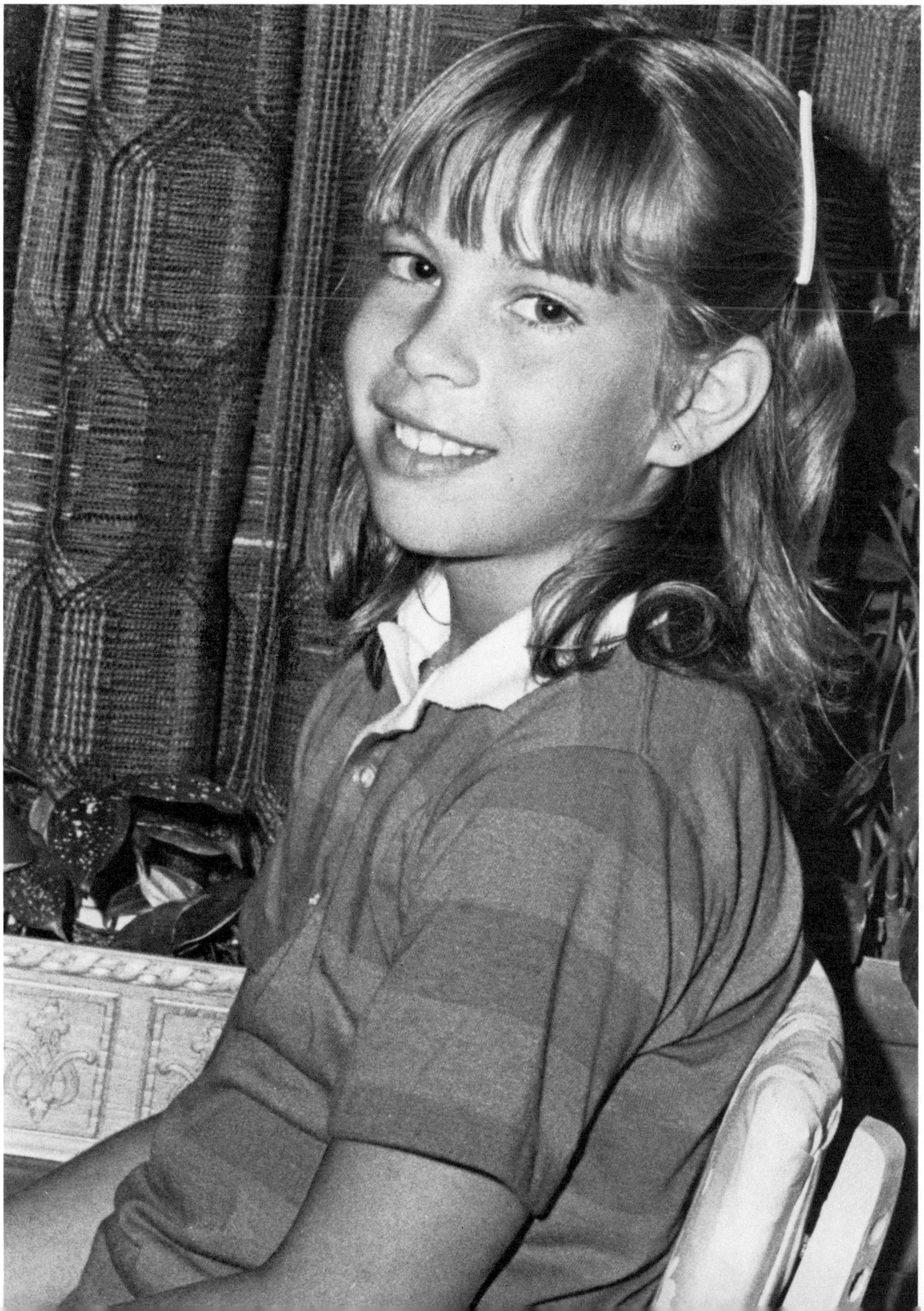

SPECIAL EFFECTS: LENS ATTACHMENTS

The notion that "the camera doesn't lie" must have been proven untrue almost immediately after Louis Daguerre produced the first practical photographs in 1839. Ever since, people have been tinkering with the photographic process in an attempt to produce what never was.

They've done it in the camera with double exposures, special films, and optical devices that multiply or fracture or distort images. They've done it in the darkroom with multiple printing, solarizing, and a dozen special tricks that go far beyond the straight-forward recording of an image.

They've even done it in front of the camera by deliberate distortion of props or backgrounds, by false perspective, by combining miniature models with full-sized objects, and by devices like projecting the Eiffel Tower behind models who have never been in Paris.

Since Daguerre, still photographers and cinematographers have compiled an enormous bag of tricks by which they can deceive audiences into believing they are seeing something they are not. In the process they produce bizarre, dreamlike images, defy the laws of optics, and manufacture their own photographic realities.

Some of these tricks require skill and equipment beyond the reach of amateurs. But many of them don't and there's not reason why you can't adopt some of them to give your own photographs a little novelty.

First, therefore, some ideas for special effects you can produce in your camera as you shoot the picture.

Dozens of image-altering devices may be attached to the front of your lens to produce an infinite variety of visual effects. Some of them are prisms that repeat an image several times on the same piece of film. Other break it up into fragments to produce a kaleidoscopic effect. And still others repeat the full image on half the film area, with several parallel secondary images on the other half.

There are attachments to vignette pictures, producing a sharply focused center and softly diffused outer edges. There are gadgets that will provide the effect of moonlight in the daytime, and others that will soften harsh edges and flatter portrait subjects. Still others will give highlights in your photographs (streetlights, jewelry, reflections off water) a star-like quality.

All of these attachments are relatively inexpensive, and all of them are available for 35mm single-lens-reflex cameras and for many other cameras. They work equally well with color or black-and-white film.

In addition, there is a whole catalog of special filters for use with color films to produce prismatic effects: rainbows, streaks, stars, and bursts or points of color wherever you want them in your picture.

There are filters that subtract haze and others that add it. There are some that allow you to modify or alter the normal color into practically anything you might imagine.

Most camera stores carry the attachments I've described or can get them for you. Amphoto publishes a book, *Amphoto Guide to Lenses*, which explains which lens to use for a particular special effect. Also, Spiratone, Inc., 135-06 Northern Boulevard, Flushing, N.Y. 11354, has an eight-page brochure describing their filters and special lens attachments.

In a word: the business of being creative with your camera may be a lot easier (and a lot less expensive) than you think. Of the many ways of producing special visual effects, these add-on lens attachments are the easiest to use and will serve the purpose if you're interested in adding punch to your pictures.

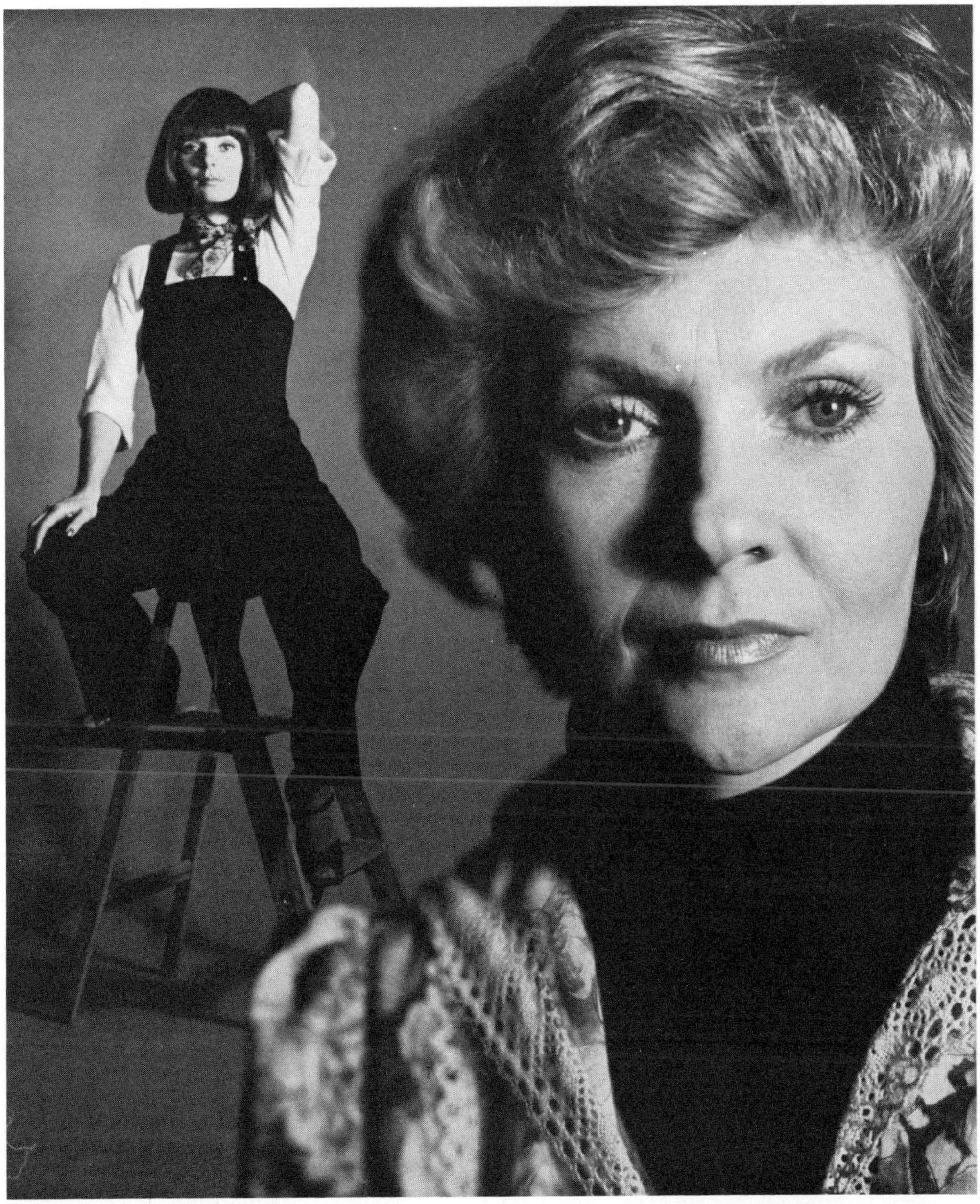

Above: A split-field attachment will let you get optically "impossible" pictures like this one.

Right: The split-field close-up attachment is an image modifying lens which permits the photographer to combine a long shot and an extreme closeup in a single frame. It produces a faintly fuzzy line at the point of demarcation: the trick is to rotate the attachment until the dividing line becomes as unobtrusive as possible.

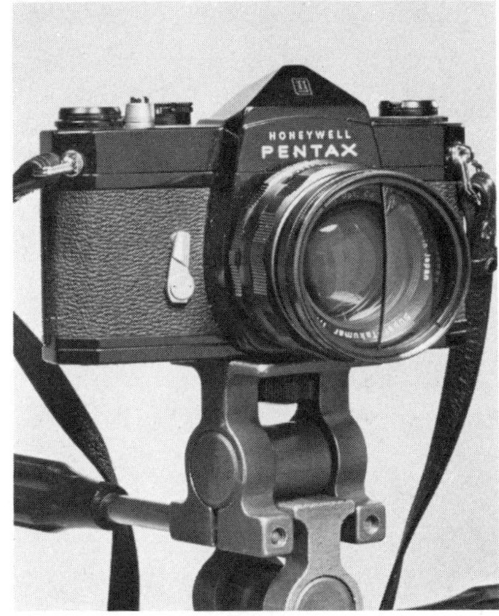

COLOR GALLERY

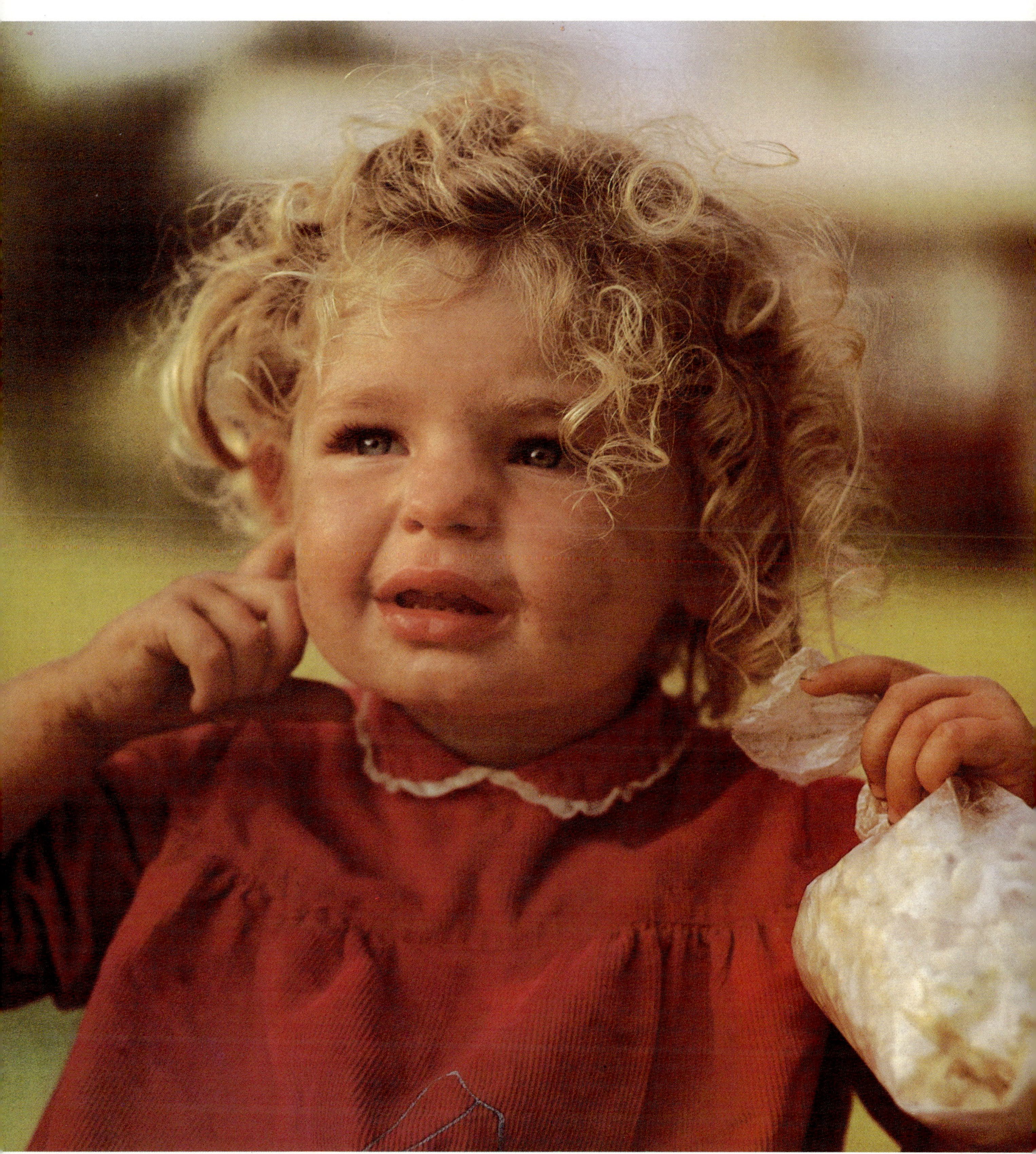

CANDID PORTRAITS OF CHILDREN demand that you be ready for the brief, fleeting expression. Required are equal parts of patience, preparation, and luck.

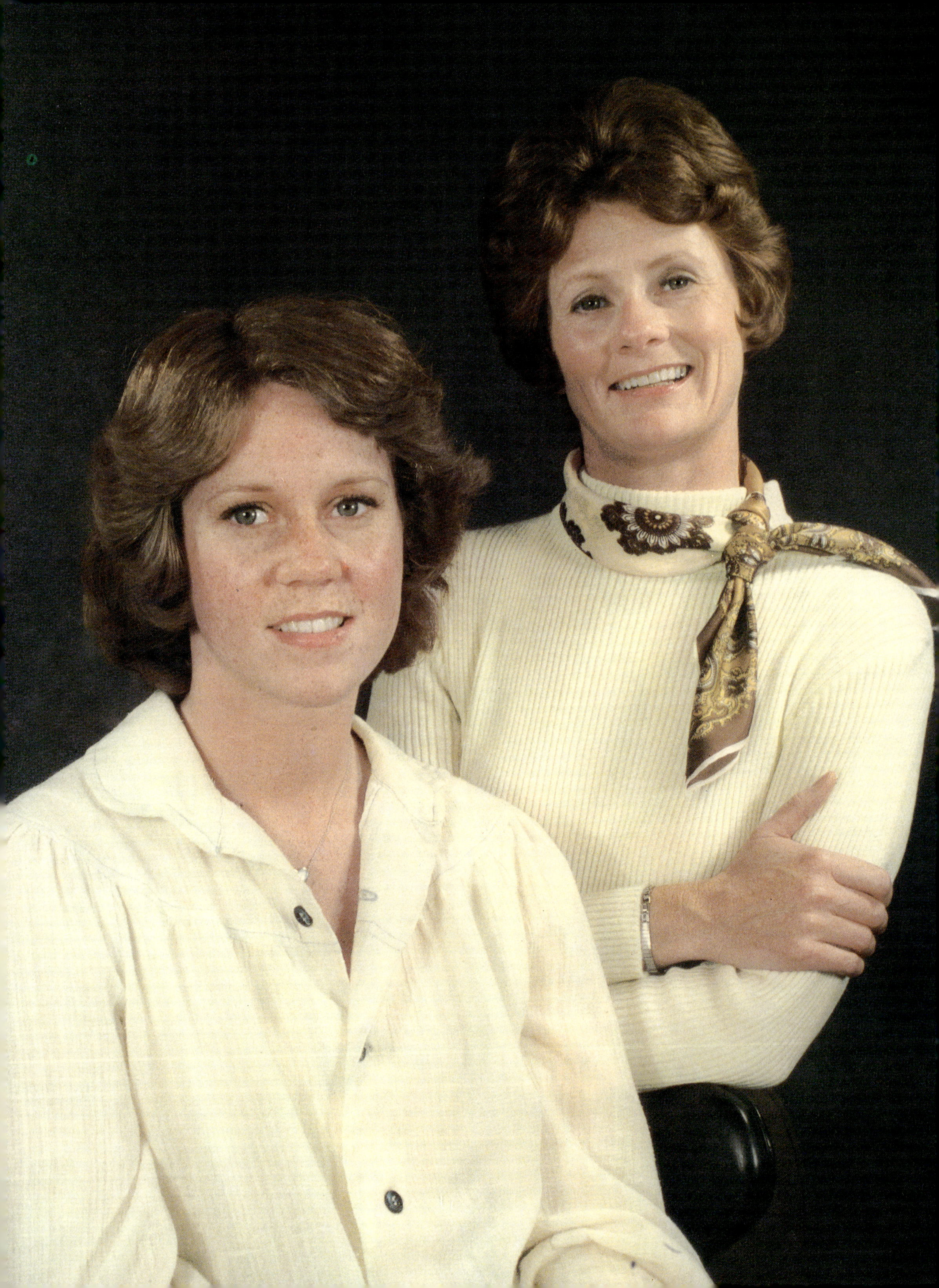

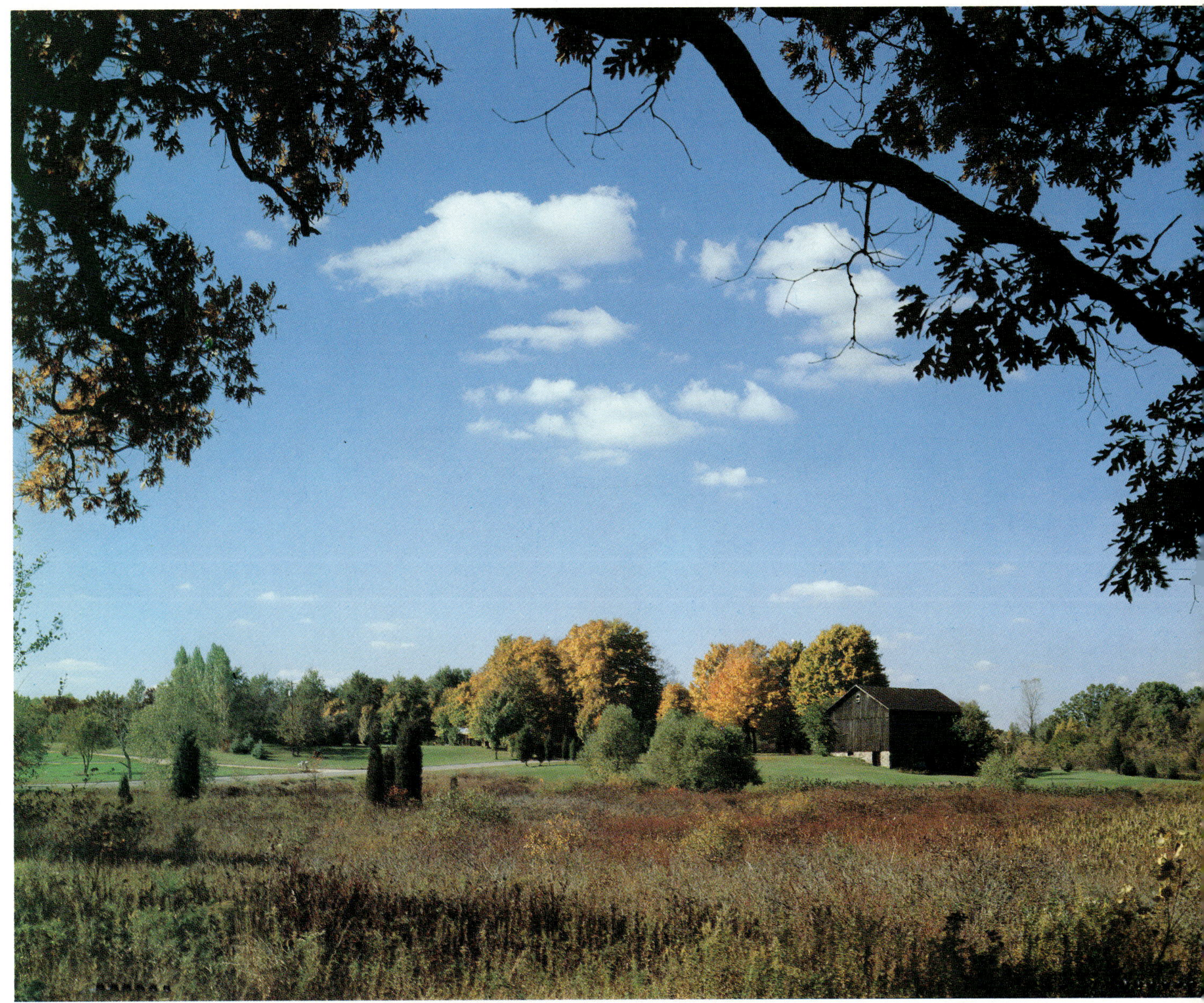

THIS FORMAL MOTHER-AND-DAUGHTER PORTRAIT was made with the simplest materials: a neutral background, a single high-backed stool, and four photoflood lamps. Two of the floods are high, one to each side, to light the subjects' hair. Two more are lower and are used to illuminate the models themselves.

WHEN SHOOTING COLOR SCENICS it's important to remember that there are significant changes in the quality of the light during the course of the day. In the early morning and late afternoon there is more warm, yellow-orange present than there is at midday. Your eye may discount it, but the film will not.

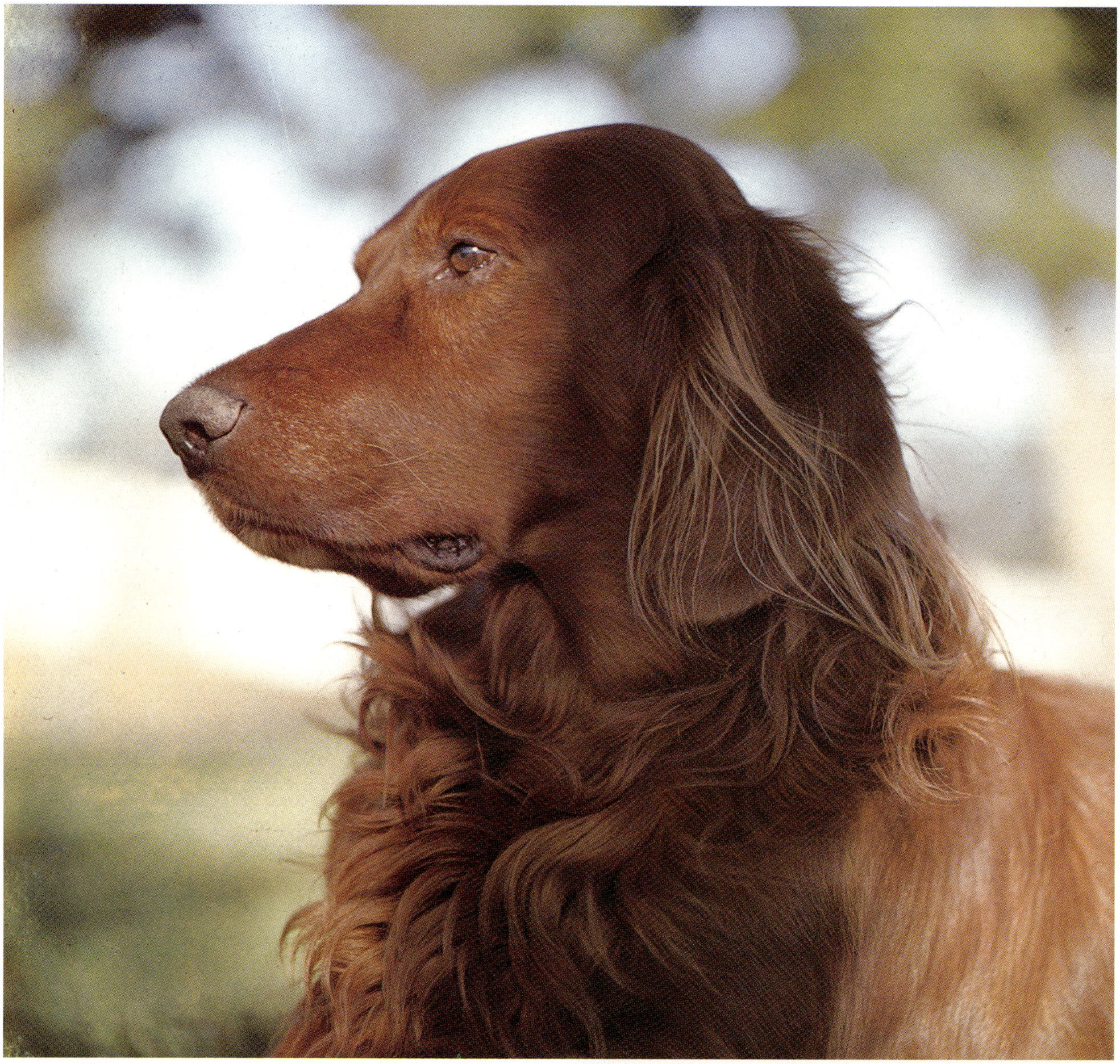

In Pet Portraiture, a shallow depth of field helps when the background is too busy and many interfere with the main subject. Here, a wide lens opening keeps the animal in focus but lets the background fade into a pleasant, unobtrusive blur.

In Shooting Animal Portraits Outdoors, a fast film and a quiet shutter are practically mandatory. This squirrel was photographed with a twin-lens reflex and a shutter speed of 1/500 sec., using a color film rated at ASA 400.

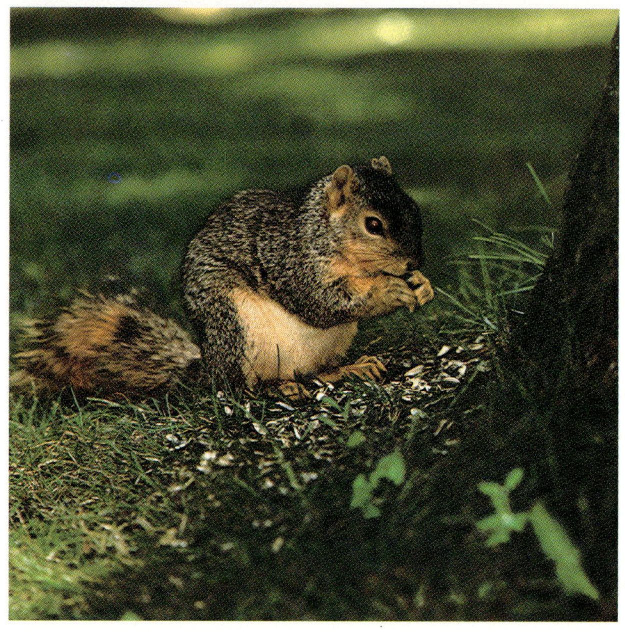

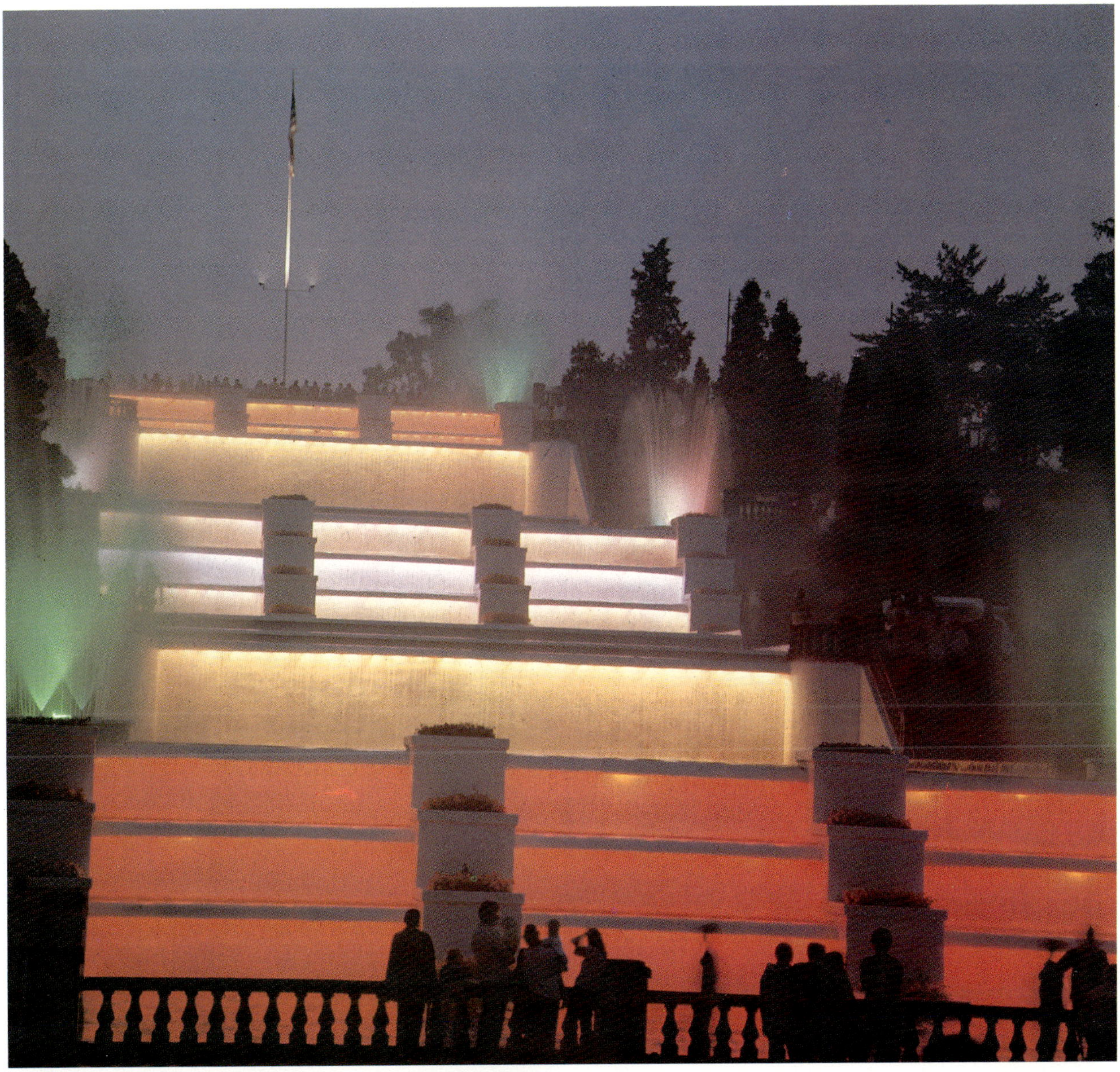

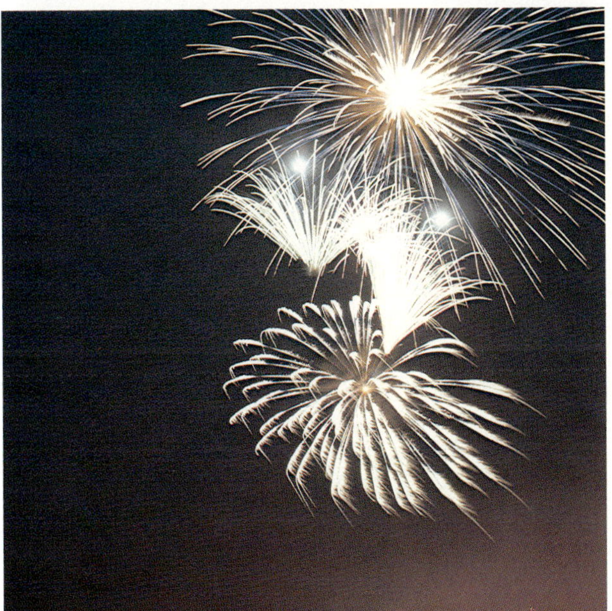

Cascade Falls, Jackson, Michigan is photographed here on a fast, daylight color balanced film. A tripod is a valuable asset for this kind of picture which requires a slow exposure.

These Fourth of July Fireworks were photographed by putting the camera on a tripod and using a cable release to prevent "camera shake."

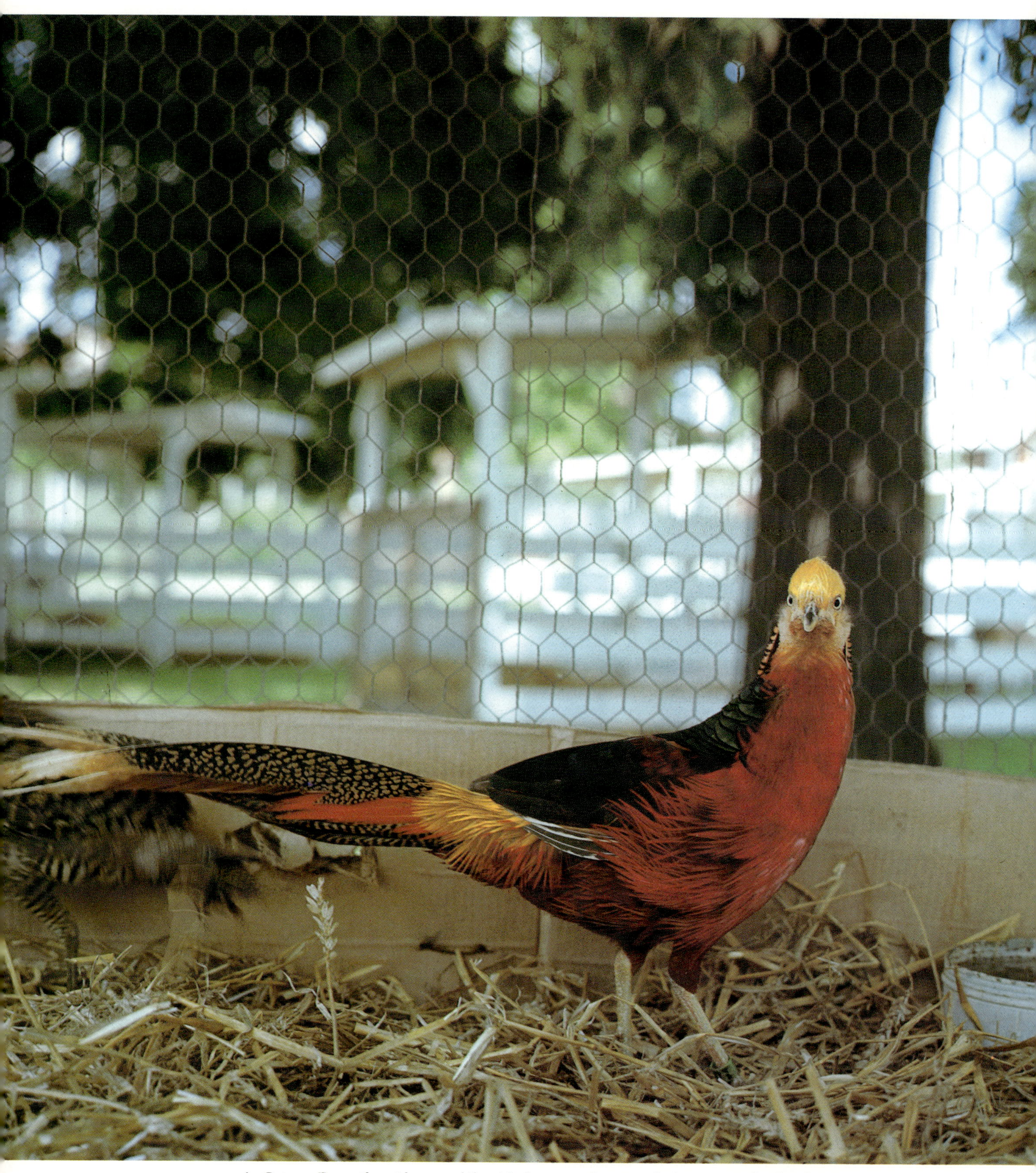

At County Fairs, the midway and the sideshows are the most obvious targets for the photographer. But don't overlook the animal and poultry exhibits, which offer their own kind of color, such as this bird of a dramatically different feather. It's a golden pheasant.

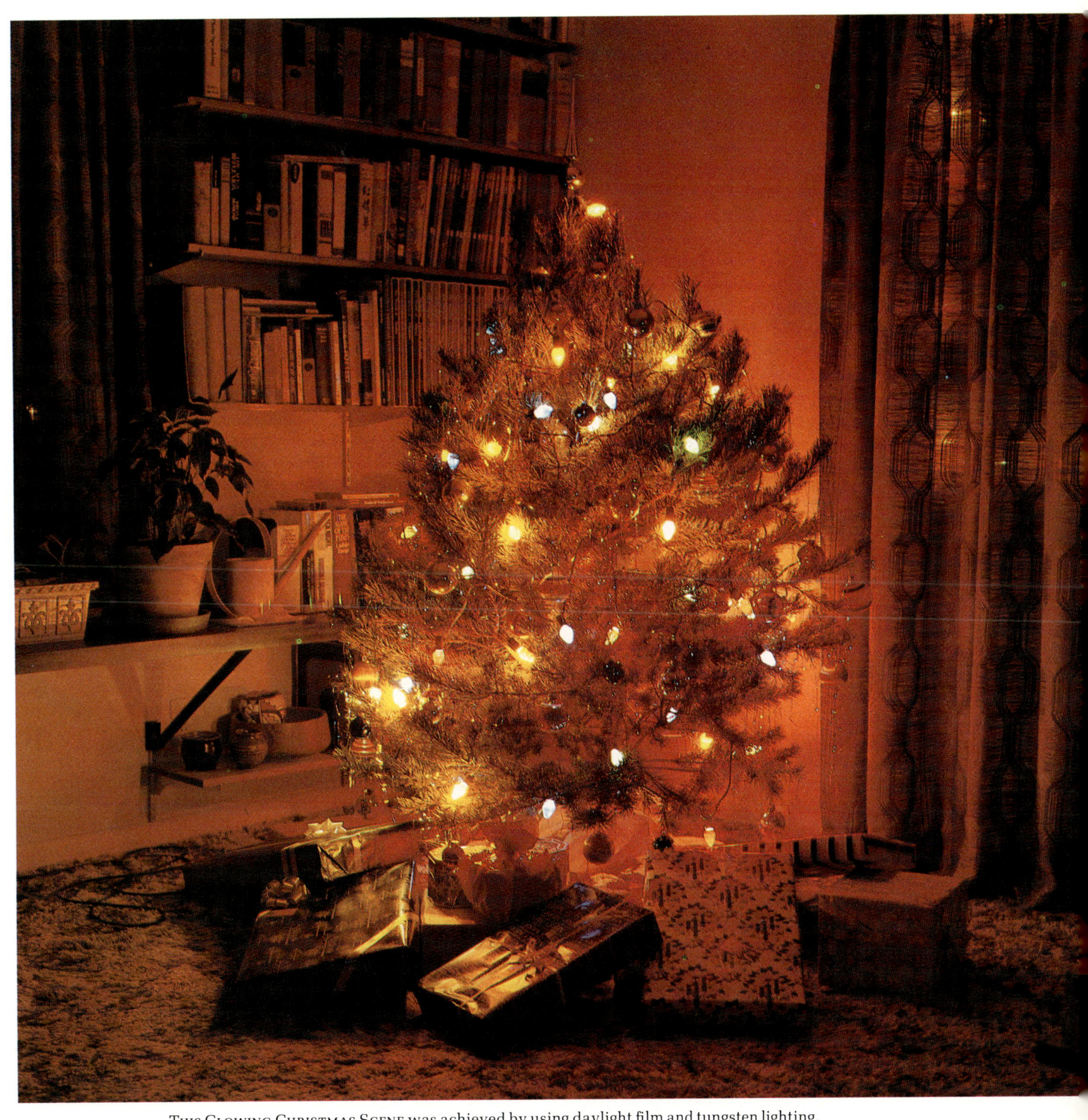

THIS GLOWING CHRISTMAS SCENE was achieved by using daylight film and tungsten lighting.

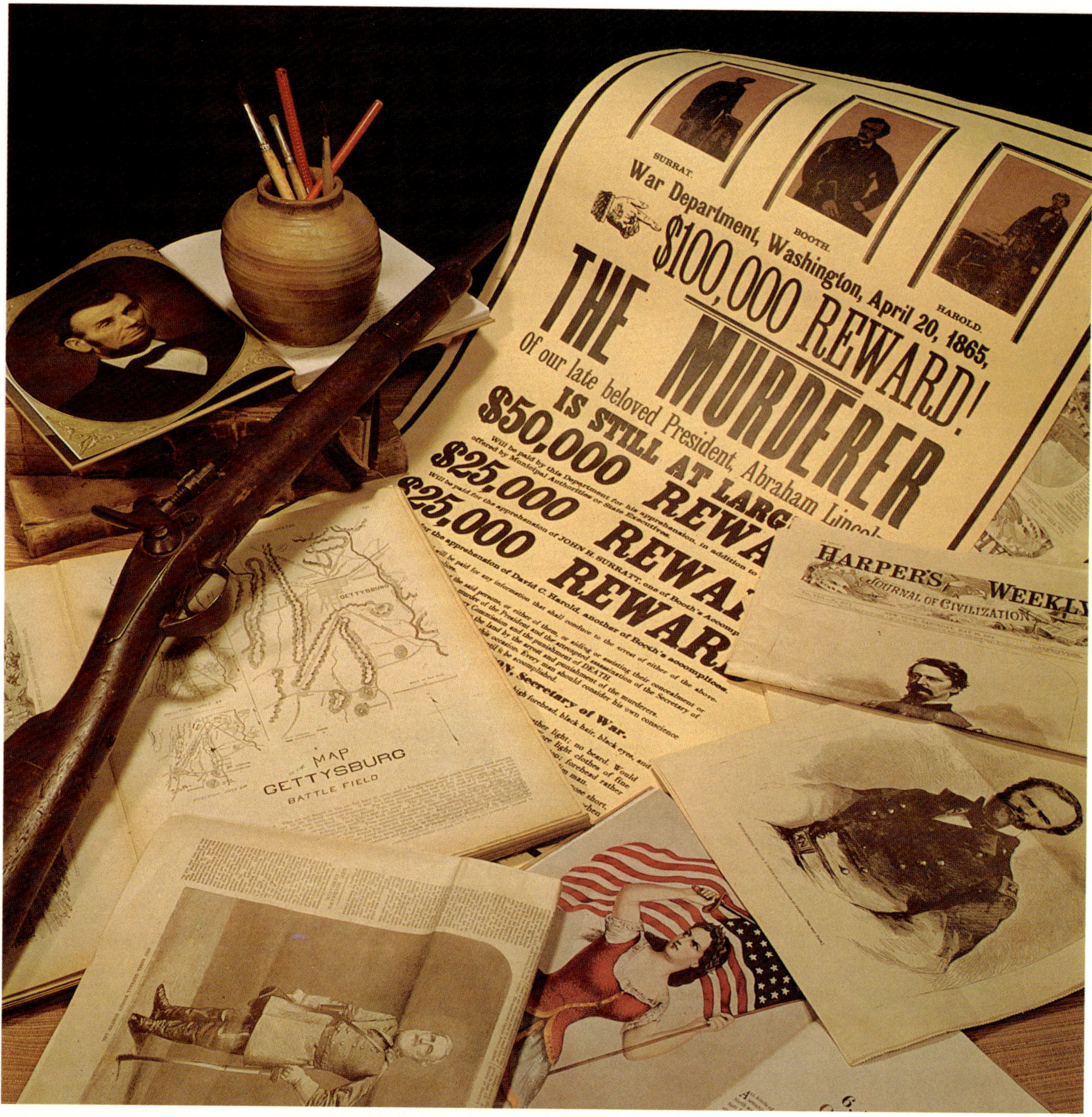

A STILL LIFE PHOTOGRAPH with an historical theme. All of the elements in the picture were chosen for their association with the American Civil War and the death of President Lincoln. Lighting and precision of focus are important considerations because there are many small details which must be clearly perceptible. Use your smallest lens opening, and check the depth-of-field scale on your lens to make sure everything falls within it.

THIS COLORFUL STILL LIFE was achieved by using a small lens opening and seamless background paper.

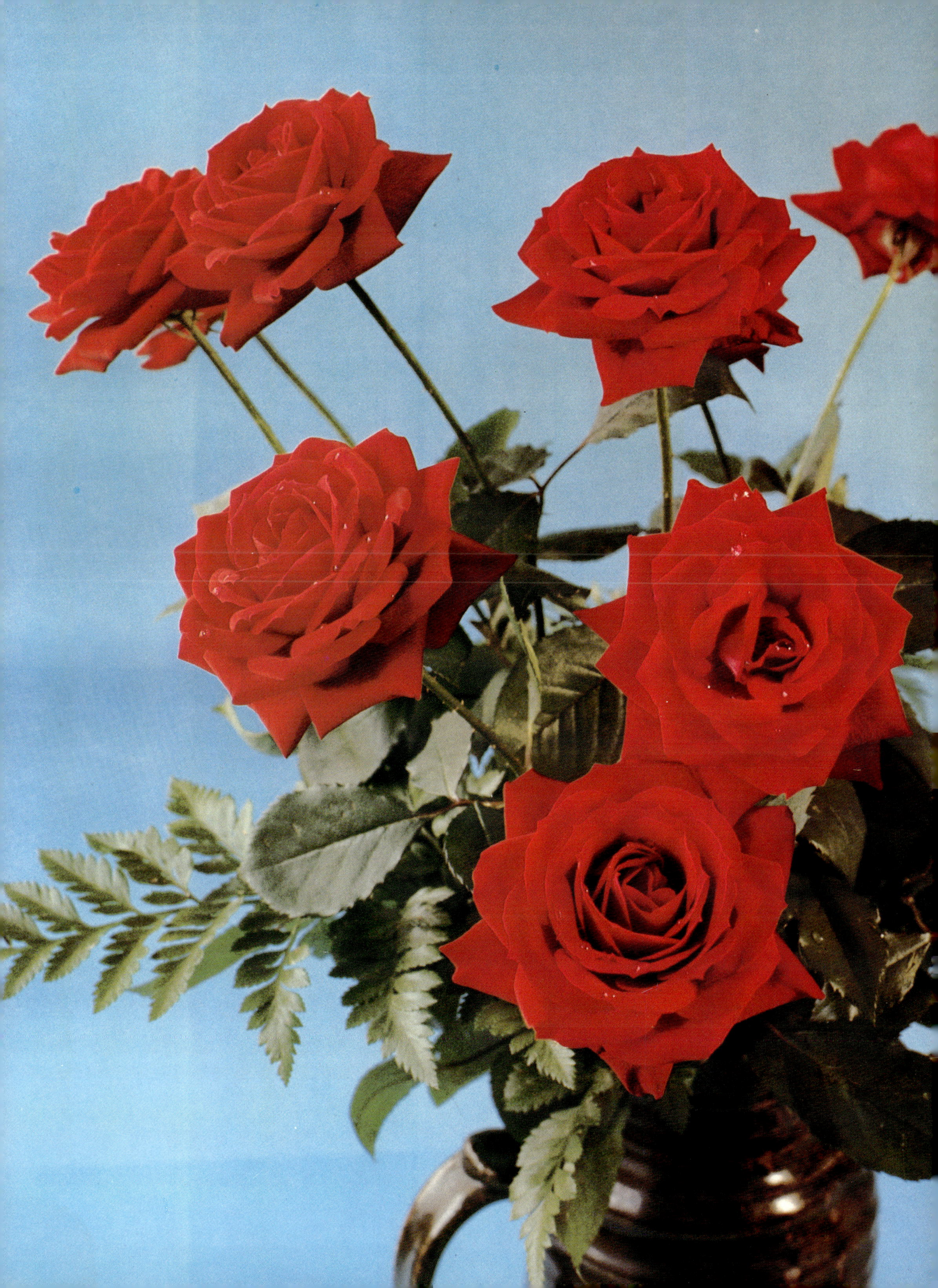

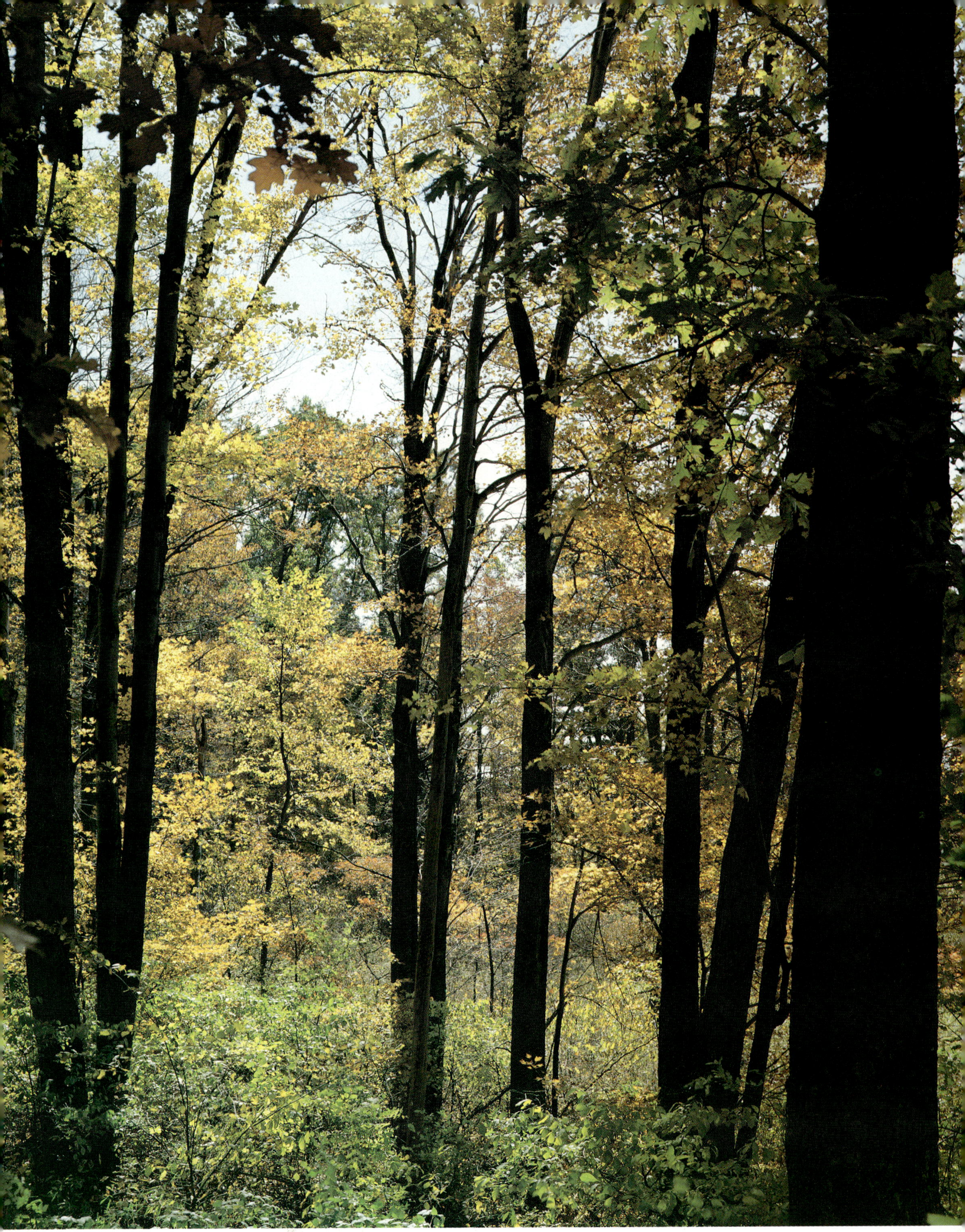

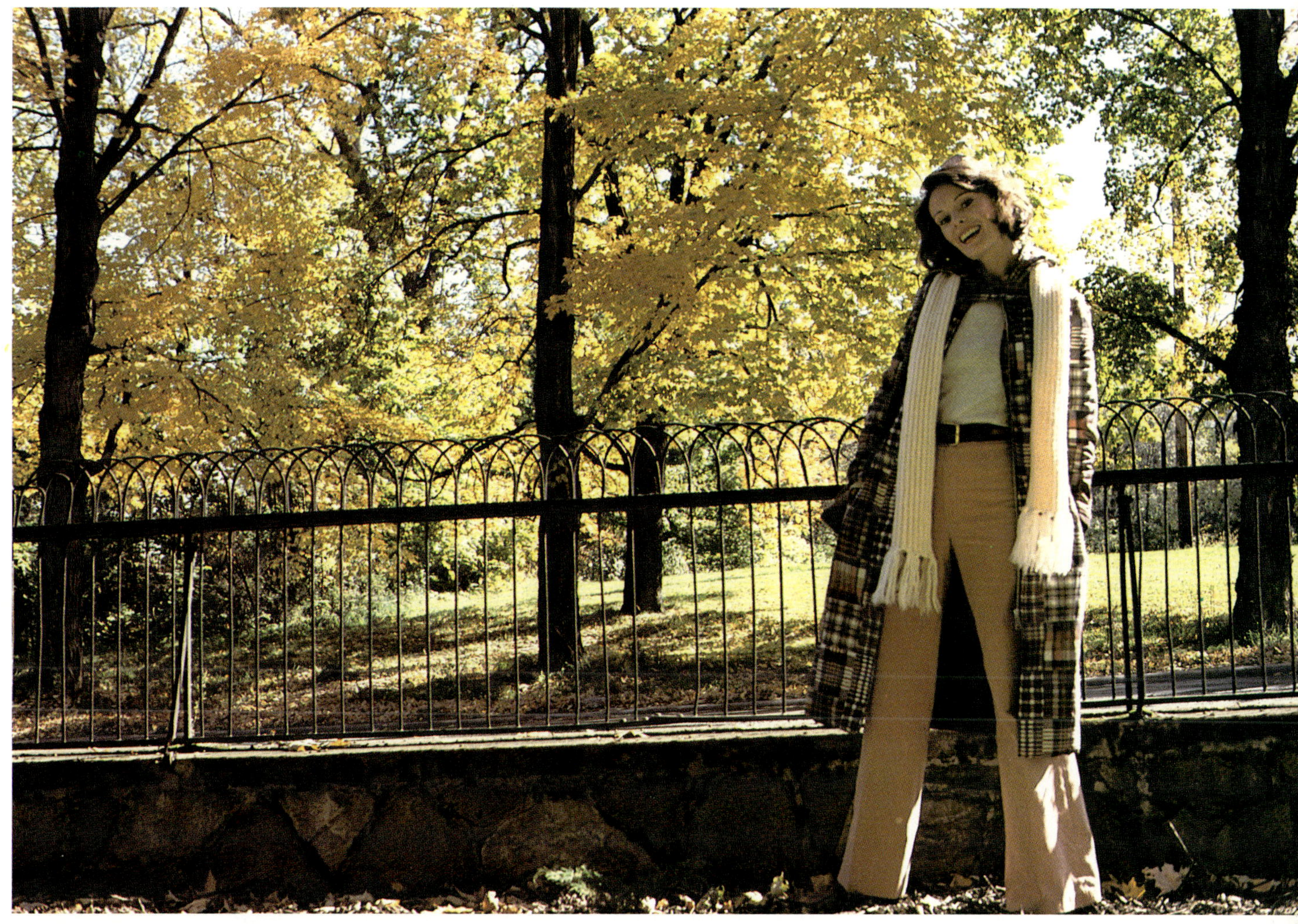

IN LANDSCAPE PHOTOGRAPHY the time of day is often critical. Photographed in the early afternoon, this forest glade is warmly lit and inviting. Three hours later the shadows will be long, leaves and branches will merge in the gloom, and the entire mood of the picture will change.

THE SUNLIT BACKGROUND is an important element in this informal outdoor portrait. For that reason, it was necessary to make the exposure at a lens opening small enough to provide sufficient depth of focus to allow both the model and the trees behind her to show clearly.

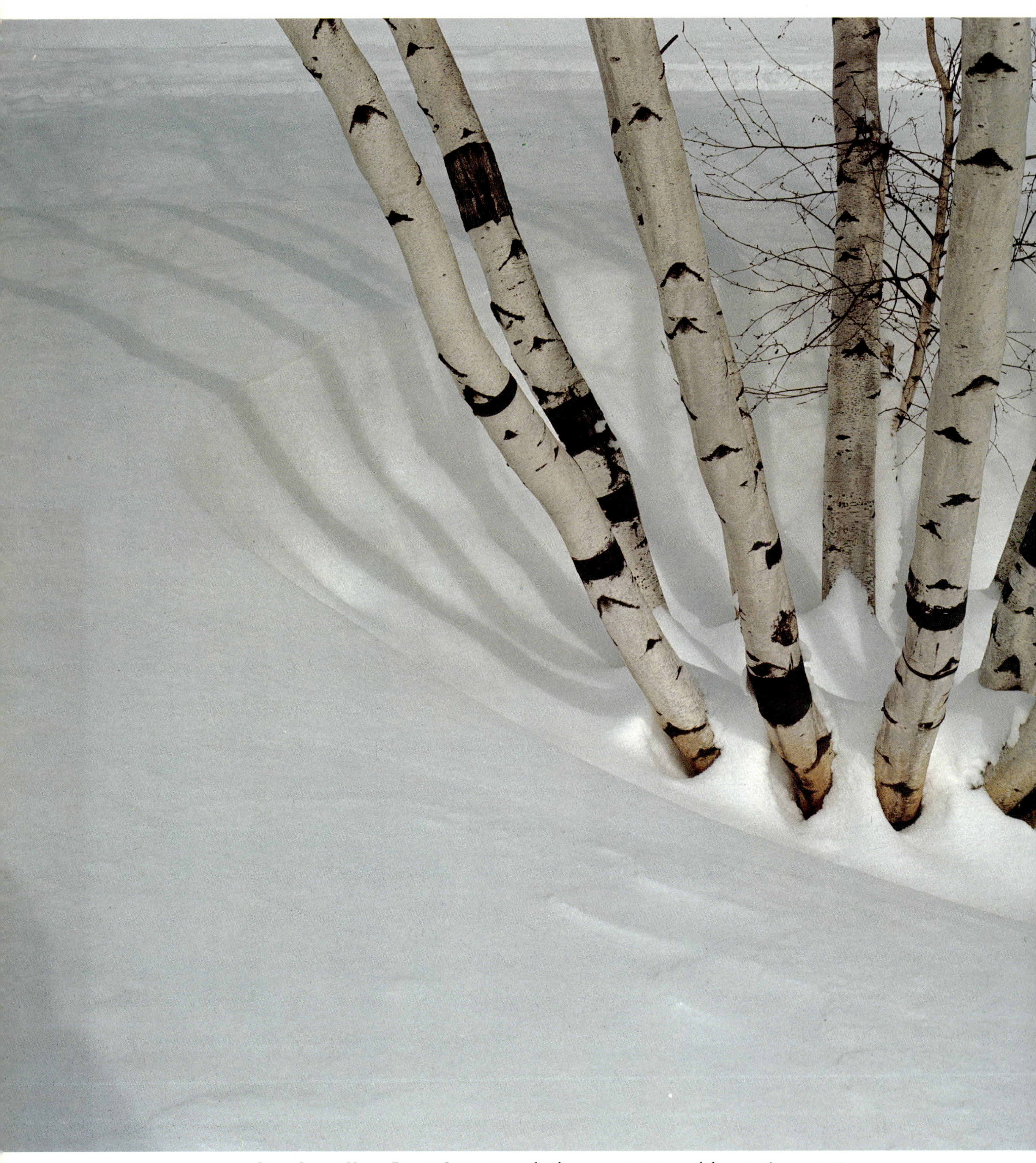

SNOW SCENES UNDER BRIGHT SUNLIGHT tend to be very contrasty, and they require more attention than exposures made on overcast days. But the shadows are essential to the composition of this picture, and it had to be shot while the sun was out. Therefore, exposure was based primarily on the snow.

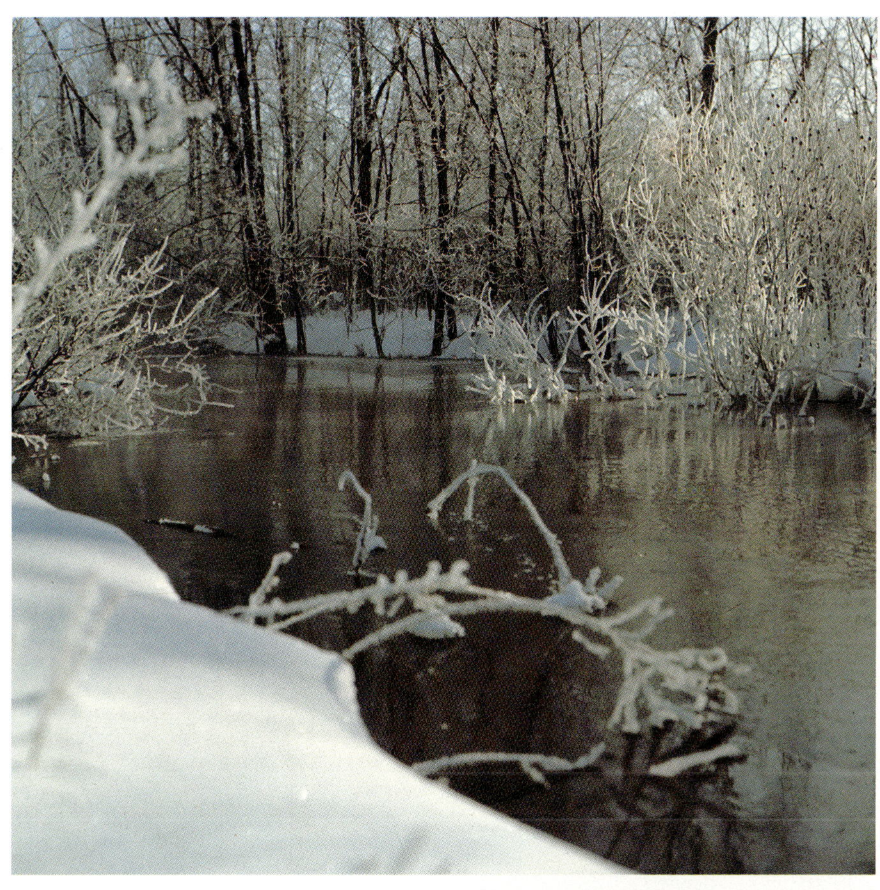

WINTER SCENICS require careful exposure calculation, especially when they include strong lights and darks, as this one does. Considerable attention to depth of focus is required, too, if objects in the foreground and distant background are to appear with equal clarity.

IN THIS WINTERY SCENE, the burst of light immediately draws the viewer's eye to the center of the photograph.

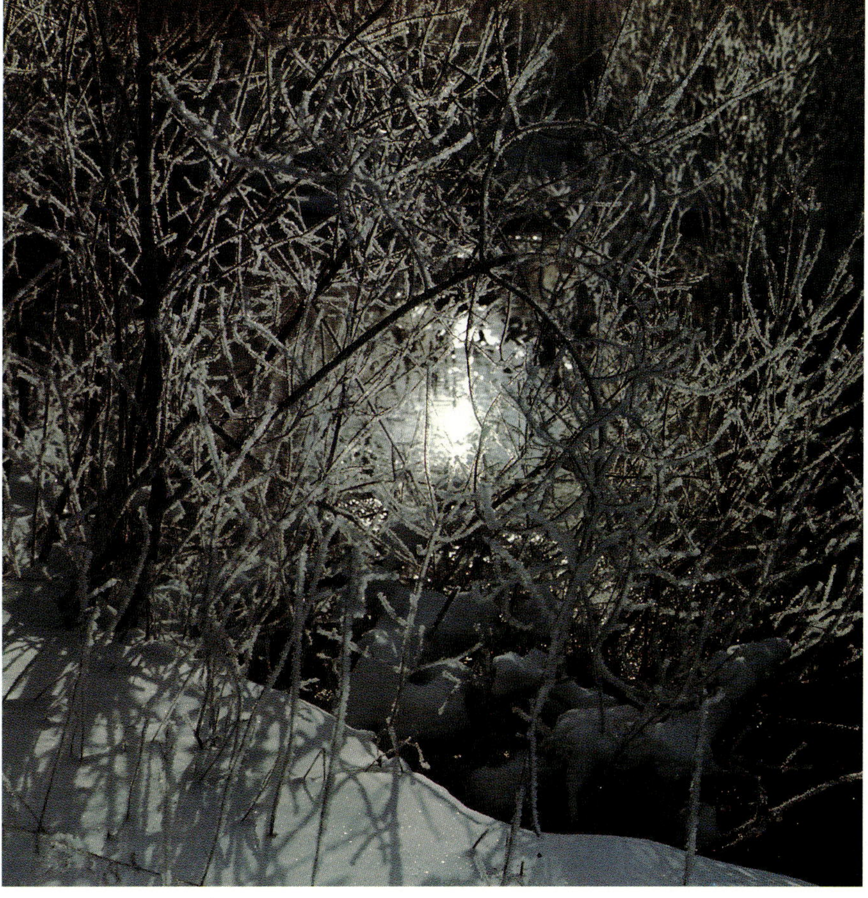

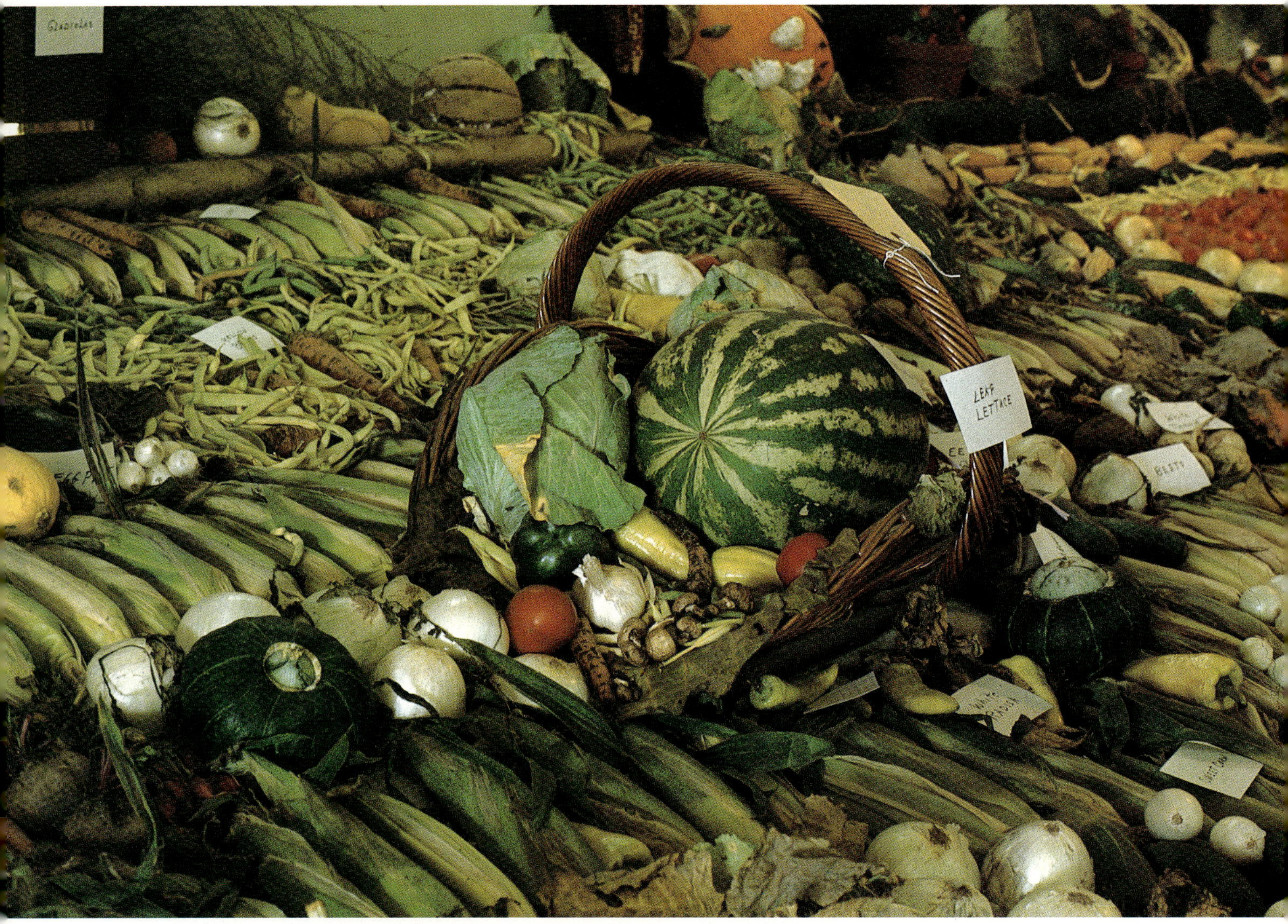

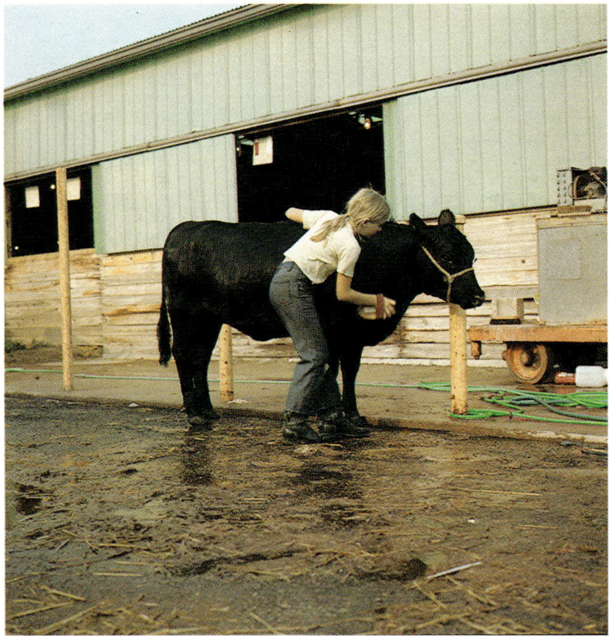

Prize-Winning Produce at an Agricultural Exhibit offers the photographer a wide range of subtly-differentiated colors. The picture was made indoors, but there was a great deal of daylight present, which made it possible to use daylight film.

At Fairs, look behind the scenes for subject matter—for the unglamorous, just plain hard work that has to be done before the show can go on. This picture is quieter than one made along the midway, but it may be more revealing.

A Ferris Wheel's Height is exaggerated even more by the tilted camera, which causes vertical lines in the composition to converge toward the top of the picture. In this picture the effect is desirable; in an exterior view of a tall building it might prove unacceptable.

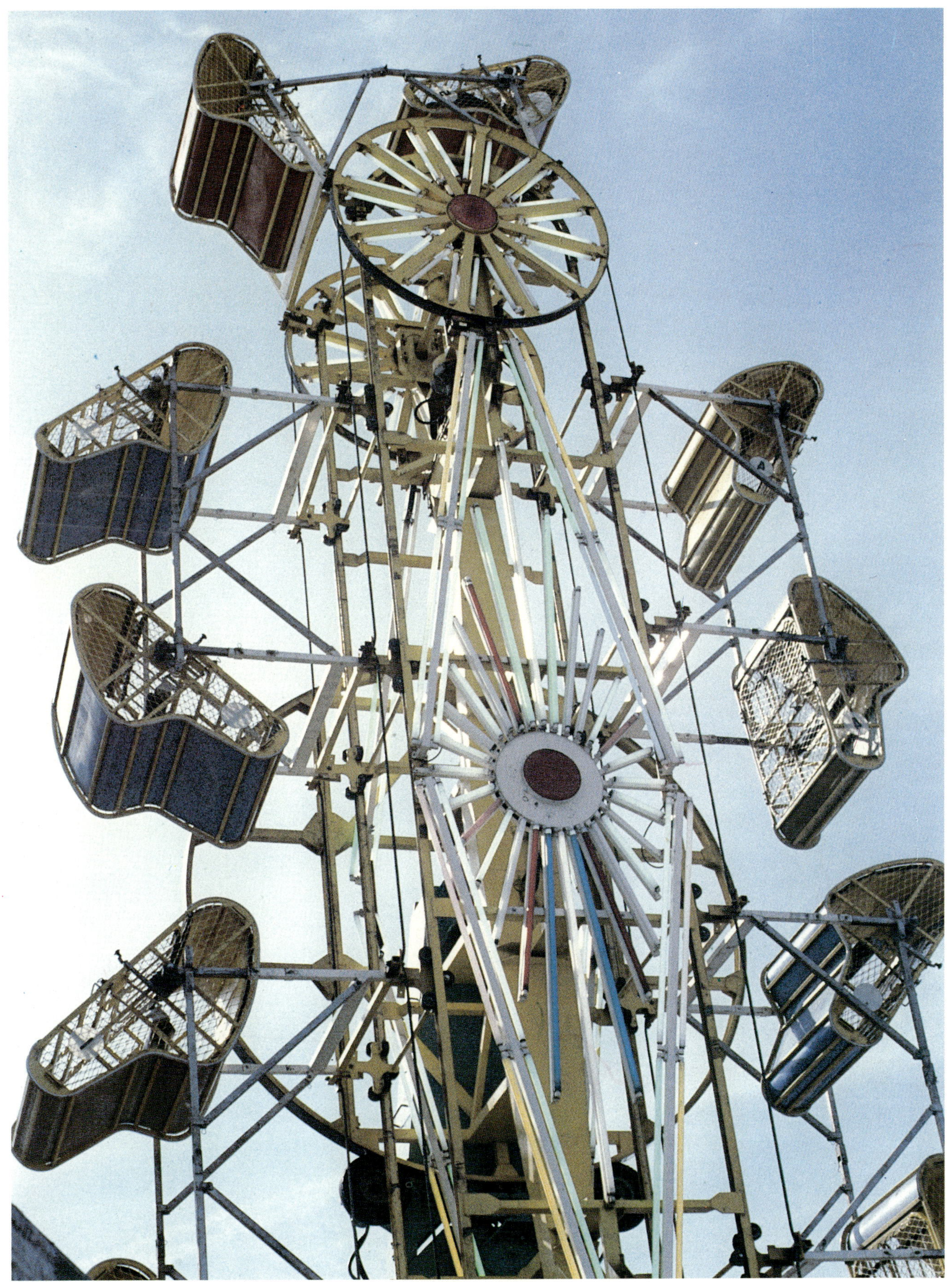

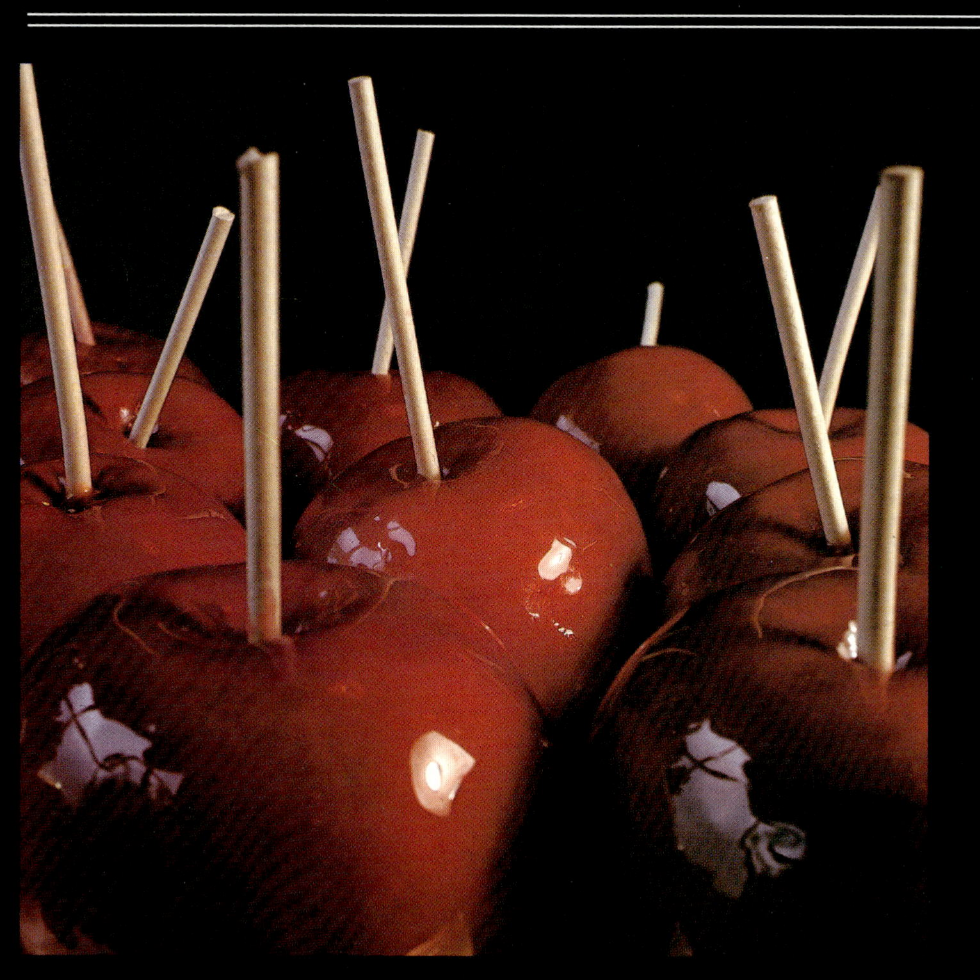

Chapter 3

EVERYDAY PICTURE-TAKING

The chapter that follows is the longest one in this book, and for good reason. It is about the most common uses to which you put the family camera.

Included here are sections on formal and informal portraiture, including groups; on photographing children and pets; on holidays and family get-togethers; on how to stop action and how to photograph still lifes; on landscapes and scenics; after-dark photography; and how to be ready to take pictures on short notice.

There are also sections on the most common seasonal problems the amateur photographer is likely to run into: how to deal with cold weather and snow, and how to cope with large expanses of reflective water and sand when you're taking pictures at the beach.

You will also find information in this chapter on dealing with light: how to use available light instead of flash and, in the section on "Exposing Against the Light," what to do when there seems to be too much of it altogether.

AVAILABLE-LIGHT PHOTOGRAPHY

Back in the early fifties two important technical advances in photography came together to produce a certain amount of excitement among camera fans.

First, there was the wide availability of fast lenses for small cameras—lenses capable of opening up to larger apertures to admit more light, permitting photography under marginal lighting conditions. Second, there were new advances in the film itself. Manufacturers were introducing films of increasing sensitivity, again making it easier to take pictures under low-light conditions.

Serious photographers were quick to see what these two developments meant. It had become possible to make indoor exposures in situations where, hitherto, you'd have needed flash or floodlights to get satisfactory results.

The technique was (and is) called "available-light photography"—photography by whatever light happens to be handy. Professionals began going out on assignment leaving their flash equipment behind, confident that they would not only get the picture, but that the picture they got would have an interesting, understated, natural look.

It had been done before, of course. Photographers, even with the most primitive equipment, have always been able to contrive ways of getting pictures under adverse lighting conditions. But now, with the new fast lenses and extremely sensitive films, it had become easy. And now you could use faster shutter speeds under the most miserable lighting: you could stop action, a thing that had never been possible before.

By now the technique has become routine among professionals and serious amateurs but not among occasional photographers. Most amateurs still think "flash" when they think of shooting pictures indoors.

The purpose of this preamble is, of course, to nudge you a little. If you have not tried available-light photography yourself, you ought to. A little experimentation on your part can give your pictures a whole new feeling.

To do it properly, you'll need to use a camera that offers you some choice among lens openings and shutter speeds, so that you can try different combinations. The lowest-priced compact cartridge-loaded cameras, for all their simplicity and convenience, won't let you do this. Some of the more advanced models combine a relatively fast lens with a range of shutter speeds. If you load with a fast (ASA 400) film, you may find that, if there's enough ambient light, the camera will permit you to shoot without flash.

But for real control over your experiment with available light you'll do best with a not-so-automatic rangefinder or single-lens-reflex—either a 35mm or a 2¼" x 2¼". They offer you fast lenses, a variety of shutter speeds, and the chance to select the combinations yourself.

There are many medium-fast and fast films available these days. They're all very good, and any of them will work perfectly well, but for starters, I'd suggest you try Eastman Kodak's Kodacolor 400 color-print film. It produces warm, accurate colors without the need for compensating filters, even when you're working with a weird mixture of daylight, fluorescent, and tungsten light. Along with your light meter, an important accessory you should have with you when experimenting with available-light photography is a tripod, because you can't ever be sure of the shutter speed you're likely to be using.

In a brightly lighted room you may be able to make your exposures at 1/125 sec. or faster, in which case hand-holding the camera may be adequate. But more often than not you'll find the meter telling you to shoot at 1/60 sec. or slower, and that's when you'll need the tripod.

It is a fundamental photographic truth that whenever pictures turn out fuzzy it usually isn't because the subject moved, but because *you* did.

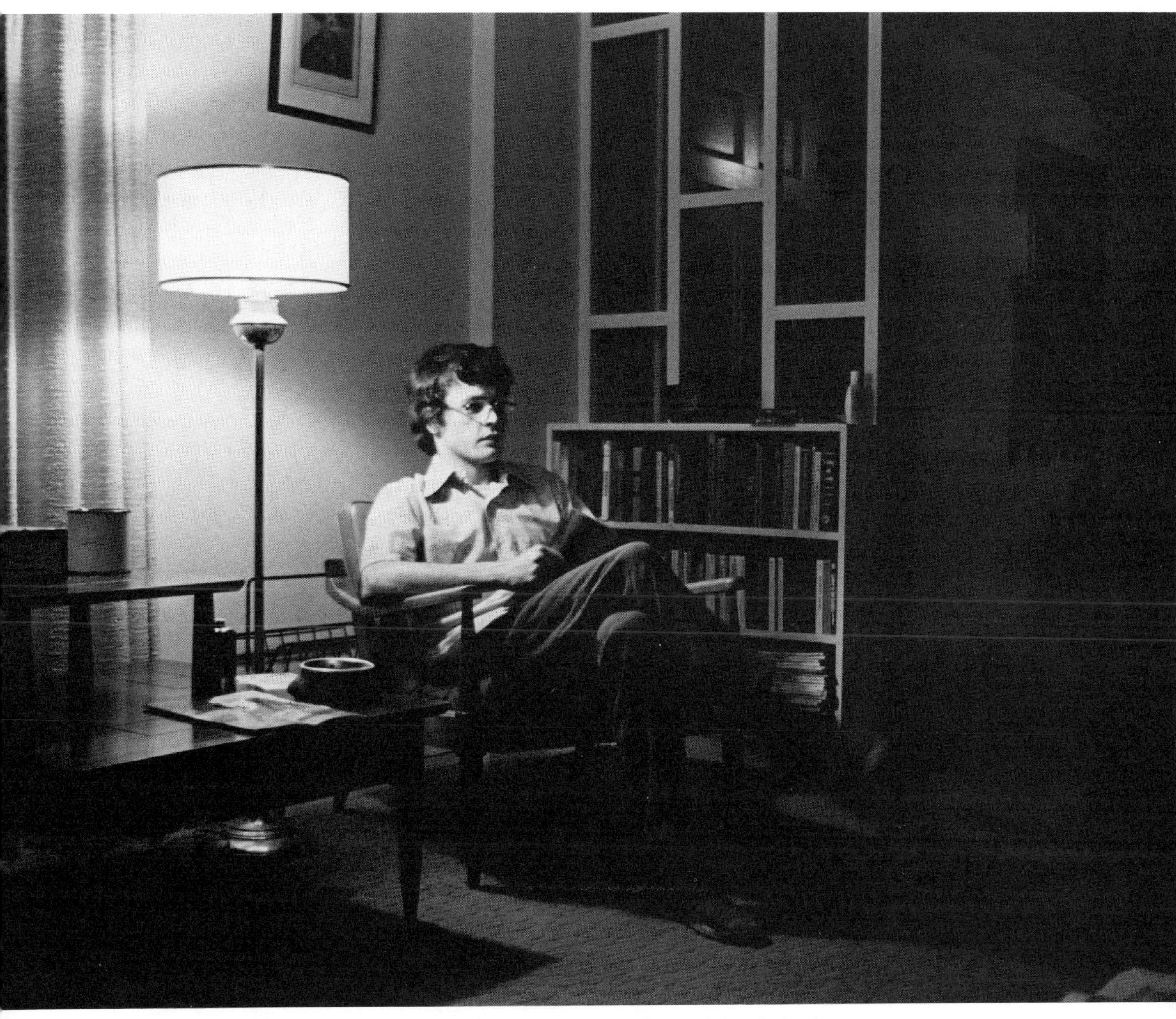

This available-light shot shows the wide range of tones possible with a carefully-calculated exposure. There are very white whites, some extremely black blacks, and a subtle distribution of grays. Moreover, there is a warm, moody atmosphere impossible to catch with straight, head-on flash.

If the subject is a person, and if the person can be persuaded to move across the room to a sunny window or a brightly lighted corner, you'll find that, assuming you're using a fast film, calculating the exposure will be relatively easy because of the increase in available light. If your camera is equipped with a meter, it will do the figuring for you and you have only to do what it tells you to do. If it's one of the newer, fully-automated cameras it will be even easier. You just point and shoot.

One of the things you should be conscious of, however, even when there's lots of light, is the direction from which it's coming. Often, especially in public places like conference rooms, offices, stores and arenas, the only source of light is overhead. This means that the tops of people's heads and their shoulders tend to get most of the direct light, while their eyes and other recessed portions of their faces disappear into shadow. In shooting people under available light, you must train yourself to look for moments when their faces are evenly illuminated.

In homes, where there are likely to be floor lamps and table lamps providing some sidelighting, avoiding these extremes of contrast is much easier. You can often move the light sources around to provide softer, more even illumination; you can replace bulbs of low wattage with more powerful ones; and you can turn overhead lights on and off as they are needed.

For this kind of photography you may often find that, even when you've done everything you can to boost available illumination, the level of light is still too low to budge your meter's needle. But this doesn't mean you can't get a picture. It just means that you'll have to settle for slower shutter speeds.

And this is where you'll need a camera that will let you select shutter speeds of 1/8 sec. or even slower. Many of the automated cameras, as helpful as they are when light levels are high, have no provision for overriding the system and choosing your own combination of lens opening and shutter speed. Check your owner's manual to see if, and how, you can make exposures at these slow speeds.

If people are included in your picture, and if you're shooting at speeds slower than 1/60 sec., look for moments of inaction before hitting the shutter button. If you're setting up a portrait, ask your subject to find a comfortable position and hold it for the duration of the exposure. Even a full second requires no undue effort.

If the picture you're after is an important one, bracket your exposure to insure a good choice.

This available-light portrait was made indoors by natural light coming from two large windows, one on each side of the subject so that both sides of the face received equal amounts of light.

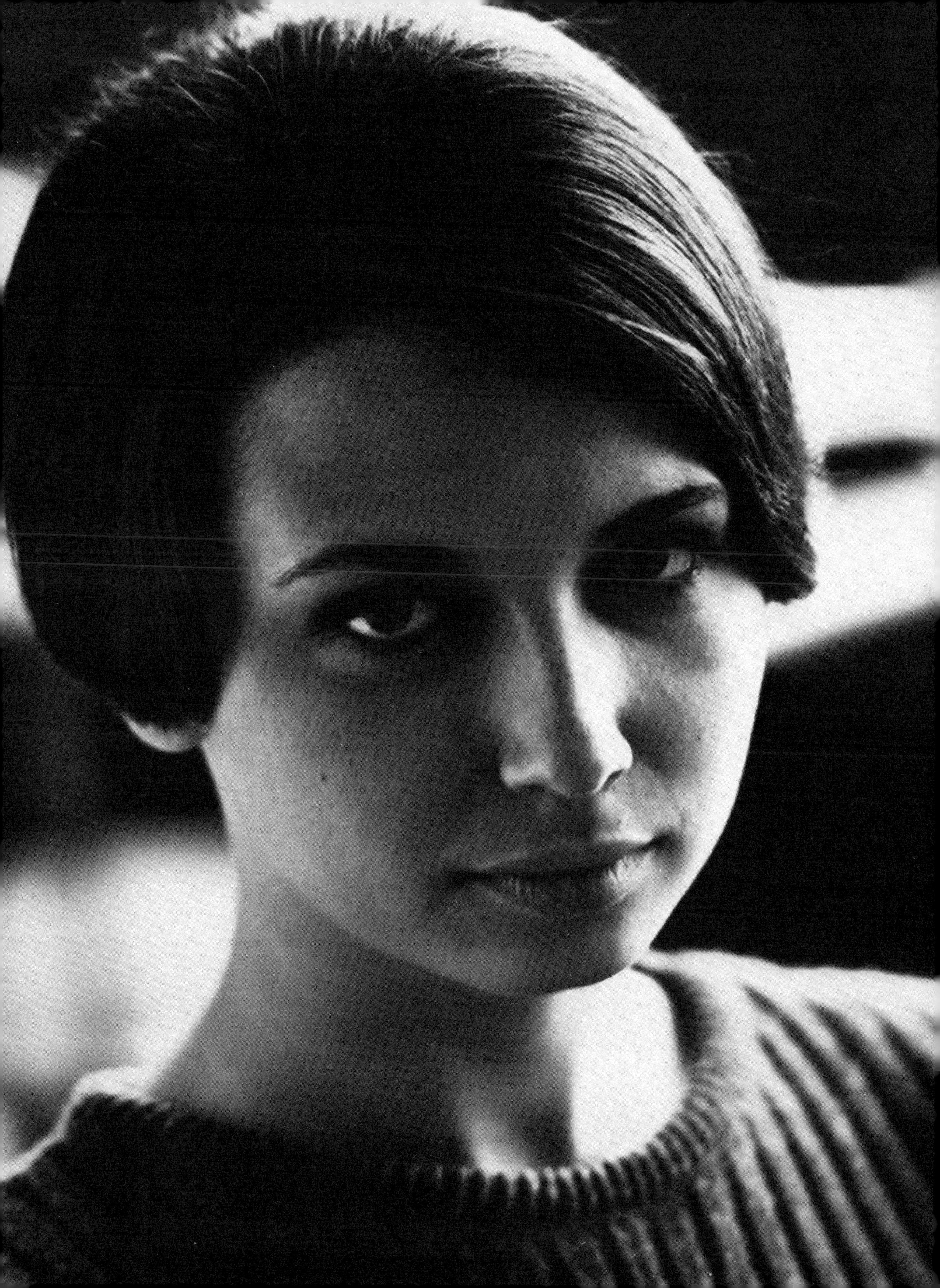

PORTRAITS: PLANNING THE PICTURE

There will come a time when you become impatient with taking casual snapshots of people and decide to move in a little closer to your model, eliminate pictorial irrelevancies, and try to say something about your subject's personality. Portraits can be formal or informal, but always they must offer the viewer some insight into the real nature of the subject.

For this reason the best portraits usually avoid unnecessary props or elaborate costumes, so that nothing distracts from the individual subject. Lighting is subdued to the same purpose and so is posing: the sitter should not appear rigid and uncomfortable and, if he's doing something it should be a logical extension of his nature. What he's doing should never be allowed to be more interesting than who is doing it.

All of which calls for planning, patience, imagination, and considerable attention to the technicalities of lighting and exposure. It makes portraiture one of the most difficult of the photographic disciplines, but also one of the most creative and rewarding ones.

Attention to lighting is fundamental. It can be natural light: outdoors in the open shade, for example. Or indoors in a sunny room near a window. It can be a combination of natural light and artificial light. Or it can be entirely artificial: floodlights, flashbulbs, or electronic flash. Having picked the model and the pose, the photographer must note carefully what the light is doing to his subject.

Direct outdoor sunlight is not very successful. It produces harsh shadows under the eyes and nose, it accentuates wrinkles and blemishes, it makes the subject squint, and it washes out areas where there should be subtlety of tone. Open shade works very well, but if you're shooting color slides keep a skylight filter over your lens to reduce the bluishness present in such light. Your film, in such circumstances, should be the kind that's balanced for daylight.

Many photographers like to do their portrait-making indoors under more controlled conditions. Lighting, for example, can be manipulated more precisely, there is likely to be more privacy, and there are no problems with gusts of wind and sudden overcasts.

If you're combining daylight, which is blue, with artificial light, remember to use blue flashbulbs or electronic flash for proper color balance. If you're using white floodlights, use tungsten film. In all cases, be sure to read the manufacturer's instructions packed with the film that specify the right lights to use.

If you have the sort of camera that can be fitted with a variety of lenses, and if a moderate telephoto lens is available to you, you might try it for your experiment in portraiture. It will permit you to maintain a comfortable distance from your subject and still fill your viewfinder with face and shoulders. For many other cameras, portrait attachments are available that fit in front of the existing lens.

It's a good idea to use a tripod, especially if you're using floodlights. You're likely to be shooting at fairly slow shutter speeds, like 1/60 sec. or 1/30 sec., or even slower. If you try hand-holding the camera at such speeds you'll probably get a shaky image—not because the subject moved, but because the camera did. The secret of good, crisp images usually turns out to be a firm support for the camera.

Once you've got your subject posed more or less to your satisfaction, adjust your lighting—which is much more easily said than done. Indeed, books enough to fill a library have been written on lighting for portraiture. But if you keep in mind certain basic guidelines, you'll find yourself gaining in confidence as you gain in experience.

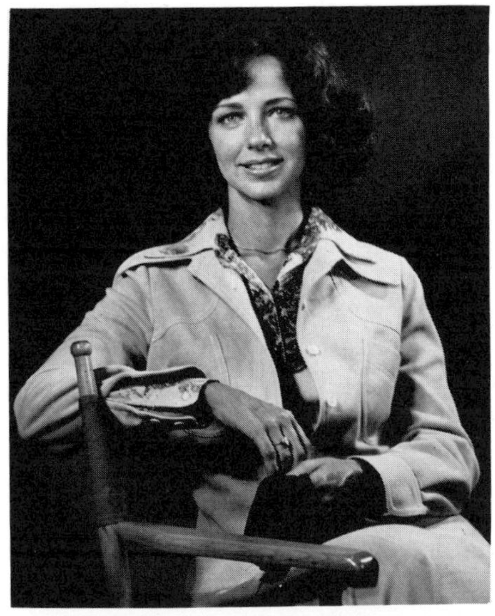

This formal indoor portrait of Robbie Timmons, anchorwoman for a Detroit television station, was made with minimal lighting. There is one light above and to the right, to put a few highlights in the hair. The main light is on the left, with a small fill-light on the right.

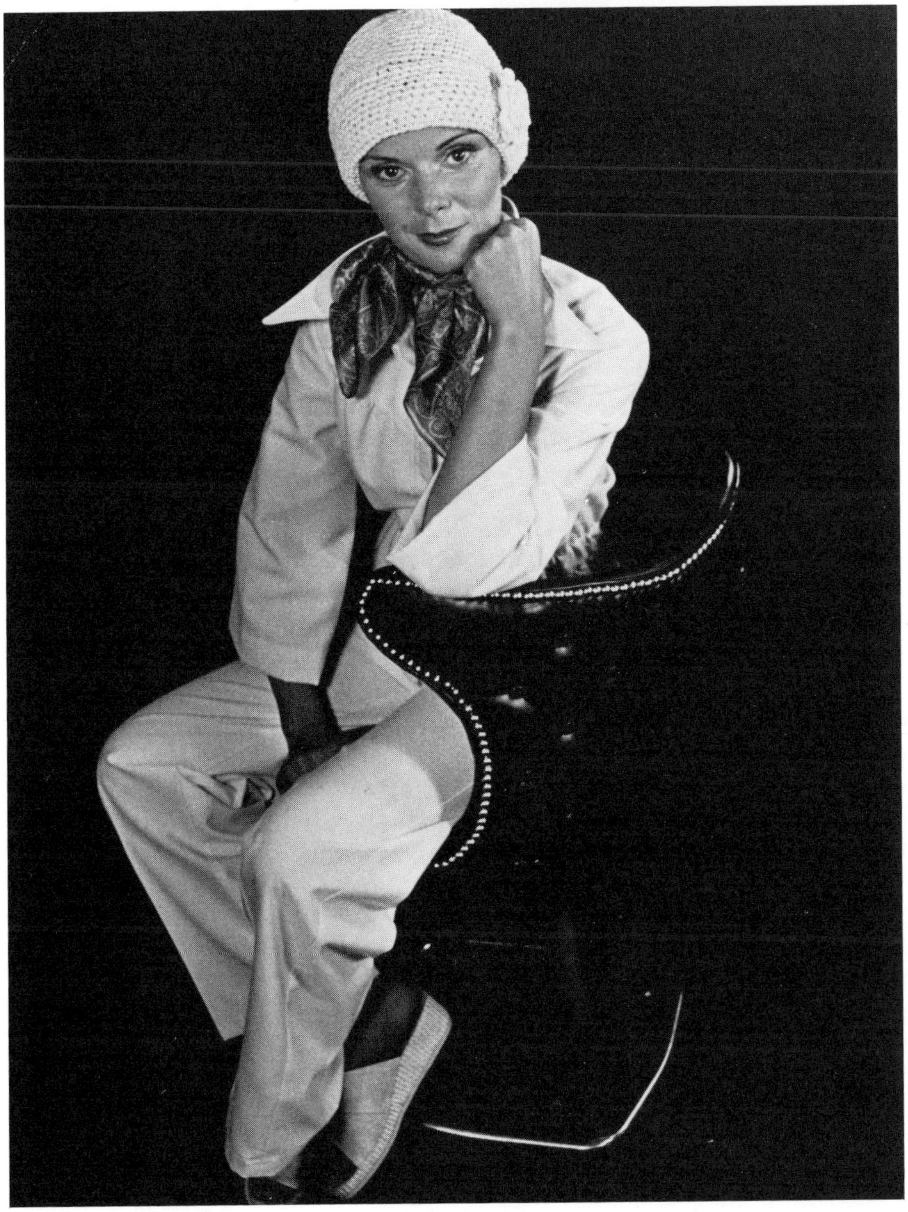

Another important thing to remember when taking portraits is the use of props. This chair adds an interesting compositional element to this portrait.

PORTRAITS: BASIC LIGHTING

You'll want a light three or four feet above and almost behind your subject, directed downward toward the head and shoulders. Its purpose is to separate the subject from the background and to add some highlights to the hair. Another light—the main light—should be located in front of, and a little to one side of, the subject. It should be directed to illuminate the face and torso. This is likely to produce a face well-lit on one side, but with shadows building up on the side farthest from the light. To cancel out this unbalanced look, a third light is used to fill in some of these dark areas. This fill-in light should be of lesser intensity than the main light: use either a smaller bulb, or one of the same intensity located at a greater distance from the subject. The ratio between the main light and the fill-in light should be about two to one. The idea is to produce a naturally modeled face, with normal shadows occurring where they ought to occur, and with no contrasty too-dark and too-light areas.

If you use floodlight bulbs, they should be in metal reflectors screwed into a clamp-on socket. Or you may want to try floodlights that have their own built-in reflectors. In either case, clamp-on sockets will let you move the lights readily.

Don't be reluctant to experiment a bit with these lighting combinations. Sometimes, for example, you may find that a fill-in light can be replaced with a white reflective cardboard positioned to catch some of the illumination from the main light and bounce it back into the dark side of the face. It may be enough to open up the dark areas without a third light.

If there is something in the background that you want to be visible in the picture (a bookshelf, for example, or a painting), you must give it special attention. It may require a light of its own: just enough to make it clear, but not enough to let it become a too-important part of the picture.

Electronic flash or flashbulbs can be used successfully for portraits, too. Their light is of such short duration, however, that it's hard to tell exactly where the shadows will fall on the subject. Some electronic flash units are equipped with modeling lights which provide a sort of preview. But most aren't, and you'll have to depend upon experience and experimentation to get the light to fall where you want it.

If you use flash and a fairly sophisticated camera, remember that the light need not remain stuck at the top of the camera. Extension cords, available at little cost, enable you to operate the light at a distance from the camera, and this opens up all sorts of creative possibilities. Try moving the light in toward your subject and, instead of hitting the subject with head-on illumination, bounce the light off a white card or sheet. The resulting reflected light will surround your subject with a more natural-looking and more flattering illumination, and it will reduce contrasty highs and lows.

As an alternative, you can try head-on flash, but with a sheet hung between the light and the subject. This will spread and soften the light, too. In either case, remember that when you illuminate your subject by indirection much of the light is lost *en route*. You'll need to compensate by opening up your lens one, two or three stops, depending upon the amount of light loss.

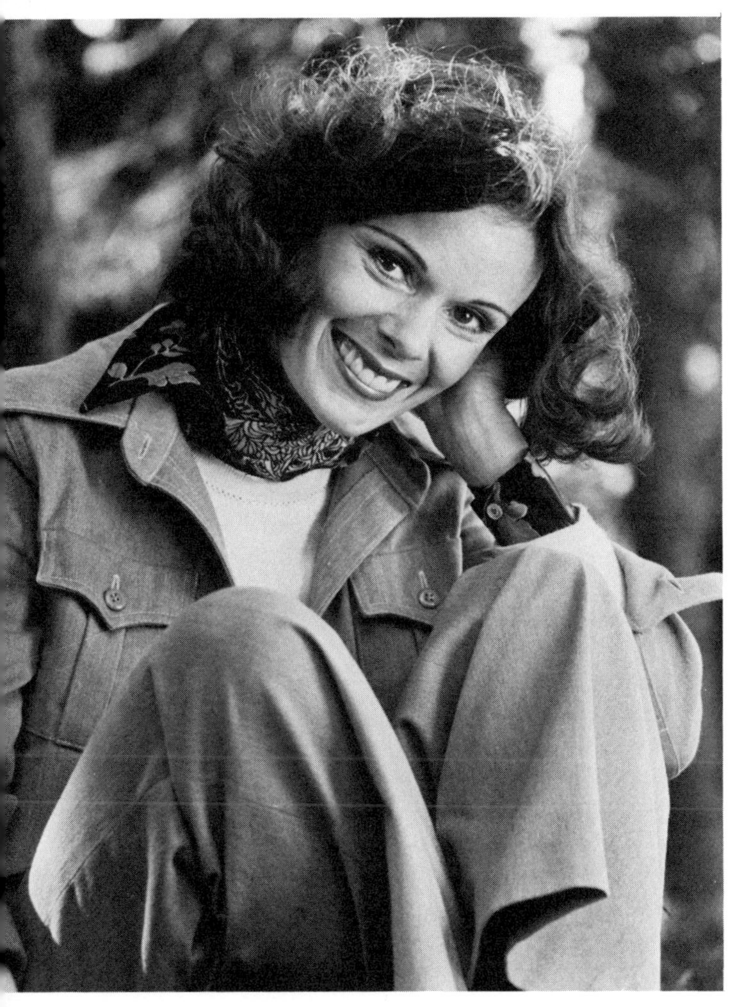

This informal outdoor portrait takes advantage of the soft light of open shade. A lens opening of f/5.6 provides a fairly shallow depth of field, turning the foliage behind the subject into a pleasantly indistinct background. The subject is professional model Loren Daniels.

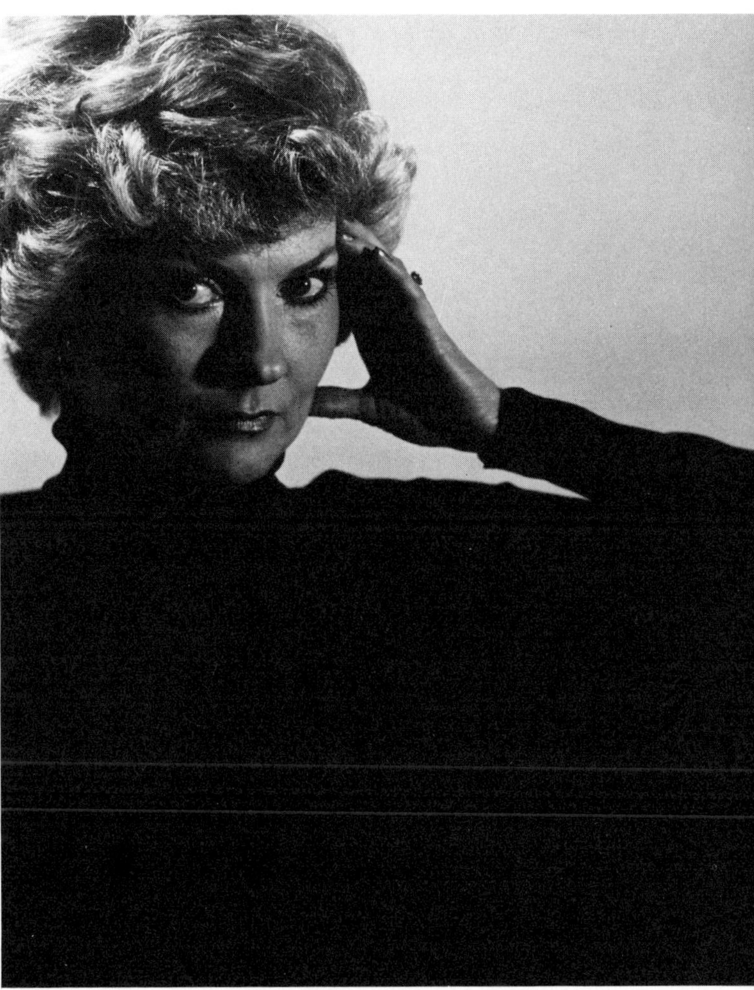

You can add mood to your portrait by deliberately introducing shadows, providing you don't let them obscure important details. In this example there is a floodlight behind the model, directed against the white backdrop to provide a strong silhouette. Another light is located above the subject and to the viewer's left, to illuminate the hair. The main light is on your right, lighting the left side of the face. The usual fill-in light is omitted, permitting the right side to disappear into shadow. The subject is professional model Bev Uselton.

PORTRAITS: POSING YOUR SUBJECT

Working with portrait subjects is another matter for a library full of books. But, again, there are some basic principles that all photographers agree on, and which can help give your pictures a professional look.

Taking your time is one of these principles. Time to get your model relaxed and time to make mistakes and then correct them, and to fuss with lighting and exposure. If the atmosphere is casual, if the mood is cooperative, and if no one feels pressed, the pictures you take will show it. Models who are new to you will need time to get beyond the initial stiffness and formality of a picture-taking session. Sitters who know you won't require this softening-up process.

Costuming and makeup are other areas where you must take charge. It is important that trendy hairdoes and costuming should be avoided: a look at any fifteen- or twenty-year-old high school yearbook will illustrate the point. All those beehive hairstyles and neck chains and Nehru jackets and harlequin glasses date portraits badly and give them, even after a few short years, a quaint and curious look. Today we view them with tolerant amusement, but we never get around to seeing the subject, except as a prop for the adornments. Stay clear of such faddish hairstyles or clothing unless you *want* a period look.

Bizarre lighting and artificial poses have the same effect. A good portraitist, professional or amateur, is always careful to see that nothing about the picture, including his own photography, becomes more attention-getting than the subject's face and personality.

There are, of course, such things as group portraits, and posing problems multiply when you're trying to arrange several people into a collective and attractive whole. Some of them will fall easily into a natural-looking pose, but others will require attention. Some will end up on the outer edges of the picture, and so you may have to see that they're getting the right amount of light. Others will blink or look away just as you hit the shutter button. All of them will have to be told what to do with their hands.

The same rules apply, with perhaps one other: make lots of exposures. You're fighting greatly increased odds when you're shooting a group, and it's no time to be sparing of film or time. Unlike the professional, you have the luxury of taking as long as you want, and you should take advantage of it.

Finally, you're ready to make your exposure, and this, as always, is the easiest part. As a rule, it's a good idea to shoot portraits at a fairly wide lens opening: around f/5.6, for example. This is because the opening will produce a somewhat shallow depth of field. The eyes, face and nose will be in sharp focus, while objects behind the head will quickly become pleasantly fuzzy and unobtrusive, the head emerging from the background clearly and separately. If you use a smaller lens opening, say f/8 or f/11, remember that you are greatly increasing the field in which things are in focus, and details in the background will be brought out more sharply.

Inspect the picture you've composed through your viewfinder. Is the pose a good one? If the hands show, are they logically positioned? Are there any unwanted shadows under the nose or brows, or falling across the face? Are those things buttoned that should be buttoned? Is everything that doesn't belong in the picture out of it, like light cords or floodlight supports?

Then shoot, using the eyes as a point to focus on. Then, for safety's sake, bracket your exposure by opening up one lens stop and making a second exposure, then closing down one stop and making a third.

Finally: vary the pose and shoot some more. Shoot the entire roll of film. You'll find as you go along that your subject will relax—and so will you. The result will be a multiple choice, and among them will be some portraits you hadn't thought you were capable of making.

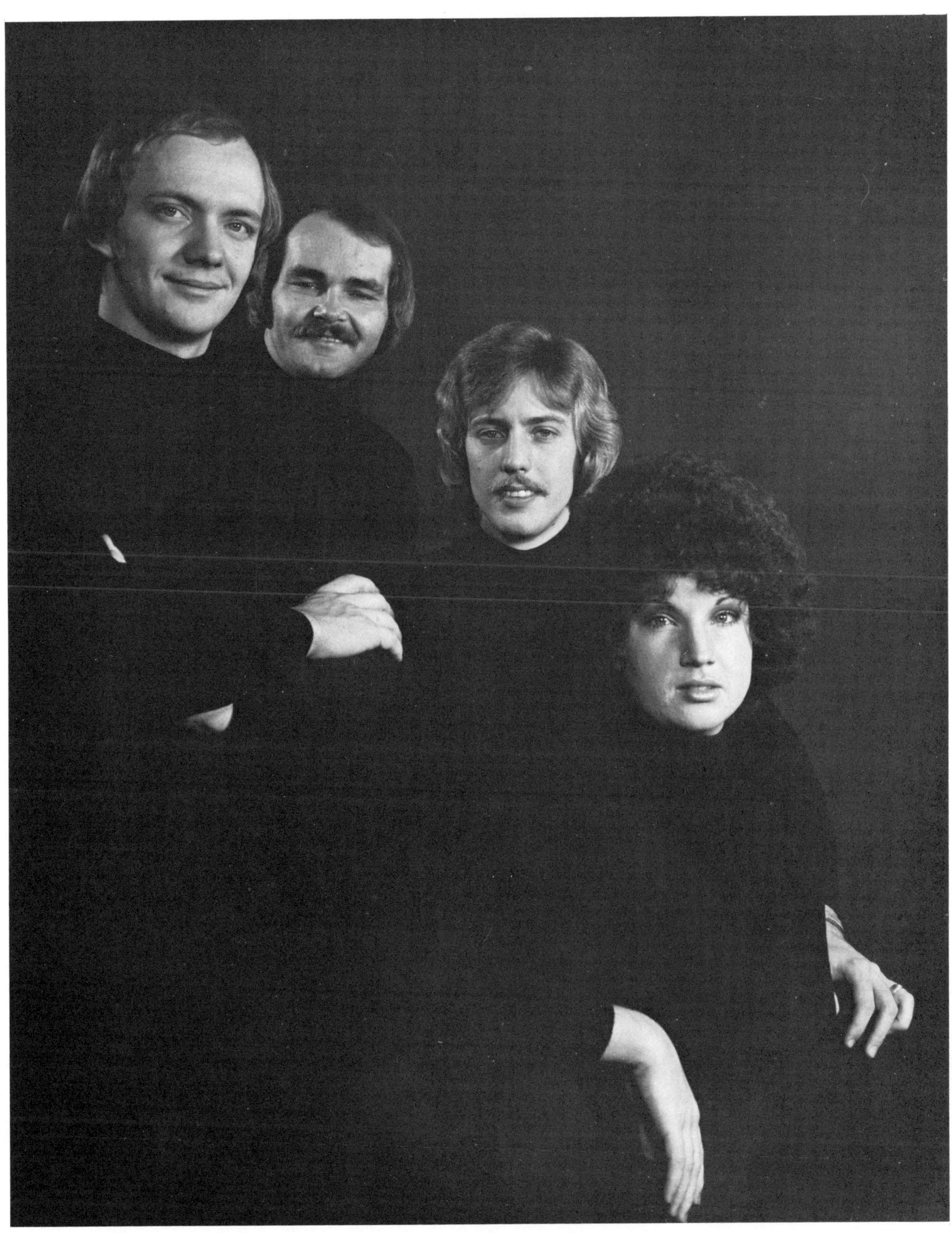

Group portraiture presents problems of its own in lighting and posing. Composition is important, too: in this example, a great deal of attention has been paid to the placement of the hands, which are almost as important to the design as are the faces. This is a musical group called "The Arrangement."

INFORMAL PORTRAITS OF CHILDREN: THE ADVANTAGES OF OUTDOOR LIGHT

At least half the pictures in most family albums are of children. It's not surprising, since children are still what a family is for, and most parents come equipped with a strong urge to record on film the growth of the child from infancy to the teens.

Even so, too many parents, after they've acquired a camera especially for the purpose, never get beyond the "for-the-record" snapshot: young Buster, a little too far away from the camera, a little blurry, and sometimes difficult to sort out from the surrounding scenery. In most cases it's all they expect from themselves and their equipment, and they rely on infrequent formal studio portraits for a clear look at what Buster looked like at three or eight or twelve.

It's too bad, because twenty years later it's the informal portrait that seems to remind you mostly poignantly of what the child was really like, and not the formally posed studio picture. Too bad, too, because both parent and camera are really capable of better pictures.

Why not try it, before Buster grows up? You'll need a camera, film, patience, and sunlight. If your camera is a single-lens reflex, you can remove the normal lens and replace it with a moderate telephoto. This is an advantage because it lets you keep some distance from the child and still get fairly tight closeups. Inexpensive portrait attachments are available for many cameras with built-in lenses. If close-up lenses are not available, however, you can do perfectly well with the normal lens. You'll just have to be a little craftier about getting close to your subject without distracting him.

For a first attempt at child portraits, try going outdoors on a good day. You won't have to fuss with artificial lights and you can concentrate on the youngster. You'll do better in open shade than bright sunlight because it eliminates heavy shadows and squinting eyes.

If your camera permits, try a faster shutter speed than you might normally use, say 1/250 sec. It will compensate for your own unsteady hand and, because children move unexpectedly and quickly, it'll freeze their action. But remember that when you opt for a faster shutter speed you should open up your lens to compensate for the resulting loss of light. Today's fully automatic cameras will do the whole thing for you. Some cameras with meters will indicate the setting to use. If you have no meter, check to find out what the instruction sheet packed with your film has to say about exposures in open shade.

If you are shooting color slide film, you may want to be sure that your lens is fitted with a skylight filter. They are very useful in open shade, since they subtract a lot of the blue inherent in daylight. They also minimize the excess blue reflected from snow, and they reduce the bluishness of distant scenes. Camera stores carry them, they're not expensive, and they will not affect your lens settings.

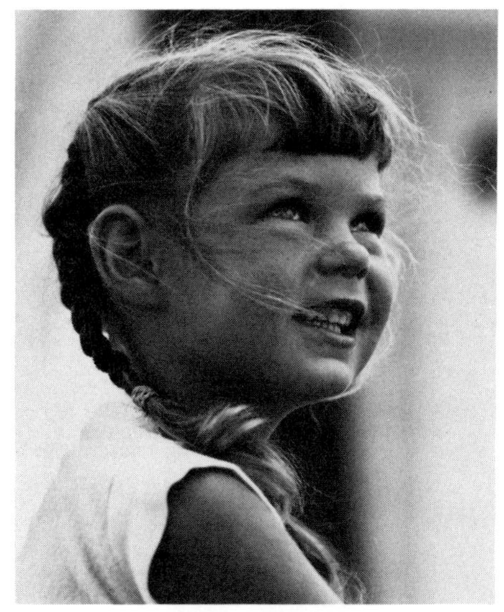

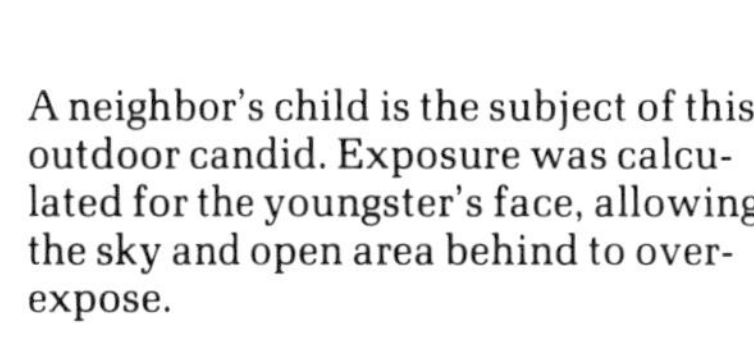

A neighbor's child is the subject of this outdoor candid. Exposure was calculated for the youngster's face, allowing the sky and open area behind to overexpose.

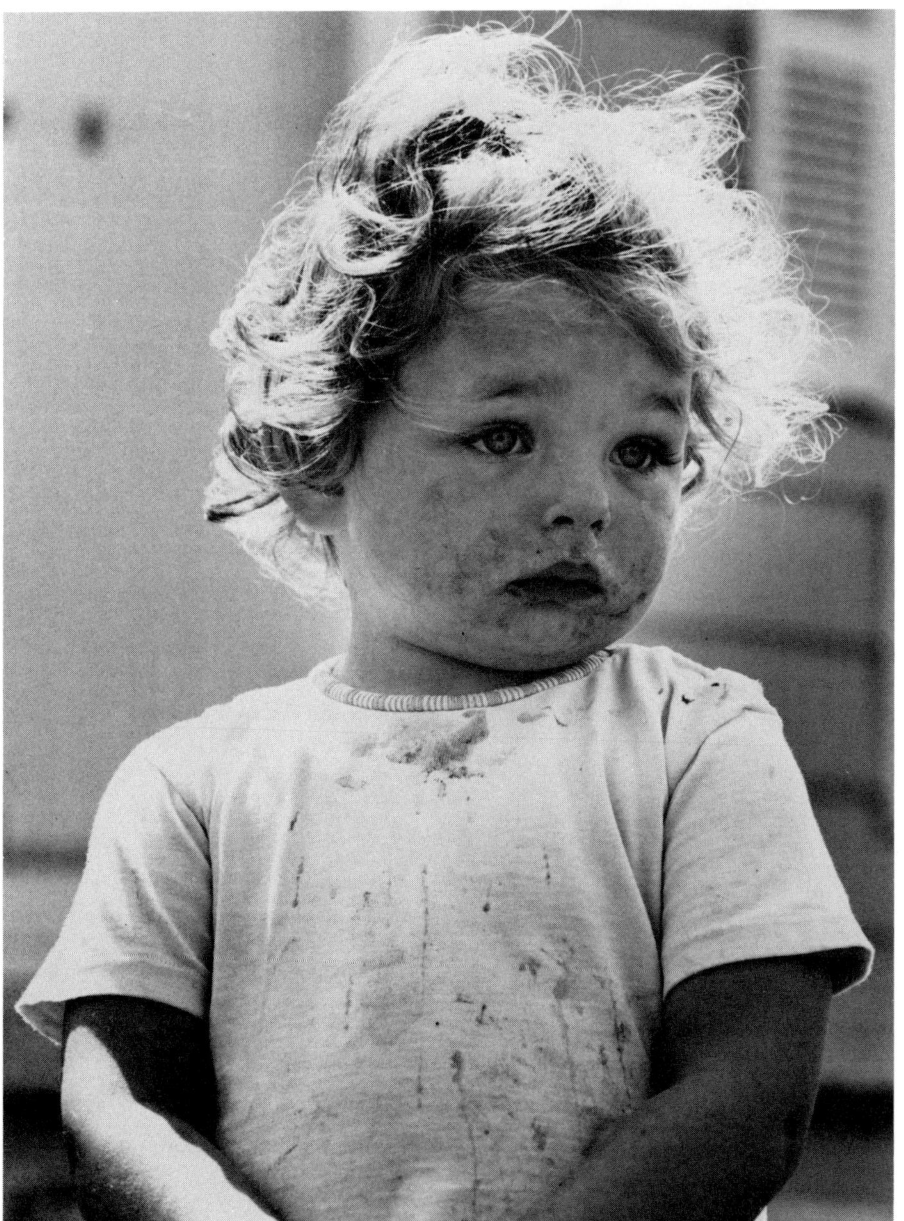

Nowhere is it written that children must be well-scrubbed and dressed up to have their pictures taken. Every family album needs pictures like this one as a counterbalance to those solemn, stiffly-posed formal portraits that really tell very little about how your child is different from other, ordinary kids.

INFORMAL PORTRAITS OF CHILDREN: COMPOSING THE PICTURE AND MAKING THE EXPOSURE

Your manner with the child is important. A quiet, unhurried confidence should mark everything you do. Let your subject get used to your presence and to the fact that you're carrying a camera. If you don't make an event out of it, the youngster will soon lose interest in you and get around to more important matters.

The younger the child, the less attempt should be made to "pose" him. Indeed, if the picture is to be candid, let it be candid. Posed pictures of children usually have a peculiarly manipulated look, and they reveal the child not as he naturally looks but as some adult thought he ought to look.

In framing, try to fill the viewfinder with the picture you want. This will tend to eliminate much extraneous clutter—foreground and background, trees and telephone poles—that have no business in the picture. Look for nice, neutral backgrounds, like walls or bushes that will sort of fade back and not interfere with the subject. Focus and frame with care. If your camera won't permit focusing, keep at least about five feet from your subject—any closer and you'll get a fuzzy image. If your camera is a rangefinder type, with one lens to view through and another to shoot the picture through, you must remember that parallax becomes critical as you get closer to your subject. The views through the "taking" lens and the "viewing" lens can't converge at close distances, and so the picture seen in the viewfinder is not precisely the same as the one you're actually getting. Some rangefinders correct for this automatically and others have lines etched in the viewfinder to help in framing closeups. With a single-lens reflex, of course, you won't have to think about it, since what you see in the viewfinder is exactly what you get on film.

As the child settles down and becomes preoccupied with other things, watch for your chance. Older children can be give a minimal amount of direction, like. "Can you see that bird on the branch over there?" which serves to get them looking where you'd like them to look. But with younger children you must wait for your opportunity.

Plan on shooting your entire roll of film. The cost of film and processing is minimal compared with the results you can get. Make lots of exposures. If you're in any doubt about lens openings, do it again at another setting before the chance is lost. All professionals do that: they shoot at the aperture their meter suggests; then, as a kind of insurance, they open up one stop and shoot again. Finally, they close down one stop below the meter recommendation and shoot again. It's called "bracketing," and it helps make certain that one of the three exposures will be exactly right.

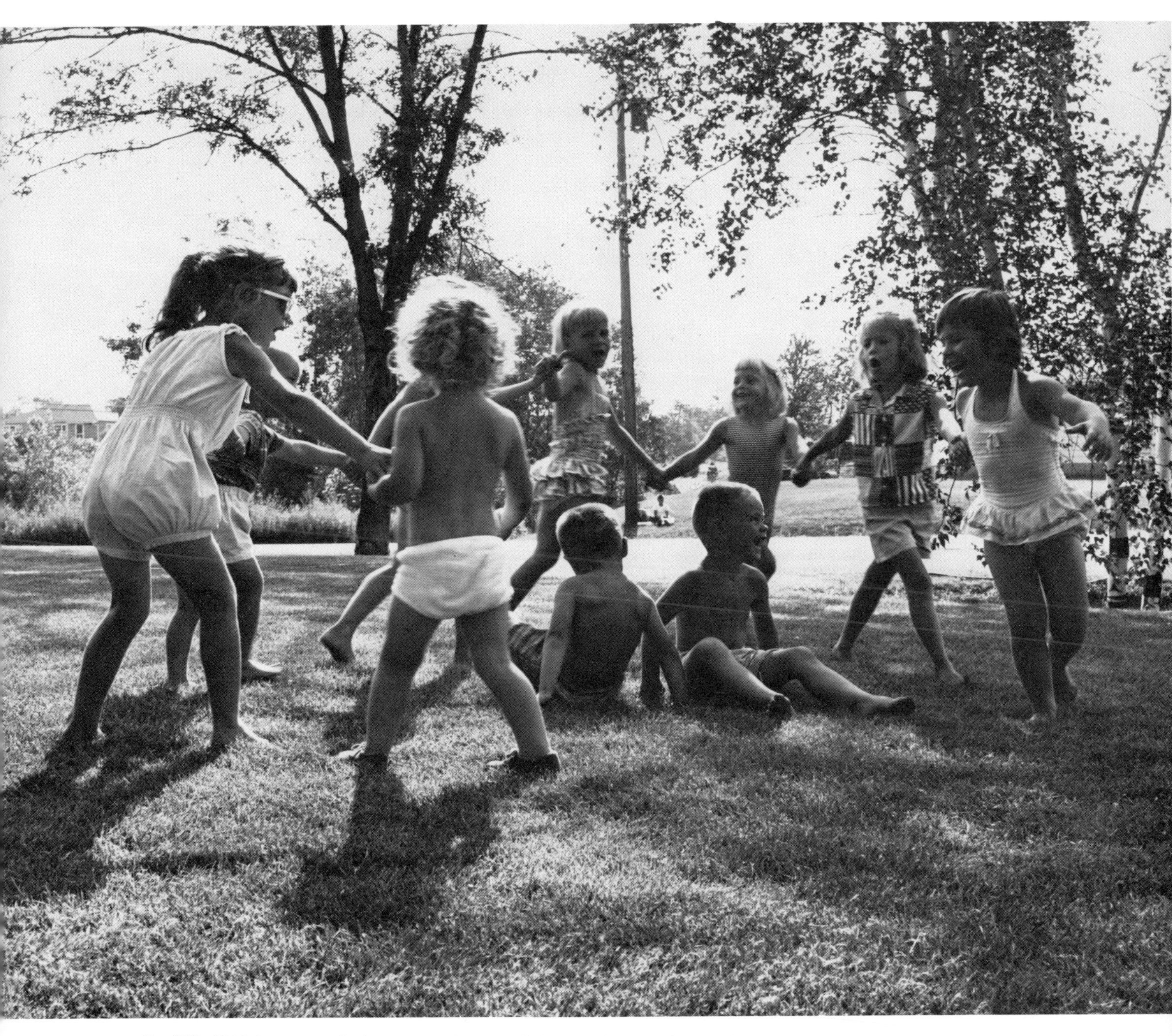

You'll find kids in groups a little easier to photograph than singly, since they tend to divert each other and forget you more quickly. For this sort of action you'll need a shutter speed of 1/125 sec. or faster.

PET PORTRAITURE

Much of what is true about photographing children is also true about photographing pets. You need a great deal of patience if you want more than a mere over-the-shoulder snapshot. At the same time you must be prepared to shoot at an opportune moment, recognizing that children and animals move abruptly and unpredictably.

If you're outdoors, open shade provides a good, soft lighting for animal candids, and it eliminates extreme lights-and-darks in which the subtle details of coloring can be lost. If you're indoors, try to photograph your subject by indirect light for the same reason.

Electronic flash or flashbulbs do not work very well for animal portraiture unless the light is reflected off a low ceiling or a nearby wall. Direct, head-on flash tends to wash out the area closest to the camera, while the more distant portions go dark. It also often produces a round circle of light in the center of the subject's eye, the result of light being reflected from the choroid layer behind the retina. In humans it's a red dot, and the phenomenon is termed "red eye" by photographers. In animals, the effect is to make their eyes look like Little Orphan Annie's.

If you use flash, turn it away from the animal and direct it toward a wall or ceiling. This will surround your subject with light and produce a much more natural, three-dimensional effect. Note, however, that if the wall or ceiling is colored, the light can pick up the color and it may affect the color of your picture. Also, since the light must travel farther to reach the subject, you must compensate by opening up your lens. The amount of compensation is determined by the intensity of your flash unit and the distance the light must travel to get from its starting point to the reflector and then to the subject.

But the truth is that animal portraits look much more logical when taken outdoors against natural backgrounds. Use a relatively fast shutter speed if you're employing natural light: 1/125 or 1/250 sec. If your camera can be fitted with a moderate telephoto lens, use it. It will enable you to get in tight on the animal without approaching him closely, and it has the added advantage of causing the background to blur into unobtrusive shapes and colors.

Now, about patience. Let the animal get used to your presence. Allow it to sniff around for awhile as you maintain a discreet distance. Avoid ordering it around or trying to fit it into a pose. Sooner or later it will settle down and, while its attention is occupied by something else, you'll be ready.

If you're using a light meter, remember to take your reading off the animal: exclude the light behind him. And shoot several exposures, varying your lens opening by one or two stops. This will increase your chances of getting the perfect pose and the perfect exposure.

If possible, look for a chance to photograph your subject against a neutral, uncluttered background—a fence, a wall, or some bushes. And try to get down to the animal's level: a "person's-eye view" of a dog or cat tends to show much of the animal's back and the ground, but it doesn't offer much information about the creature's personality.

Finally, take your time and shoot the whole roll of film during the photo session. The animal will lose interest in you and your camera, and the odds in favor of a salon-style portrait will increase. Then have the completed roll processed promptly. Don't leave it in the camera or on a shelf because the latent image is degraded by time and heat.

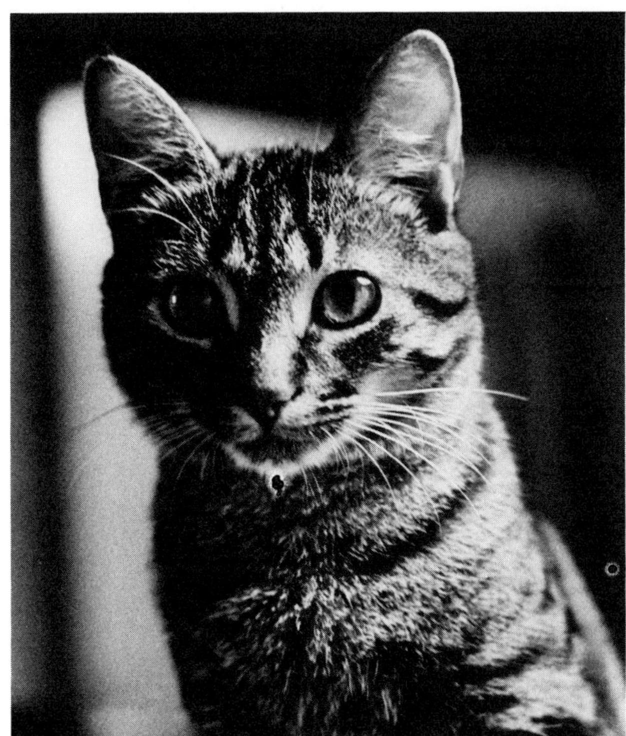

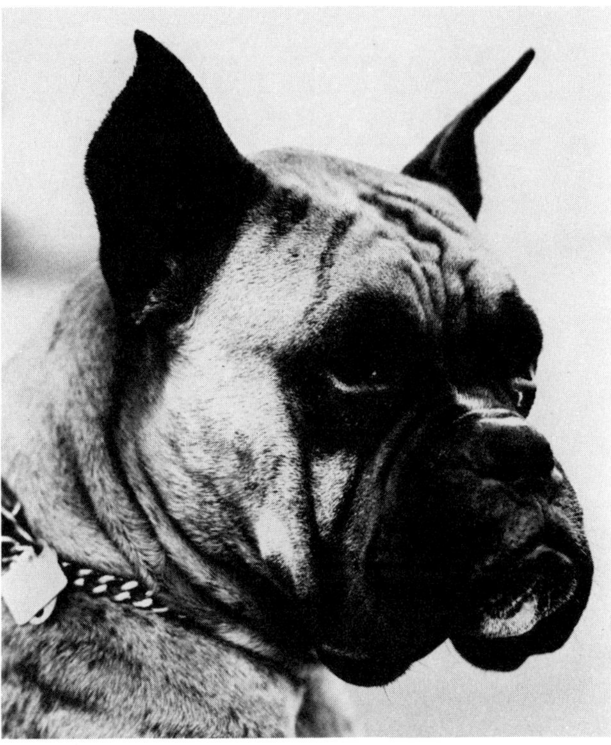

Left: "Red eye" in your animal pictures can be avoided by eliminating flash and using available light. This cat was photographed indoors by the light from a window. There was not much of it, however; which meant that the picture had to be made at a very slow shutter speed and at the lens' widest opening. *Right*: An adult animal's character, like a person's, is in its face. Don't hesitate to move in as close as your camera will let you.

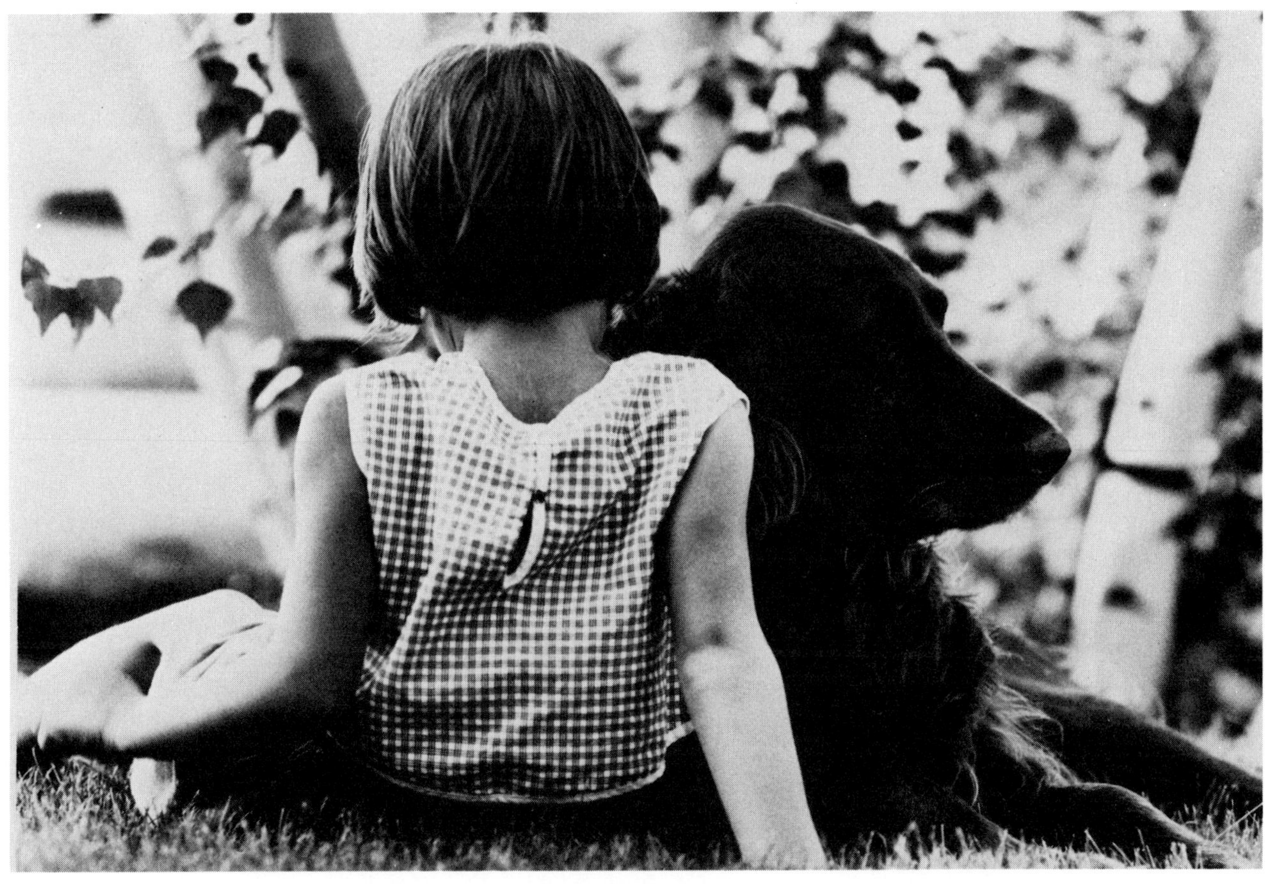

Animals and children are a photographic cliché, but they're an irresistible cliché. You'll do best if you avoid giving directions. Just be patient, and look for your chance.

HOLIDAYS: SOME GENERAL SUGGESTIONS

Many amateurs tend to think of their cameras only when special events occur. Holidays, for example: after Christmas and Thanksgiving the amount of developing and printing done by commercial film processing laboratories increases markedly for a while, and then it tapers back to normal until the next holiday.

A high percentage of these pictures are what you might expect: the Christmas tree, visiting relatives at Thanksgiving, the kids in their Halloween costumes. They're all good subjects, of course, and they deserve their place in the family album, but there's no reason why you shouldn't look for new ways to document these traditional events. Here are a few suggestions.

Be ready for the holiday. Mostly, this means being sure you've got plenty of film. If you intend to project your pictures on a screen, slide film is what you'll need, but remember that excellent prints can be made from your favorite slides. It works the other way, too: if prints are what you're after, you should use negative film—but if you decide you need them, you can have slides made from the negatives at little cost.

A good, all-purpose negative film is Kodak's Kodacolor 400. It works very well in situations where you have no control over the lighting. You can mix daylight, which is blue, with warm tungsten and cold fluorescents and still get warm, convincing colors.

Take care that your flash attachments are in good working order, with fresh batteries, because you may find yourself in situations where a fast film won't be enough to let you get the picture without supplementary light.

When you're using flash, remember to check your background before making the exposure. If there's a window, a mirror or a highly varnished door or wall behind the subject, you can wind up with unpleasant highlights just where you don't want them. The light from your flash can bounce off the shiny surface and back into your lens, producing a big patch of reflected light right in the middle of your picture.

And watch out for "red eye," which occurs when your subject is looking directly at the camera. It's best avoided by bouncing the light off the ceiling, by removing the flash from the camera and directing it at your subject from an angle or, easiest of all, by having your subject look at something other than the camera.

If you're trying to photograph a large area, such as a room full of people, try the bouncelight method. Just point the light at a nearby wall, or at the ceiling between you and your subject, so that the light is reflected back on the scene you're shooting. It will spread the light over a much broader area and provide a much more natural look.

But remember that when you do this you're making the light travel much farther to reach the subject. Much of it will get lost on the way, so you must compensate by opening up your lens to a larger aperture. The exact opening will depend upon the flash-to-subject distance. But play it safe, if the picture's an important one, by bracketing your shot: make the exposure, but then make two more, one at an f-stop higher and another at an f-stop lower than the first.

Will you be photographing children? Kids are an important part of any holiday, and it would be surprising if some of them didn't show up in your pictures. You can improve your kid pictures immensely by keeping a few ideas in mind.

FIRST: GET DOWN TO THEIR LEVEL. A six-foot adult photographing a three-foot child produces a peculiarly truncated view unless he gets eye-to-eye with his subject. Bend a little.

SECOND: DON'T POSE THEM. You'll get a livelier, more natural shot if you simply stalk your subject until you see what you want and then shoot. In this context,

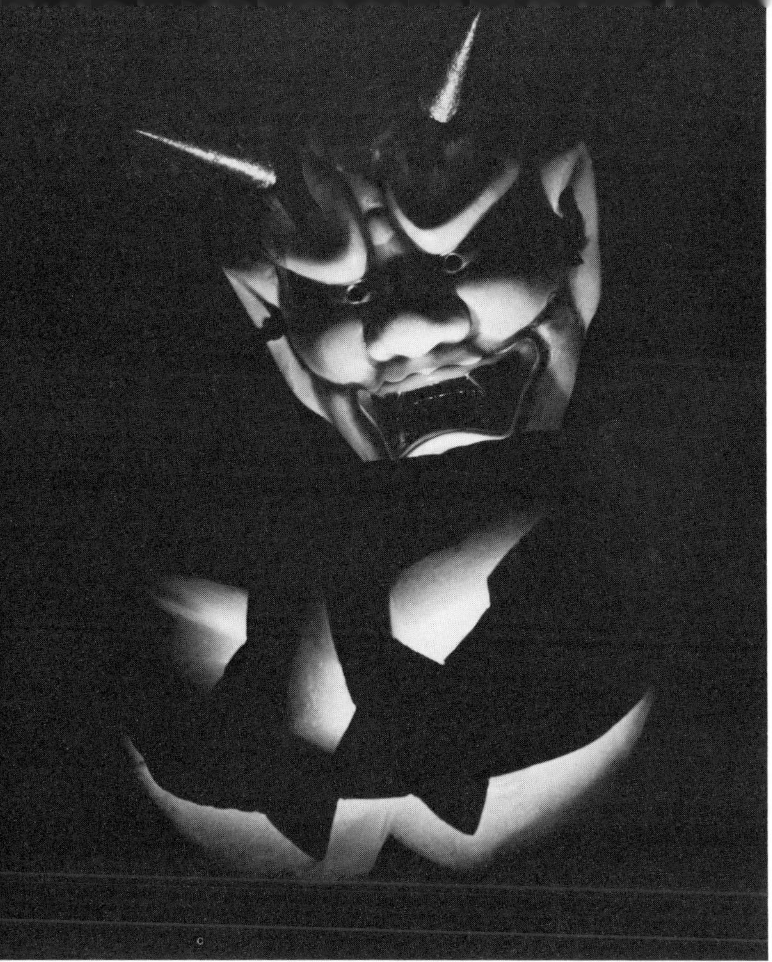

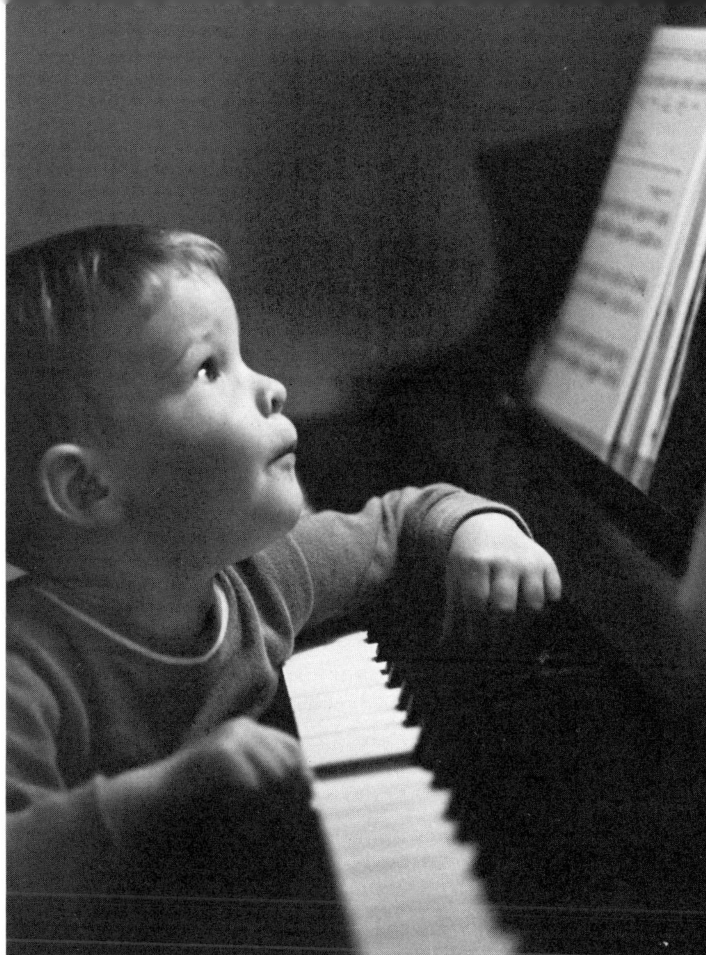

Left: You can build effective holiday pictures from props common to the season. In this case, a Japanese mask and a jack-o'-lantern were combined to make a simple but dramatic picture. The only light used came from the candle in the pumpkin. The picture required a fast film and a two-second exposure, with the camera resting on a firm support. *Right*: Children get up to all sorts of things at parties and family get-togethers. This one wandered away from the crowd and found a piano, and gave the photographer the chance for a very simple, very quiet picture.

incidentally, there's something else to be said: beware of the hovering parent who will spot what you're doing and rush forward to give the child directions. "Smile, Mary Ann!" the parent will say. "Hold still! Straighten your dress! Uncle Sidney wants to take your picture!"

Send that parent to his or her room until you've got the picture you want.

THIRD: GET IN CLOSE UNTIL WHAT YOU SEE IN YOUR VIEWFINDER IS EXACTLY RIGHT. This sounds obvious, and it is, but it has to be thought about. When you're planning a picture you tend not to see the odds and ends surrounding your subject, and in your mind's eye you see only the subject itself. But the camera can't do that. It will dutifully record everything in front of it. It is you who must do the editing. You must frame your picture so that the irrelevancies are not there in the first place. This usually means moving in tightly, trying several angles until you find the right one, and checking to be sure the background is neutral and unobtrusive. Otherwise, you'll lose the child amid all the clutter.

Will you be photographing groups? Does it have to be one big group, or can you break it down into clusters of three or four? Often you'll get a better, more complete record of the festivities if you fragment the job instead of trying to record everything in one or two grand, comprehensive shots. Make sure that you get everyone in one or another of the pictures, but go for a mosaic rather than a panorama.

Speaking of group shots there's no reason to leave yourself out of them. If your camera's equipped with a time delay, use it. Just set the camera on its tripod, frame the picture carefully, set the shutter delay, press the exposure button, and give yourself ten or twenty seconds to take your own position in the picture.

HOLIDAYS: SOME SPECIFIC SUGGESTIONS

CHRISTMAS. There is no holiday more productive of good picture-taking opportunities than Christmas. Even so, most of us remain pretty haphazard about it, and if we get any good pictures during the season it's mostly luck.

Maybe we'll shoot one or two pictures of visiting relatives if we think of it. Or we might get a picture of the kids opening their presents. And does anybody remember whether there's film in this camera, and what kind it is, and how long it has been there?

There's probably a party or two scheduled over the year-end, but maybe somebody else will remember to bring a camera, and if they get anything good we can get a print made from their negative. Right?

Wrong. If you want to sit down twenty years from now and enjoy looking at pictures showing how it was in the good old days, you'll have to remember that, sooner or later, *these* are the good old days. If you want pictures of them, you'd better count on doing it yourself.

Try to exercise a little imagination in documenting Christmas holidays. Certain subjects are obvious: the tree, the kids, guests, and the Christmas gifts. But be on the lookout for the little things that make the season memorable, too: a snow-covered créche, the litter left under the tree after the packages are opened, or a child's preoccupation with a Christmas-tree ornament.

You can give the tree an uncommon look by putting the flash attachment away, turning off the room lights, and photographing it by its own lights. The camera will need an extremely steady support for the prolonged exposure called for: use a tripod or rest the camera on a firm table. If you're using color film, try the kind that's balanced for daylight. The lights of the tree will register warmer in tone and be more pleasing than the colder effect produced by tungsten film.

You can get colorful, almost abstract effects by moving in closer to the tree and limiting your shot to one or two lights, some ornaments, and perhaps a bit of tinsel in the background. Try several angles before you make the exposure to see what happens in your viewfinder to the shapes and colors picked up by your lens.

THE FOURTH OF JULY. This holiday affords a once-in-a-year chance to photograph fireworks after dark. Again: support your camera on a tripod. Set your lens at infinity and aim at the area in the sky where the fireworks are appearing. Then merely open your lens and leave it open while several displays are set off. You'll catch a series of unpredictable but very dramatic patterns on a single frame of film.

Remember that the "B" setting on your camera opens the shutter and leaves it open until you release the pressure, and that the "T" setting lets you open it and leave it open until you press the button a second time. If you don't have "B" or "T" settings, try giving the first display of fireworks a one-second exposure. Then, without advancing the film, re-cock the shutter, wait for the next display, and give it another second on the same piece of film. And then a third and a fourth exposure.

If your camera is one that won't let you double expose deliberately, consult your owner's manual. There is almost always a way to permit intentional double exposures. With most 35mm cameras you can do it by pressing in the rewind button under the camera while operating the film-advance lever. This cocks the shutter, but prevents the film from moving forward in the camera.

EASTER. This holiday offers you an obvious opportunity to preserve photographically the flower arrangements or potted plants common to the season. Shoot the pictures by a sunny window (floodlights are hard on flowers). Use a white card, off-camera, to bounce some sunlight back into the shady side of the subject. Or see what happens when you put a colored sheet or card behind the floral arrangement to provide a complementary, neutral background.

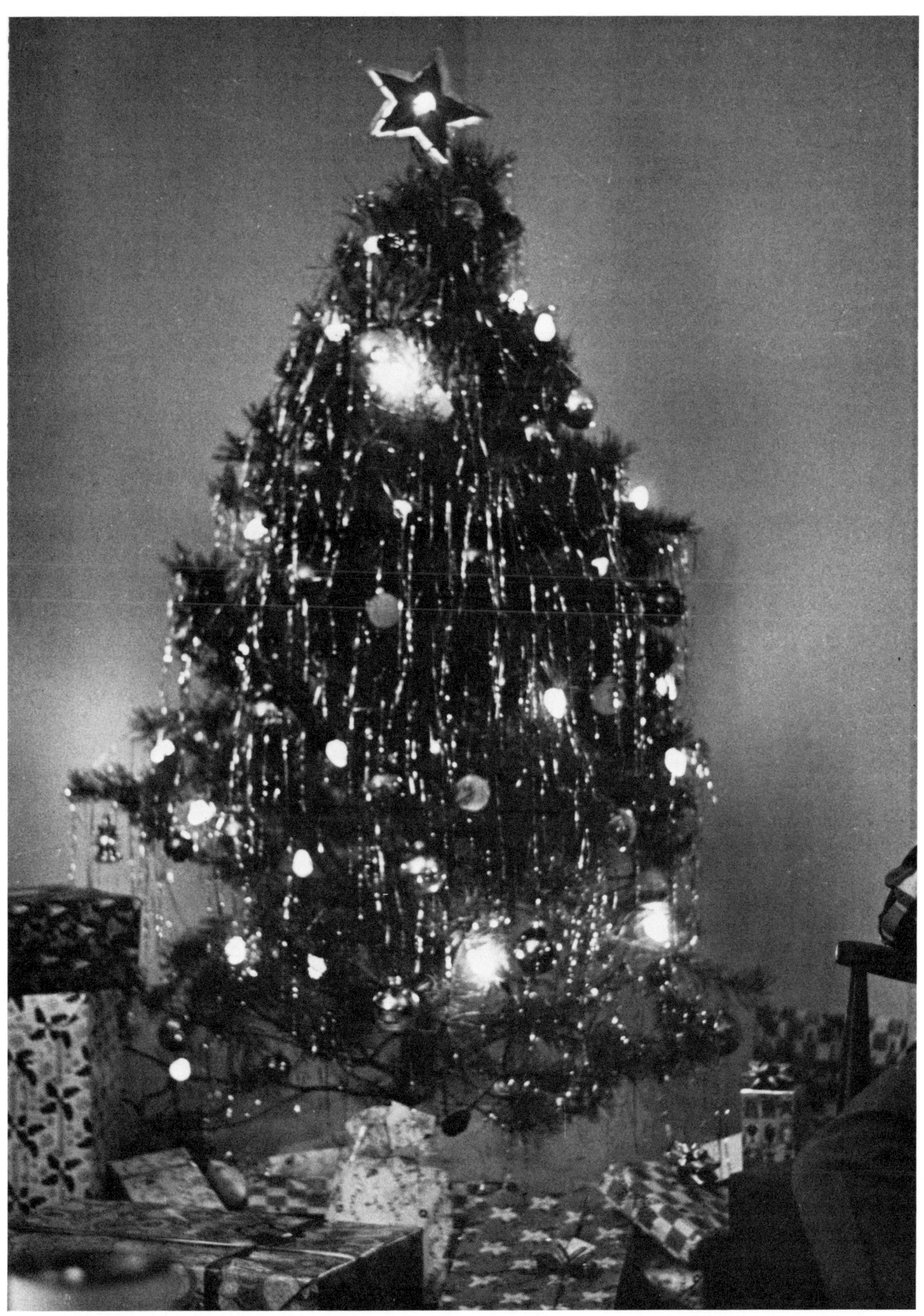

When photographing the Christmas tree, give the tree an uncommon look by photographing it by its own lights.

PHOTOGRAPHING ACTION: HOW TO STOP MOVEMENT

When you leaf through a book of nineteenth-century photographs you're likely to be struck by the forbidding appearance of the people who appear in it. There they stand or sit, rigid, remote and unsmiling. "They were different than we are," you think. "They were more serious, more austere. They were a sterner, no-nonsense generation."

Not really. You must remember as you look at them that they were having their pictures taken, and that they had just been told to compose themselves, to hold perfectly still, and not to blink.

That's the way it had to be. Film emulsions were slower and time exposures were necessarily longer. Everyone had to hold still if they didn't want to come out blurred. In the old family photographs it's usually the children who show up a little fuzzy. They didn't take orders as well as the adults, and they often moved during the exposure.

But it has been a long time since "Hold it!" was a necessary part of the photographer's instructions to his subjects. Films are faster, cameras are smaller and more sophisticated, and all sorts of supplementary lights are available. Today even the simplest cameras are capable of capturing movement. All the photographer needs to know is how to take advantage of the fact.

Most simple cameras with a fixed, or non-adjustable, shutter speed are set at somewhere between 1/50 and 1/125 sec.—fast enough to stop moderate motion. 1/125 sec. for example, is enough to freeze the pace of a person moving slowly.

A more sophisticated camera will offer a range of shutter speeds, often from one second to 1/500 or 1/1000 sec. To stop a diver in midair or a shortstop fielding a fast grounder 1/1000 sec. is enough.

Cameras equipped with electronic flash (often called "strobes") will permit even briefer exposures. When you use strobe, it is the light and not the shutter that determines the duration of the exposure, and most strobes range between 1/1000 and 1/10,000 sec.—a speed fast enough to stop a bird in flight.

Strobe lights and fast shutter settings make it easy for even the most unskilled photographer to freeze almost any kind of movement if he'll take the trouble to use the equipment properly. But even without such equipment, movement, and excitement can be added to pictures by keeping in mind a couple of rudimentary facts about photographing action.

For one thing: *the closer the moving object is to you the faster the shutter speed you'll need.* A racehorse passing you at a distance of fifty feet might require a shutter speed of 1/250 sec. to stop the movement satisfactorily. At ten feet, however, you might need 1/1000 sec.

For another thing: *objects coming toward you or going away from you do not require as fast an exposure as those moving at an angle to your camera.* A bicyclist heading toward you can be stopped without excessive blur at a much slower shutter speed than one crossing your line of sight.

A third thing: *with some movements there is a peak of action at which movement is momentarily slowed and during which it is possible to arrest motion at a slower shutter speed.* A diver, for example, reaches a point at which upward movement ceases and downward motion begins. There is a split second when direction changes. At that point, action can be stopped with relatively slower shutter settings.

Some action, however, has no such peak points. This is where you must have recourse to faster shutter speeds, or, as we shall see, other devices.

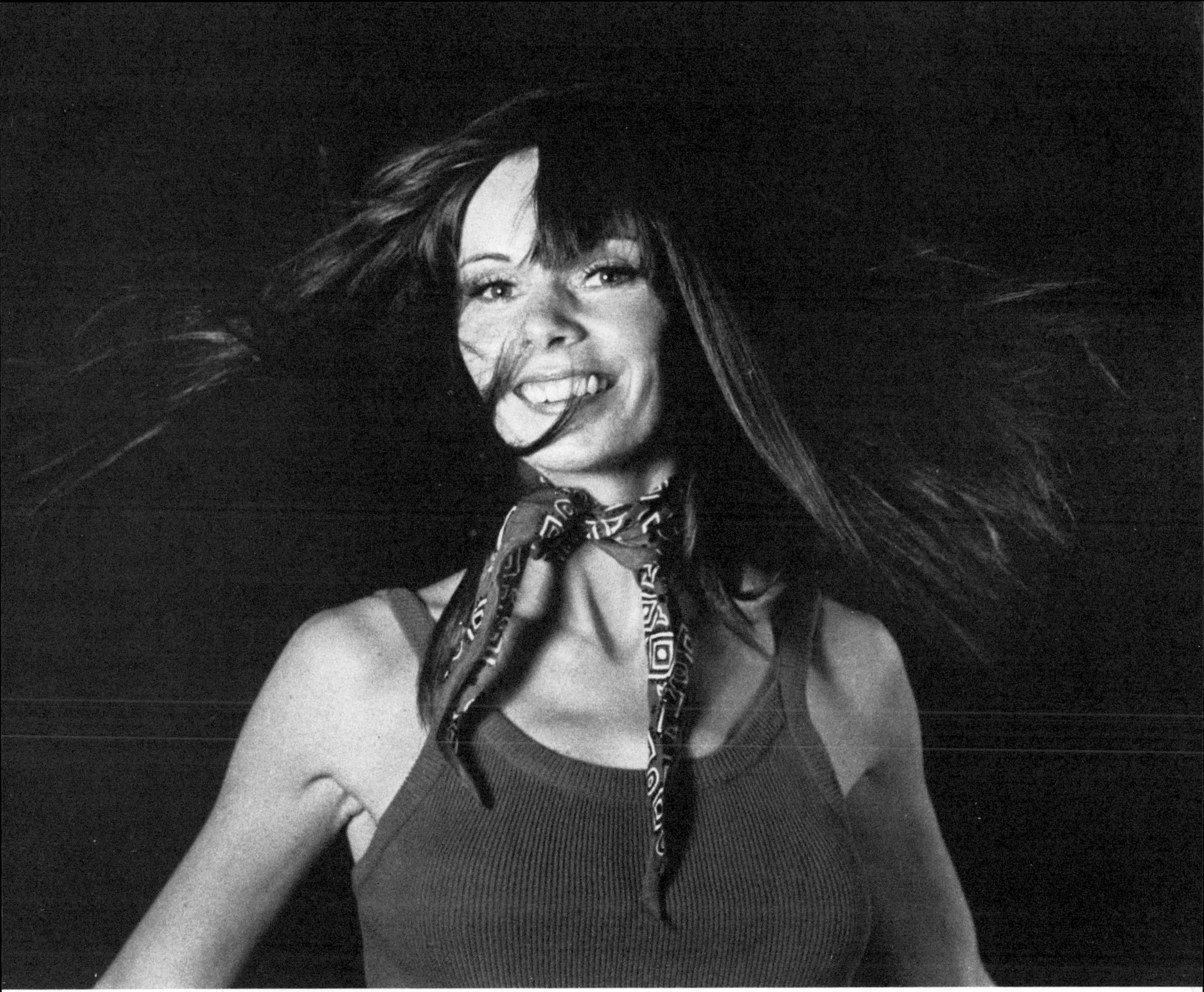

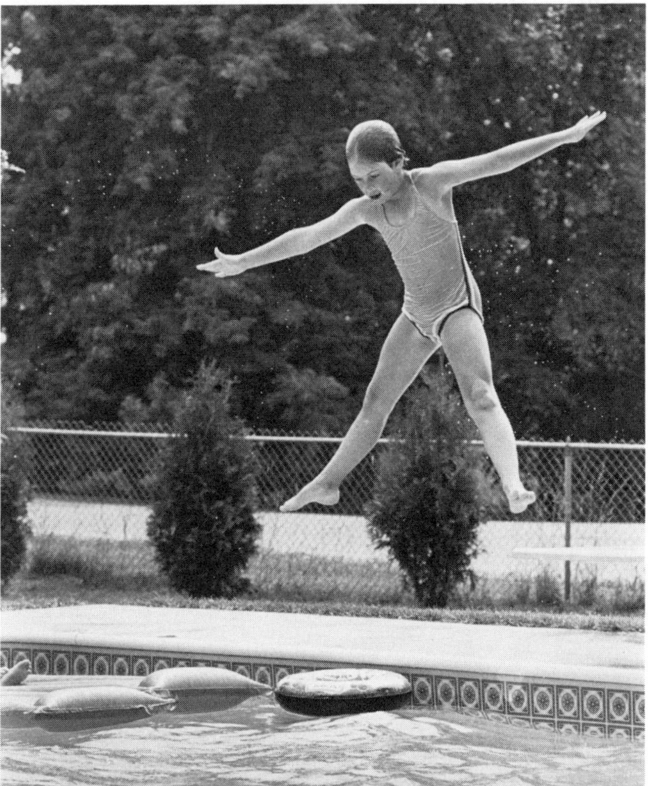

Left: This action photo of a young swimmer demonstrates how a fast shutter speed combined with fast film can stop movement in mid-flight. The shutter speed was 1/1000 sec. *Above*: Electronic flash permits exposures of 1/1000 a sec. or faster—enough to stop the movement of model Loren Daniels' hair and freeze the expression on her face.

PHOTOGRAPHING ACTION: CREATIVE USE OF BLURRED IMAGES

It is important, when you're photographing movement, to ask yourself how frozen the action really ought to be. With electronic flash or fast shutter settings it is relatively easy to bring everything in your picture to a dead halt. But is "dead" what you want? Detail might be desirable in photographing a hummingbird in flight if its body structure is the point of your picture. But if you want to say something about the bird's incredible speed, you might prefer to render it just as the eye sees it, with blurred wingtips.

Similarly, a photograph of a runner crossing the finish line might communicate more of the excitement and strain of the race if his legs and arms are allowed to blur. This is the creative aspect of action photography: making your photograph do more than merely record the details of movement.

Shooting action at slower shutter speeds can be made easier if you can anticipate the pattern of the movement and station yourself in the best place to capture it on film. All professional action photographers do this as a matter of course. They will find their location, take their light readings and make their camera settings, and anticipate the exact point at which they will make their exposure.

Then they will prefocus, if possible. That is, they will let several runners pass while they focus their lens carefully as each runner passes a given point. Having done this, as the next runner enters the frame, they make the shot. The aim is not to try to focus on the runner as he moves, but to be ready for him as he comes into focus.

Extremely effective action pictures can be made at very slow shutter speeds by deliberately violating one of the old clichés of photography. Instead of holding the camera rock-steady, try panning with the subject. In other words, follow the subject as though you were shooting motion pictures. Do it smoothly, pivoting at the waist, and keeping your subject centered in the viewfinder. With this technique you can make exposures at shutter speeds as slow as 1/15 sec. Done right, the result will be a blurred background with the central subject defined clearly. This can be a very satisfying kind of action picture, since the sense of speed is communicated effectively while the blurring of the background minimizes visual distractions.

And the technique is a good one to know because you don't have to own a three-hundred-dollar camera to get the picture. Even an old Brownie box camera will do perfectly well.

Action photography, like all photography, is a matter of balancing shutter speed with the film's speed (a "fast" film is merely one more sensitive to light than a "slow" film) and the light available to you. You must remind yourself that when you increase your shutter speed you reduce the amount of light reaching the film. This in turn means that you must compensate by opening up your lens to a larger aperture to let more light in.

In action photography, all of this is made much easier by using a faster film. At your camera store ask for film that has an ASA rating of 400. And then go out and see how good an action photographer you are.

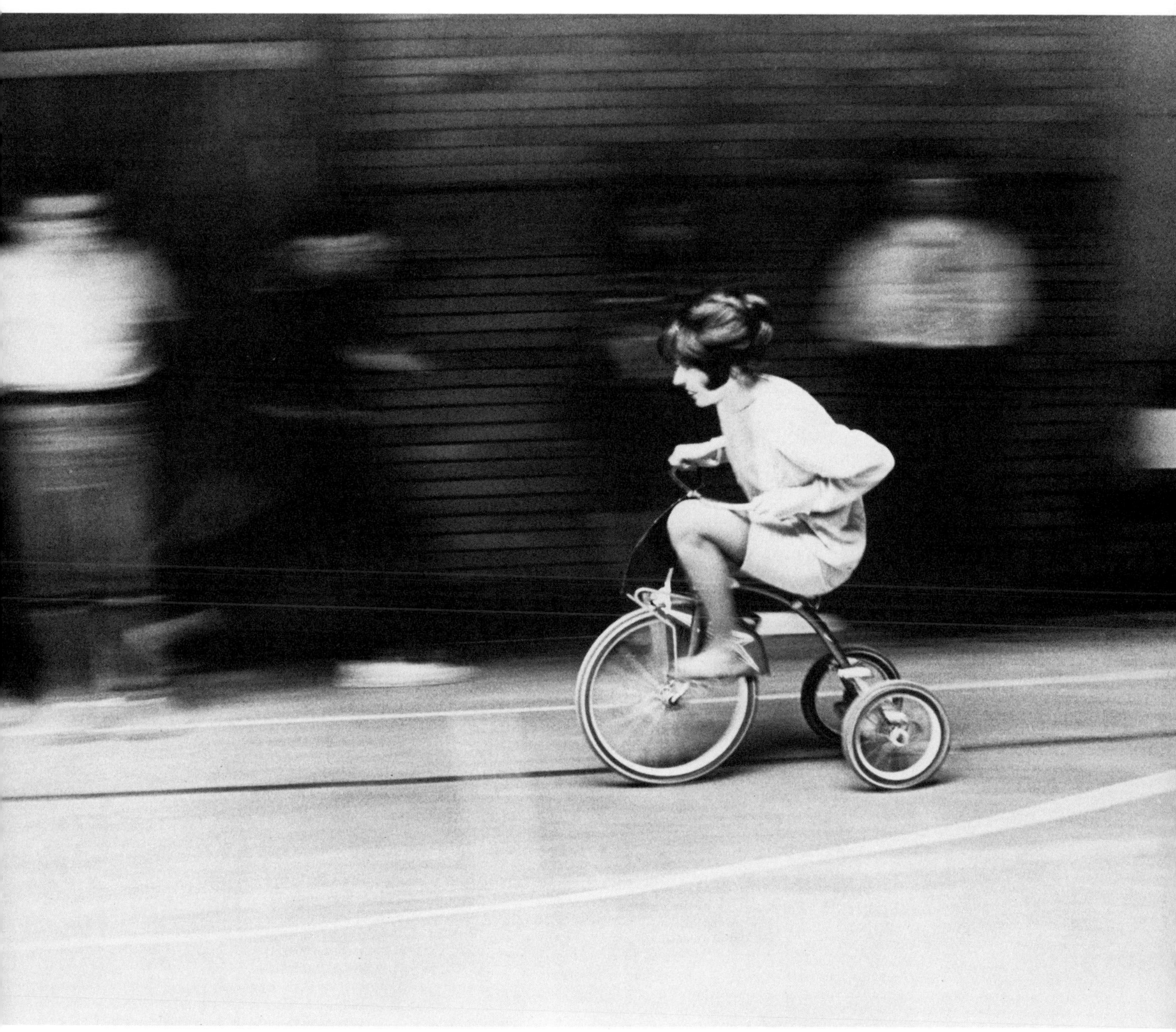

Panning with your subject allows exposures at very slow shutter speeds. This tricyclist was photographed at 1/15th sec. The blurred background enhances the impression of speed, yet the subject is acceptably sharp.

STILL-LIFE PHOTOGRAPHY: LIGHTING, COMPOSITION, EXPOSURES

Still-life photographs are often called "tabletops," and for good reason: a tabletop is a convenient place on which to set up your picture. The table should be broad enough to contain all of the elements you plan to include in your shot, and then some. You will want to be able to move your camera about as you search for the best angle, and you don't want a sudden table's edge interrupting your composition. Allow yourself plenty of space on and around the table.

You'll also need to think carefully about a background. A long roll of seamless paper can be valuable because it can be used to form the surface on which your subject will appear and also as a backdrop. You merely lay it out on the table top and then curve it upward to create the background.

A roll of fabric or carpeting can be used in the same manner if you want your background to have some texture. If you're shooting color, you'll want a background that complements the subject.

For starters, set up a floodlight on each side of the table top to illuminate the picture area. Then lay out the objects in a tentative arrangement. Pick a camera angle and study what you've got through your viewfinder.

You may need to move your camera backward or forward to frame the picture properly. Then, as you study the layout through the camera's viewfinder, you will begin to make such decisions as "that smaller piece needs to be moved forward where it can be seen, and that larger piece has to go to the rear of the layout."

Slowly an aesthetically satisfying composition should emerge. When you see in your viewfinder just about what you want, you must then turn your attention to lighting, because it is the lighting that will give your photograph depth and feeling.

The two floodlights, arranged symmetrically, will produce a flat, evenly lit picture, which may not be what you want at all. Try turning one of them off. Is the picture too light on one side and too dark on the other? What happens if you leave both lights on but move one farther away from the table? Or if you turn one off, leave the other on, and place a white cardboard just outside the picture to catch the light and reflect it back into the dark side?

What happens if you interpose a sheet of white cloth between light and subject to soften and diffuse the light? Or if you turn one or both lights *away* from the subject, using white cardboard reflectors to bounce the light back into the picture? Or if you raise or lower one light, or both, or change their positions?

The point of all this, of course, is to suggest the infinite variety of devices you can use to manipulate the light, to direct it where you want it, and to block it off from areas where you don't want it.

The best still-life photographers have always treated light as though it were plastic and malleable. They use it to give depth and texture to their pictures, and to direct the viewer's eye precisely where they want it to go. There are dozens of books available on composition and lighting for still-life photography, and they are helpful. But there is no substitute for trying it yourself.

Finally: when everything is arranged to your satisfaction, you must double-check everything in your viewfinder before making the exposure. Are shadows blocking off important parts of the picture? Are shiny surfaces reflecting things they shouldn't be reflecting? Is your lens aperture set at an opening small enough to allow sufficient depth of field, so that everything will be in sharp focus?

A great deal of patience and self-discipline is needed for successful still-life photography. If you try it, you may wind up finding out as much about yourself as about photography. If you don't try it, you'll miss an important and fundamental photographic experience.

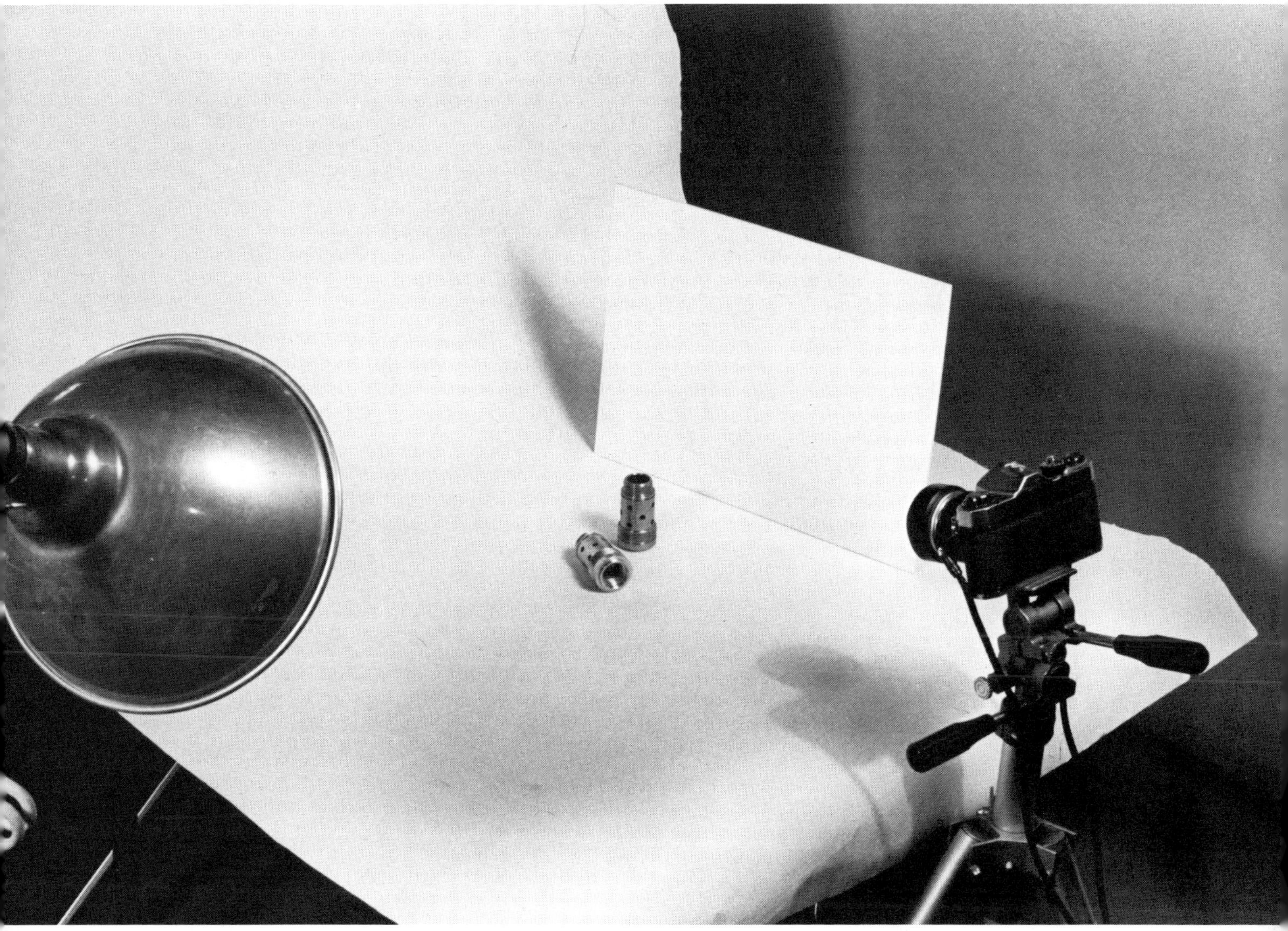

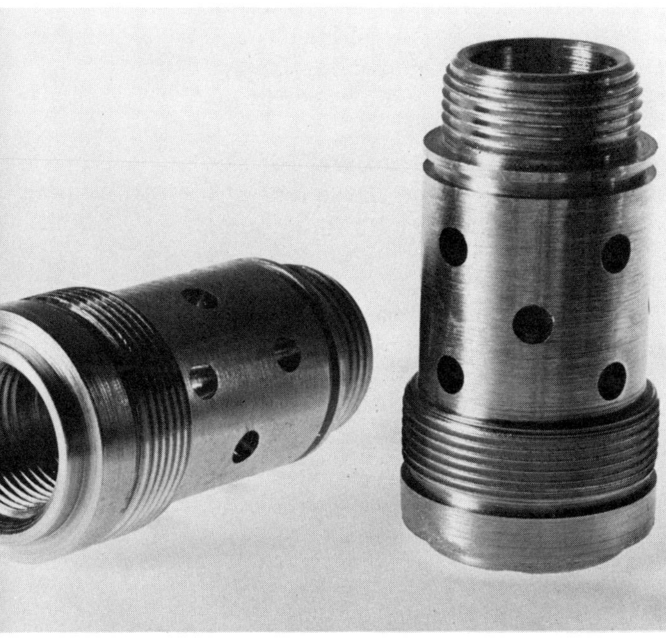

Above: This simple setup produced the accompanying still-life photo. A single lamp in a reflector is positioned to light the upper surfaces and left side of the subject, while a white card is used to bounce light back into the shaded right-hand side. *Left*: Glass and metal objects pose special problems in still-life photography because they are highly reflective. Light must be carefully controlled to eliminate unwanted shadows and highlights, and to produce a sense of depth and roundness in the subject.

LANDSCAPES AND SCENICS: WHAT YOU SEE AND WHAT YOU FEEL

To the inexperienced lensman, landscapes, and scenic views look as though they ought to be about the easiest form of photography there can be. There in front of you, after all, is the prairie or the palace or the country village you want to record on film. The sun is shining. What else is there to do but point and shoot?

But when the pictures come back from the lab, all that size and scope and color seem to have disappeared. Reduced to a small print or a slide nothing is left of the sweep of the plains or the sheer physical grandeur of the structure, and the village has become nothing but a collection of tiny buildings huddled in the distance.

Most important, the photograph utterly fails to convey anything of what you felt when you first viewed the scene and decided that anything so picturesque or so awe inspiring ought to be recorded for your album. The camera seems somehow to have trivialized what was for you an important experience.

To improve your landscapes and scenics you need to be conscious of two things: you must understand what is going on in you when you feel impelled to photograph a landscape, and you must learn what can be done, technically, to transfer as much as possible of that feeling to film.

To turn the snapshot into a memorable photograph, however, requires some serious attention to the manipulation of a number of elements.

THE TIME OF DAY. There is a world of difference between a picture of a country lane photographed at high noon and the same lane photographed at dusk. In the one picture the shadows are strong, the path is clearly defined, the trees and foliage are warm and brightly lit. In the other, the shadows are long, leaves and branches merge together in the gloom, and the path ahead fades into darkness. Everything is changed. Well, what will you have? What do you want your picture to say? Clearly, you must pick the time of day carefully, depending upon the atmosphere you want your picture to communicate. If it means getting up at six a.m. or waiting until nightfall, that's the way it must be.

COMPOSITION. In selecting the most effective point of view you must also teach yourself to examine the scene in minute detail through your camera's viewfinder. Are there power lines or telephone poles or other unwanted elements interfering with your composition? If a feeling of depth is required to give the picture space and proportion, can you use nearby elements to form a sort of frame about the picture? Or is there a path or road available that can be used to provide lines diminishing into the distance?

In composing, you need also to determine the importance of foreground and sky to the picture. A pastoral scene might require a cloud-filled sky for best effect, but an impressive waterfall might be diminished if it must compete with foreground and sky for prominence.

CAMERA ANGLE OR POINT OF VIEW. Rarely will the first view you have of your subject prove to be the best one for a photograph. For good landscapes you must be willing to examine the subject from every angle you can reach, looking for the optimum point of view. And, when you've done that, you must ask yourself whether something will be added if the view is from a very low angle, almost at ground level, or whether some elevation is needed to show the scene in its most dramatic perspective.

FOCUS. For amateurs with fixed-focus cameras there is no decision to be made about focusing. But for photographers with adjustable lenses, selecting the proper focus for landscapes is a little more complicated.

However, merely focusing on infinity will not give you the greatest *range* of sharpness available at whatever lens opening you've chosen. Instead, you should

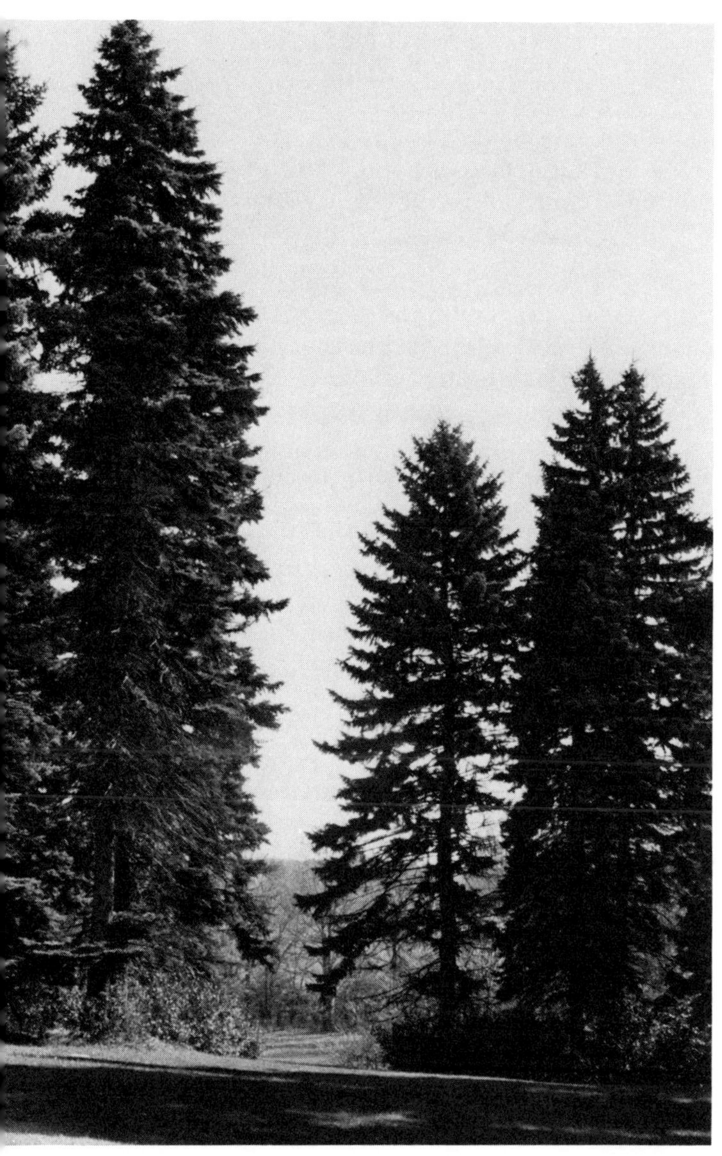

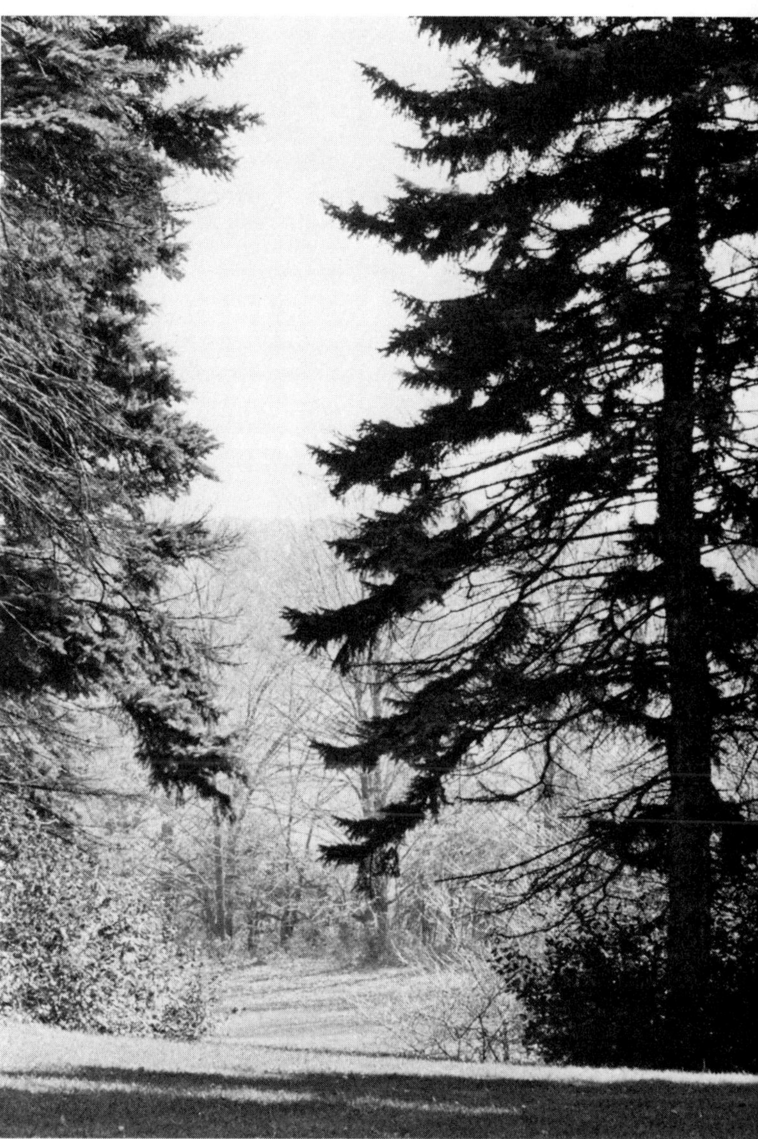

The normal lens (55mm on a 35mm camera) produces the view, above, left, which approximates what the human eye would see. This picture was made with a 135mm telephoto lens. Note that, while it pulls distant objects up closer, it also compresses the perspective, making the trees on the right and the one in the far distance look much closer than they actually are.

set your lens at its *hyperfocal distance*. To do this, you first set your lens at the "infinity" (∞) mark on the lens barrel. (On some cameras, usually those with a leaf shutter and a collapsible bellows, the focusing scale appears not on the lens but on a metal plate beside the bellows). Then read the number opposite the aperture you are using. This tells you the hyperfocal distance for that aperture. Set the lens to focus on that hyperfocal distance. Then everything in your picture will be in sharp focus from half that distance to infinity.

FILTERS. In planning landscapes and scenics, you should remember that the scene before you can be further modified by the use of filters over the lens. With color film, a polarizing filter can eliminate reflections and glare, and an ultraviolet filter can be used to reduce haze in distance shots. A skylight filter, which works only with slide film, will reduce the blue present in open shade, in snow scenes, or on overcast days.

If you're using black-and-white film, an entire range of filters is available to you. Blue skies can be darkened to make clouds stand out more prominently by the use of a deep yellow filter. A red filter will bring them out even more spectacularly, but in the process it will darken the sky almost to black. A green filter will lighten grass and leaves, and a blue filter will emphasize haze or fog.

A polarizing screen will work with both color and black and white. But filters intended for black-and-white films can't be used with color films unless, of course, you are deliberately seeking an off-beat effect. Remember, too, that when you use a filter you reduce the amount of light reaching the film, and that you must compensate by either opening up your lens to a larger aperture, or slowing your shutter speed. Each filter has its own filter factor: you multiply the exposure indicated by your meter or by the instructions packed with the film by the filter factor to get the corrected exposure. If your camera has through-the-lens metering, the meter will do the figuring for you.

LENSES. A camera that will let you replace one lens with another is a great help in scenic and landscape photography. Without changing position, you can alter the view considerably, depending upon the extra lenses you have available.

Wide angle lenses will broaden the camera's outlook, providing a feeling of expanse, of breadth and depth. Telephoto lenses produce an opposite effect: they narrow the view and pull distant objects up closer. Their effects will vary according to the focal length of the lens. The longer the lens the more it produces a sort of compacted, foreshortened look in the picture. For example, it will cause objects in the far distance and in the middle distance to appear closer together. Trees that are really quite far apart seem to be clumped together; a village located a mile from a glacier appears to be directly under it; automobiles spaced out along a highway seem to be bumper to bumper.

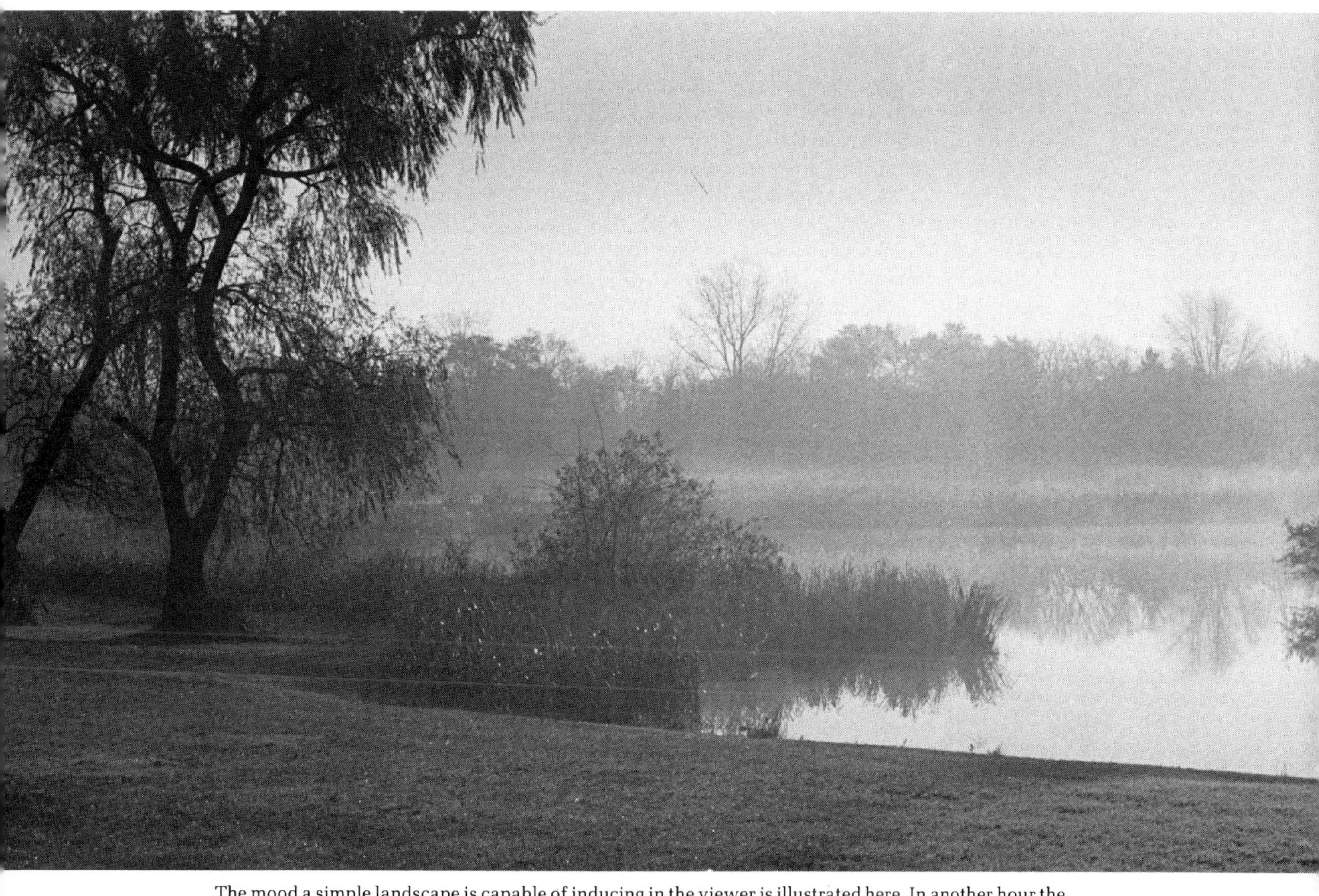

The mood a simple landscape is capable of inducing in the viewer is illustrated here. In another hour the sun will burn off the early morning mist from the surface of this pond and the scene will alter markedly. But for the moment it has the muted fragility of a Japanese watercolor.

AFTER-DARK PHOTOGRAPHY

For some reason, amateur photographers hardly ever try their hand at outdoor photography after dark. It may be that they think special experience and elaborate equipment are required, and that nighttime photography is, therefore, best left to advanced amateurs and professionals.

It's not at all true. All you really need is a good firm support for your camera (a sturdy tripod is best), a camera that permits time exposures of a second or longer, a roll or two of black-and-white or color film, and a predisposition to experiment. (If no tripod is available, the camera can be rested on a flat surface, but if you try that, use a cable release to trip the shutter. The cable release will make it possible to open and close the shutter without even touching the camera.) You won't even need a light meter, since most meters tend to get confused when confronted by lots of dark punctuated by puddles of light, and they could end up giving you wrong readings.

And nighttime exposures are very forgiving: they allow lots of latitude for error. You'll have to work hard to overexpose one.

Check out your camera first to see how to set it for exposures of one second or longer. Some cameras have a "B" (for *bulb*) setting: you set it at "B," push the shutter button and hold it down. The shutter opens and remains open as long as you keep the button down. When you release it, the shutter closes. Some cameras have a "T" (for *time*) setting: you press the release and the shutter opens. You can take your finger off the button, and it will remain open until you press the button again. It's handy when you're making exposures of several seconds, because you don't have to stand by the camera holding the button down.

Some of the newer automated cameras with built-in metering systems want to do everything for you: they read the light, figure what the exposure ought to be, and set the timing themselves. They're almost always wrong about nighttime exposures.

The trick is to outwit these marvelous electronic aids and do it your way. Consult your instruction manual to see how to by-pass the automatic metering system. Some cameras have an override switch that lets you cancel out the system and do things manually. Others have to be tricked. Sometimes you can lie to the camera about the speed of the film you're using. If the film has a fast ASA rating of 400, for example, you set the ASA dial not at 400 but at, say, 200. The camera won't know any better and it will automatically give you twice the exposure time. Or, if you set the ASA knob at 100, you'll quadruple it. (Be sure to notify the film processor how you have altered your ASA rating.)

Another way to get longer exposure time from automatic cameras that do not have a "B" or a "T" setting is to cover the CdS cell on the front of the camera with your finger. This shuts off the light to the camera's meter and lets you count off the seconds yourself.

The point is to tinker a bit with the camera at first, to see how to get extended exposures from it. A few dry runs so that you're confident about how it works, and you're ready to pick your subject and shoot.

All kinds of film are available to you: black-and-white and color; very fast, medium, or slow. For good warm color rendition in slide film, try Kodachrome II outdoor color. Ektachrome 64 works well and so does the faster High-Speed Ektachrome. Among the negative films, Kodacolor 400 combines high speed with good color reproduction. In all cases, you'll find that despite the fact that you're photographing by artificial light, the outdoor films will give you more pleasing results than tungsten (indoor) film, which delivers a colder, bluer tone.

Subject matter? City streets at night. Fairs and carnivals. Illuminated waterfalls. Open-air theater. Fireworks displays. Store windows. Signs and exhibits. Monuments. The results are often unexpectedly dramatic. Moving lights will trace patterns against black backgrounds, and lights of many colors will range from pinpoints in the distance to bright blobs of color in the foreground.

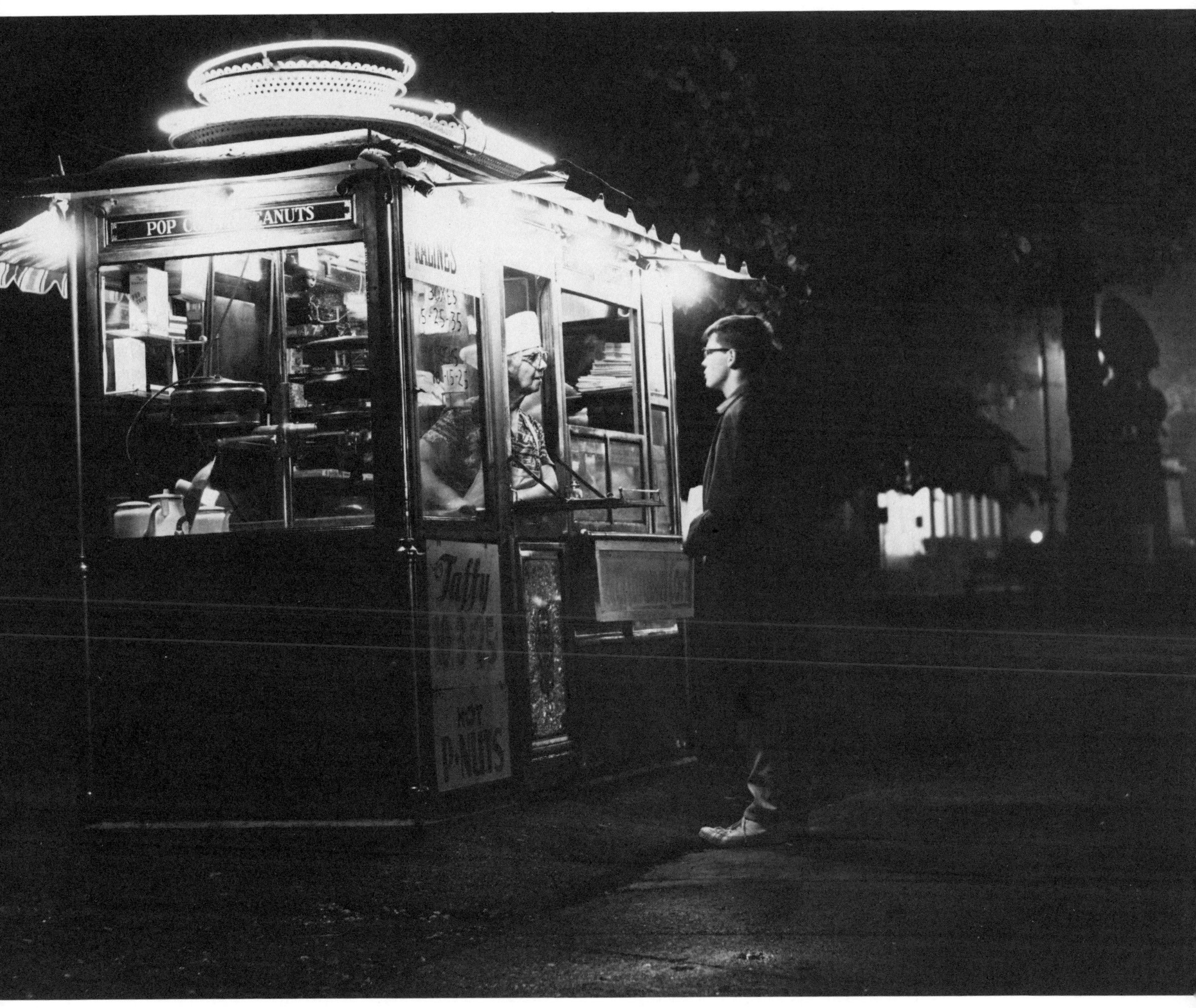

There used to be popcorn stands like this one in almost every American town. But they've almost all become part of some museum's collection—as, now, has this one. The picture was made at about ten o'clock on a summer night, and the subjects were asked to hold still for the two seconds required to make the exposure.

For starters, try framing your picture carefully with your lens opening set at f/5.6. If it's a brightly lit subject, like a busy city street, try a 1/30 sec. exposure. Then advance your film, set the time at one second, and try it again. Then again at two seconds. Then again at four, six, eight and ten seconds. If your camera will let you, try one at thirty seconds and another at one minute. And, finally, try one at two minutes. You'll have made ten exposures and, after they're processed, you're bound to be delighted with a number of them.

THE UNEXPECTED OPPORTUNITY: PICTURES ON SHORT NOTICE.

There have been times in your life when something absolutely unexpected happened—when you said to yourself, "I wish I had a picture of that!" But you didn't have your camera with you or, if you did, you couldn't get it into action in time.

And you missed the chance for what the old-time professional photographers used to call a "grabshot."

The event might have been something with no particular news value, but with a great deal of personal importance to you: a brief moment of beauty as the sun sets, or the expression of a baby's face as he meets a puppy for the first time, or the time your Uncle Sidney got his foot caught in the iron grating and they had to cut him loose with a hacksaw.

On the other hand, you might have been witness to something with genuine news (and often dollar) value. Almost daily the magazines and newspapers print photographs taken by amateurs of accidents, natural or manmade disasters, or public personalities at unguarded moments. The people who took those pictures were not professionals, but they were on the scene, they kept their heads, and they got the picture.

Often, the picture the amateur got turns out to be the only one taken of the event and, while it may not have been of professional quality, newspapers and wire services were happy to buy it.

And what if a genuine UFO showed up over your back yard and you didn't have your camera handy?

Being ready for unexpected opportunities is a relatively simple matter. You have to have your camera, loaded with film, with you. You have to be familiar enough with it to aim, focus and shoot without losing time. And you need quick reflexes and a cool head.

There may not even be time enough to take meter readings and to fiddle with lens openings and shutter speeds. Fortunately, some of the newer cameras are equipped with built-in metering, automatic lenses, automatic shutter setting, and even automatic focusing, and they'll do these things faster than you can. But even if your camera lacks these refinements you can still be prepared to grab the picture at a second's notice. Here are some suggestions:

Obviously, you must have your camera within easy reach, on the car seat beside you or on a strap around your neck. It won't help if it's packed with the luggage or stashed somewhere in the hall closet. It should be loaded and cocked. The shutter speed and lens openings should be set in anticipation of whatever might turn up.

You, of course, have no idea at all of what might turn up, so you have to make a few assumptions. You assume, for example, that the thing you'll want to photograph might be moving. Or maybe you'll be moving. Which means you'll need a fast shutter speed, about 1/250 or 1/500 sec., to stop the action.

Then you assume you won't have a lot of time for careful focusing. Therefore you'll want the smallest lens opening you can get because this will give you greater depth of field, increasing the odds that your subject will be in focus.

All of this will be made a great deal easier if you use a fast film: something with an ASA of 400, for example. It will let you combine small openings with fast shutter speeds.

It's a good idea to form the habit of resetting your camera as the light changes, going to smaller openings as it brightens or larger ones as the sun sets.

If you have a camera that offers you a choice of lenses, I'd suggest you use a wide-angle lens, if possible, since they have a greater depth of field than the longer lenses and thus will help ensure that whatever you're shooting will be in focus. A

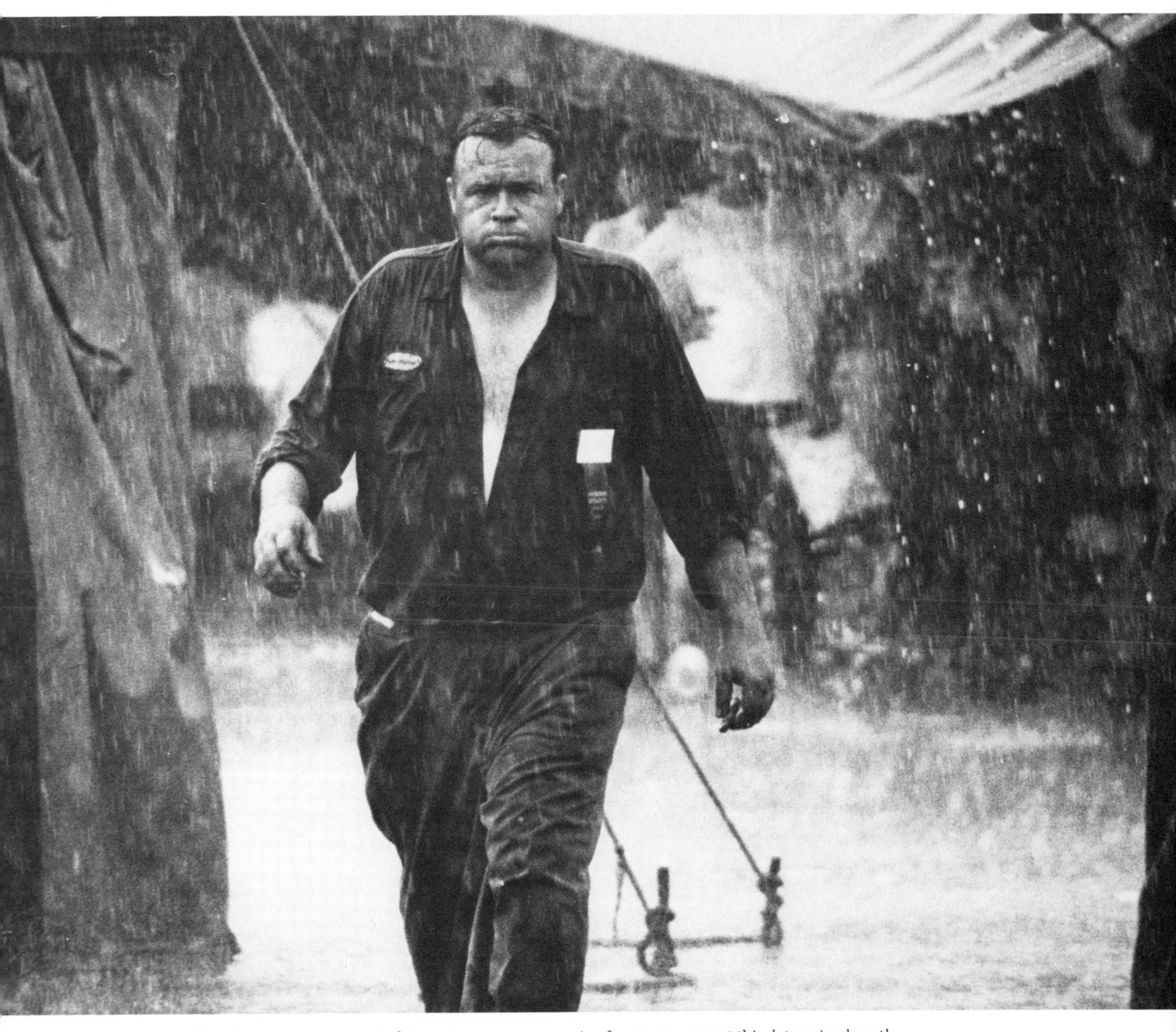

A sudden downpour at a county fair sent everyone scurrying for cover—except this determined gentleman, who declined to be put off by a little weather. It offered a brief, unexpected opportunity for an entertaining picture.

35mm wide angle has, in my experience, proved good for the purpose with a 35mm single-lens reflex.

Finally: keep cool, and keep shooting. The more exposures you can make, the greater are the odds that you'll come up with a winner. And, incidentally, if you have reason to believe that what you've shot has genuine and immediate news value, take the exposed film to the editor of your local newspaper and tell him what you've got, along with all the specific information you can give him about the people or circumstances involved in the event you've photographed.

You may wind up with a picture by-line and some unexpected cash.

EXPOSING AGAINST THE LIGHT: HOW TO BREAK THE OLD RULE

I remember very clearly when I was about ten and my parents shipped me off to summer camp for the first time. To mark the occasion they presented me with a brand-new Brownie box camera.

When I arrived at Camp Mahn-Go-Tah-See with my name inscribed in indelible ink on my underwear and everything else I owned, it turned out that *all* of us campers had a Brownie box camera. And everyone gave me the same solemn advice about taking pictures.

"The sun has to be over your shoulder," they told me.

It was the first Inflexible Photographic Rule I had ever heard. And I followed it dutifully. Today, when I look through the pictures I took that summer, I can't help noticing that everyone in them squinted a lot.

And why not? I was making them stand rigidly looking into the sun while I took their pictures. If there wasn't any sun, I didn't take any pictures. (That was Rule No. 2.)

In the intervening years I have encountered lots of Inflexible Rules about photography, and I have become persuaded that as soon as you hear a new one it becomes your bounden duty to find ways of breaking it. It is, if you're interested in giving your pictures a little more style and a little more imagination than the next person's.

Let us, for example, examine Rule No. 1 and its corollary, "Never shoot into the sun."

If the light is behind your subject you can, of course, get glare in your lens and little else . . . unless you take some simple measures to eliminate the glare and accentuate the subject. If you do that, you're likely to find that the light becomes an asset to your picture rather than a liability. It can provide a softening effect, for example, that is very flattering in portraits. Or it can separate your subject strongly from the background.

One of the easiest things you can do is to fit your lens with a sunshade. They're inexpensive and they prevent stray light from creeping in around the edges of your pictures.

Another thing you can do is move as close to your subject as you can, thus cropping out lots of daylight you don't need in the picture anyway.

And, most important: expose for the subject alone, and not the whole picture area. If you're using a hand-held light meter, walk up to your subject and read the light reflected off it. Then make your exposure accordingly. The background will overexpose into a fuzzy nothing, while the subject itself will pop out strongly against the neutral background.

If your camera is fitted with a meter that reads the light for you, do the same thing: get up close so that the only light reaching your camera's meter is the light bouncing off the subject.

If the subject is on the other side of a river or somewhere else where you can't approach it, you need only find a nearby substitute for it and meter the light reflected from the substitute. Just be sure that they're both being hit by the same light from the same angle. In photographing people from a distance, the palm of your hand works well: hold it away from you so that it's being lit as your subject is lit, take a meter reading, and do as the meter directs.

If you have no meter, the manufacturer's exposure table packed with the film sometimes offers a guide for backlit subjects. And, if you have any doubts, remember it's good practice to bracket your shots: make two more exposures, one at the next largest opening and another at the next smallest aperture.

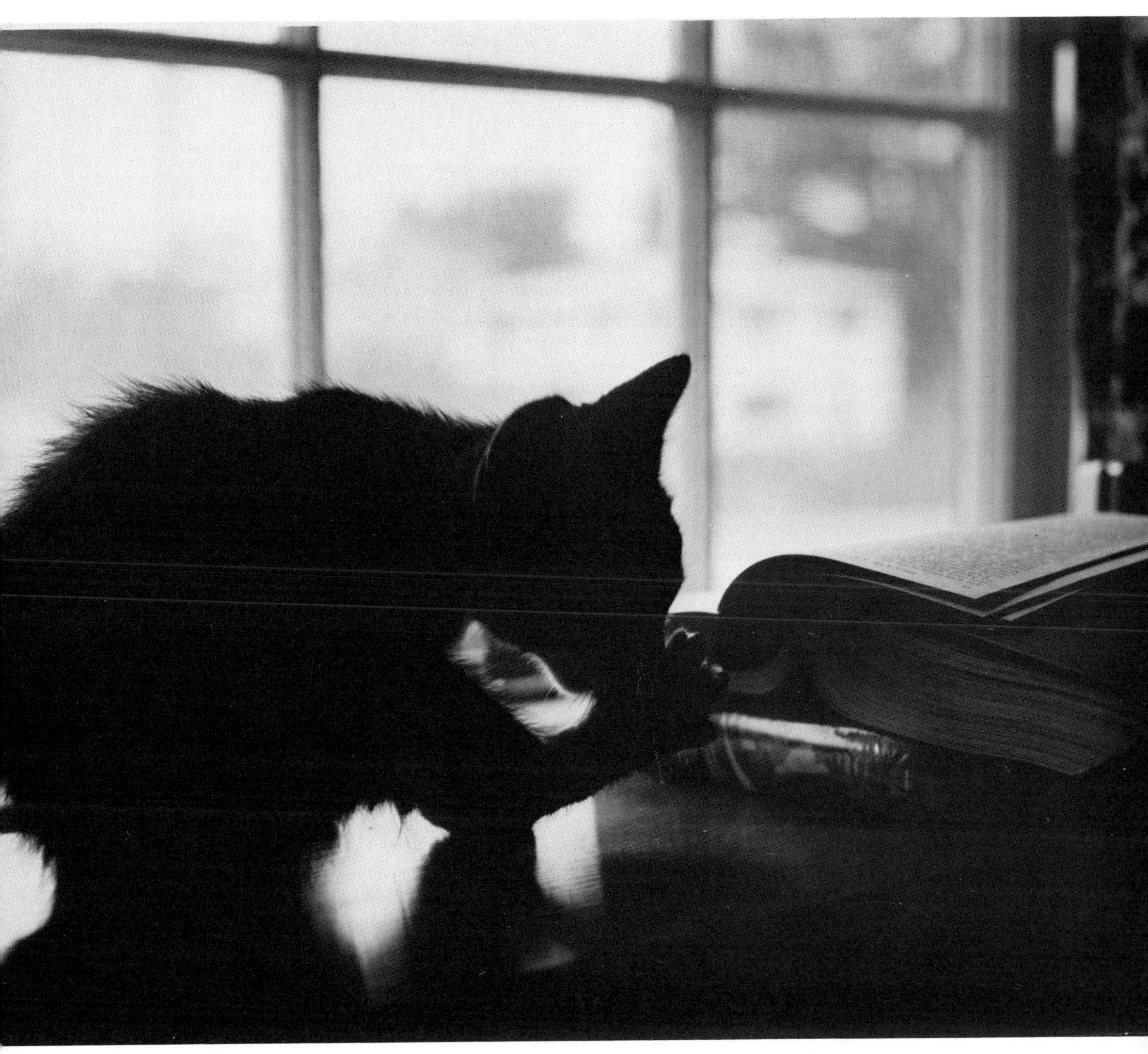

When exposing against the light, remember expose for the subject alone and not the whole picture area. If you are using a hand-held meter, walk up to your subject and read the light reflected off of it.

PICTURES IN WINTER: COMMON COLD-WEATHER CAMERA PROBLEMS

Winter may offer some spectacular photographic subjects for snapshooters, but it can also create all sorts of peculiar problems for you.

The trouble with many camera problems produced by cold weather is that you don't know you've got them until it's too late to do anything about them. A picture comes back from the lab with a sort of soft, mushy look. Or it's sprinkled with what may appear to be miniature bolts of lighting. Or it's badly overexposed, and you *know* you took the picture at the proper shutter speed.

They're all problems common to cold-weather photography, and they can be eliminated if you know why they happen and if you take a few rudimentary precautions.

The mushy look, for example, is usually the result of moisture condensing on the surfaces of your lens and then freezing. The moisture gets there when you accidentally breathe on the glass, or because you go from the cold into the warm air and then out into the cold again, or because some snowflakes get onto the glass, melt, and then freeze. You wind up by taking your pictures through a film of ice, which gives them a diffused unfocused look.

The tiny lightning streaks are the result of the dry air that accompanies cold weather, and they occur when you crank the film rapidly from one shot to the next. Static electricity is generated, and it can be recorded on the film.

The overexposures usually occur on a particularly cold day when the lubricants in your camera's shutter congeal. They become stiff and they slow up the shutter's movement, allowing more light to get to the film than is normally the case. The result will be an overexposed picture.

You can prevent ice from forming on your lens by letting the camera reach outside temperatures before you use it and by taking care that no snow or warm air reach the glass surfaces. You can prevent static electricity from forming by advancing the film very slowly through the camera. But the problem of congealing lubricants requires more attention.

The safest bet is to have a camera repair shop clean off most of the lubricant before you use it outdoors in cold weather. It is not a very complicated operation, but it should be done by an expert.

Sometimes graphite-based lubricants are used for winter photography because they are less inclined to freeze, but they are not for every camera. Let your camera shop technician determine what treatment is best for your camera: never try to remove or to add lubricants yourself. When the cold weather is past, return the camera to have the lubricant replaced.

You can also get into trouble when you bring your camera back indoors after a cold-weather shooting session. Moisture will condense on every surface and, if left alone, it can corrode the camera's innards. Prevent this by taking an airtight plastic bag with you when you go outside and, when you're finished, put the camera in the bag before going inside. Leave the camera in the bag until it reaches room temperature.

Light meters also tend to behave oddly in very cold weather, usually because they're battery-operated and batteries tend to lose their zip in the cold. Then they can give you wrong readings. The trick is to keep the batteries warm, either by keeping the entire camera next to your body until you're ready to use it or by keeping a spare set of warmed batteries handy.

These are the basic mechanical problems that come with cold-weather photography, and if you expect them you can be prepared for them.

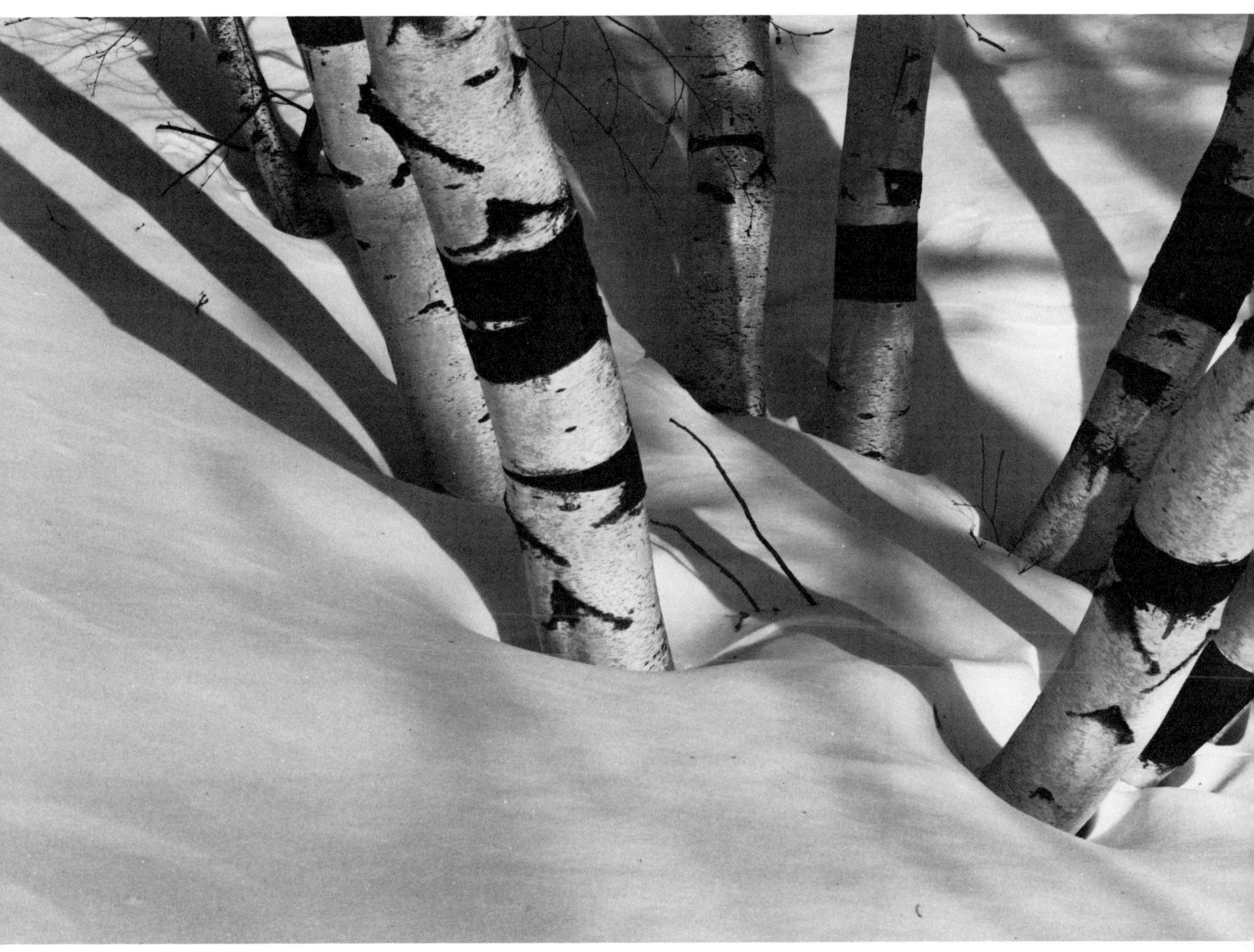

Pictures that include large areas of snow can be improved by the use of filters and by special attention to light metering. This picture, made on black-and-white film, was taken through a yellow filter to increase the contrast between the snow and the birch trees, and to preserve the texture of the snow.

PICTURES IN WINTER: DEALING WITH SNOW

In the northern states we learn to expect snow much as a farmer comes to expect chicken hawks. We may not love it, but we get used to it, and whenever possible, we try to ignore it. Which is all right most of the time: it makes February a bit more bearable. But when you're outdoors in winter, taking pictures, it pays to become acutely aware of the snow.

It can do strange things to your photographs. Sometimes they'll come out sort of bluish. Sometimes they'll be markedly overexposed or underexposed. And sometimes the snow will appear either much darker or much lighter than you had expected.

These peculiarities are the result of lots of light bouncing off sheets of snow. Like an enormous reflector, the snow picks up daylight and tosses it in all directions. In the process, the light acquires some of the blue of the sky, and this can affect the color rendering of your picture. But if you will think a little bit about what's going on you can guard against it and your winter pictures will be as professional-looking as the best.

One of the easiest things you can do is fit your camera's lens with a skylight filter (they're sometimes called an ultraviolet, or UV, filter). They're inexpensive, they won't affect your lens settings, and when you're using slide film, they do a good job of filtering out much of the blue present in snow scenes and hazy landscapes.

You can attach a skylight filter to your lens and then forget it. It won't affect any black-and-white shooting you do, and it will serve to protect the surface of your expensive lens from dust and scratching. Indeed, it is my usual practice whenever I buy a new lens to attach a skylight filter to it as a permanent part of the lens.

There's another filter you might like to try when you shoot snow scenes in color. It's called a polarizing screen, and it will enable you to darken blue skies without altering the other colors in your picture. It is also valuable for minimizing unwanted reflections from ice, water, snow, glass, or any other nonmetallic surface.

A polarizing screen costs a little more than an ordinary filter and, in use, it has to be manipulated for the best effect. It also introduces a little arithmetic in calculating exposures: you have to open up your lens 1½ or more stops to compensate for the light absorbed by the filter. But it can be a useful tool in winter photography and, if yours is the kind of camera that can be fitted with such a filter, it may be well worth looking into.

When you're using black-and-white film, a yellow or an orange filter will add dramatic effect to your pictures by darkening the sky and lightening the clouds. A dark red filter will produce an extreme example of this: the sky will go nighttime dark and the clouds will appear spectacularly white. These filters can only be used with black-and-white film, and each has its own filter factor: you multiply the exposure recommended by your meter or by the instructions packed with your film by the filter factor to get the corrected exposure. If your camera has through-the-lens metering, of course, the meter will do this arithmetic for you.

Finally, a surprisingly simple and effective step you can take to improve your winter pictures is to use a lens shade. It will prevent ambient light from creeping in around the edges of your picture and softening up the image.

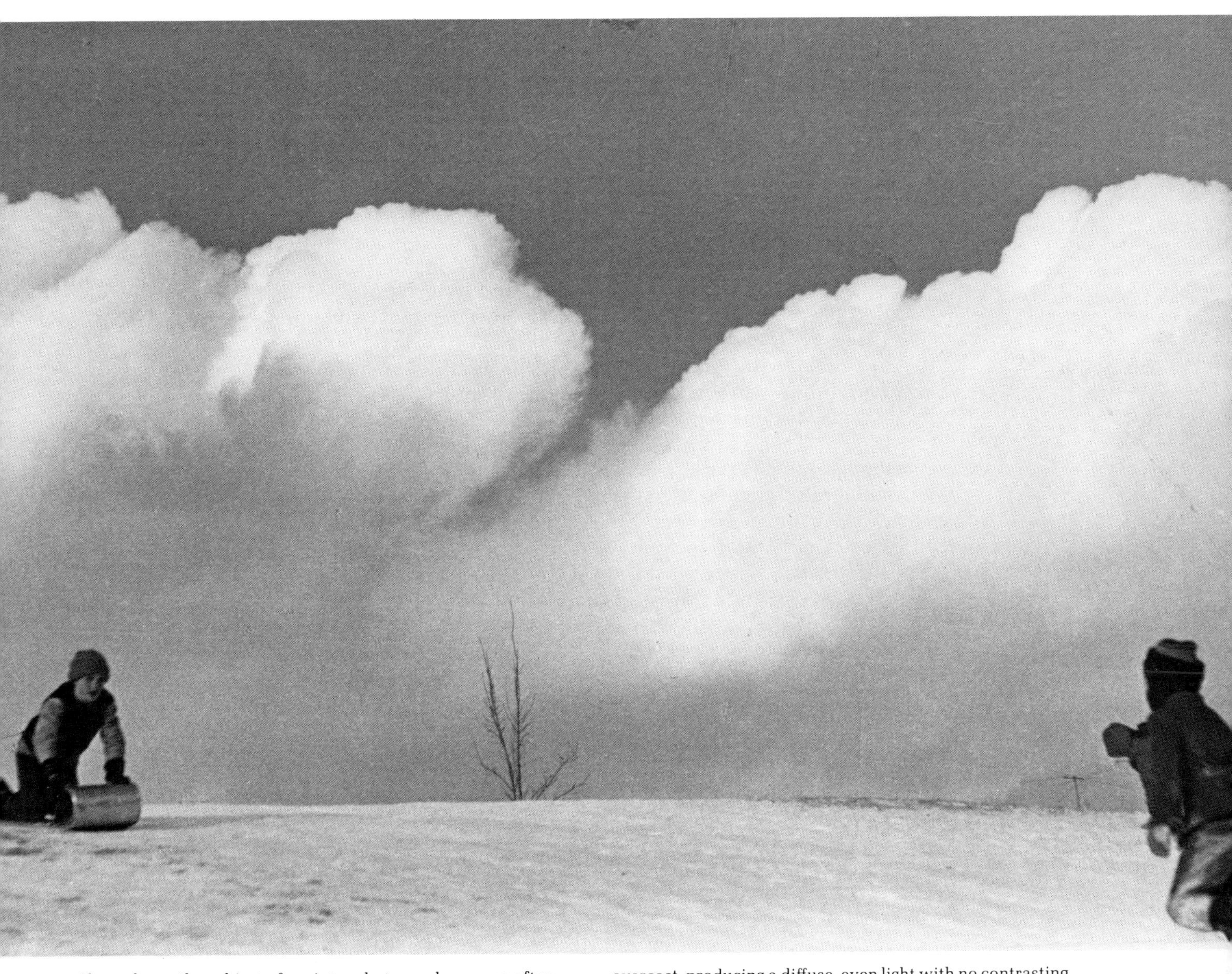

If people are the subject of a winter photograph you can often simplify your exposure calculations by excluding much of the snow and merely suggesting it. In this example the sky was overcast, producing a diffuse, even light with no contrasting lights and darks. Such light is softer and more flattering, and is excellent for outdoor portraiture.

PICTURES IN WINTER: PROBLEMS OF CONTRAST

Generally, you'll be shooting pictures of snow scenes under one of two conditions: either the sun will be out and there'll be lots of brights and darks, or the day will be overcast and the light will be soft and diffuse.

When the sun is shining you'll have some exposure problems. For example, if you're chiefly interested in photographing a person or an object, you pretty much have to decide to expose for the main subject and let the surrounding snow do what it will. And what it will do is overexpose, since it's so much more reflective than your primary subject.

If, on the other hand, it's the texture and shading of the snow that counts, you'll have to expose for that and let the persons or objects in the picture go dark.

There are ways of splitting the difference, however. You can take a light reading with your meter off the snow and then take on off your primary subject, setting your lens opening somewhere between the two extremes. Or, if your camera is equipped with flash, you may be able to direct the flash into the darker area while you expose for the lighter and thus, by combining daylight and flash, you can balance the two extremes. Both techniques take a little planning and practice, however, and so for safety's sake it's a good idea to bracket your shots: take several exposures at different lens openings.

If it's a portrait you want, it's sometimes possible to have someone hold a piece of white reflective cardboard just off-camera. Position your assistant so that some of the sunlight is caught by the reflector and bounced back into your subject's face. This is often enough to lighten up the darker areas and soften the contrast between dark and light.

The important thing to remember, wherever sun and snow are involved, is that you must be aware of them and their effects on your exposure. If your camera is equipped with a meter, be somewhat distrustful of it. Whenever you can, approach the primary subject and read the light reflected from it, rather than from the general area. If you have no meter, trust the instructions that come with your film.

Winter photography is much simpler when the sky is overcast. The light tends to even out. There are no strong shadows, people aren't squinting into the sunshine, and you have a broad latitude of exposure.

Of course, colors don't come up as vividly as they do in the sunshine. They're subtler and more muted, and photographs taken under these conditions often tend to have a quieter, moodier feeling to them. Snowy, overcast days are good days for landscapes and scenics.

Subject matter? In winter, there's no shortage of them. The effects of a fresh snowfall on human behavior, for example: people sledding or skiing or snowmobiling or shoveling. Or the silent, vacant feeling that comes when the streets and fields are deserted after a heavy snow. The new shapes that common objects like fenceposts and mailboxes acquire under a blanket of snow, or the shadow patterns cast on the white backdrop by trees and buildings.

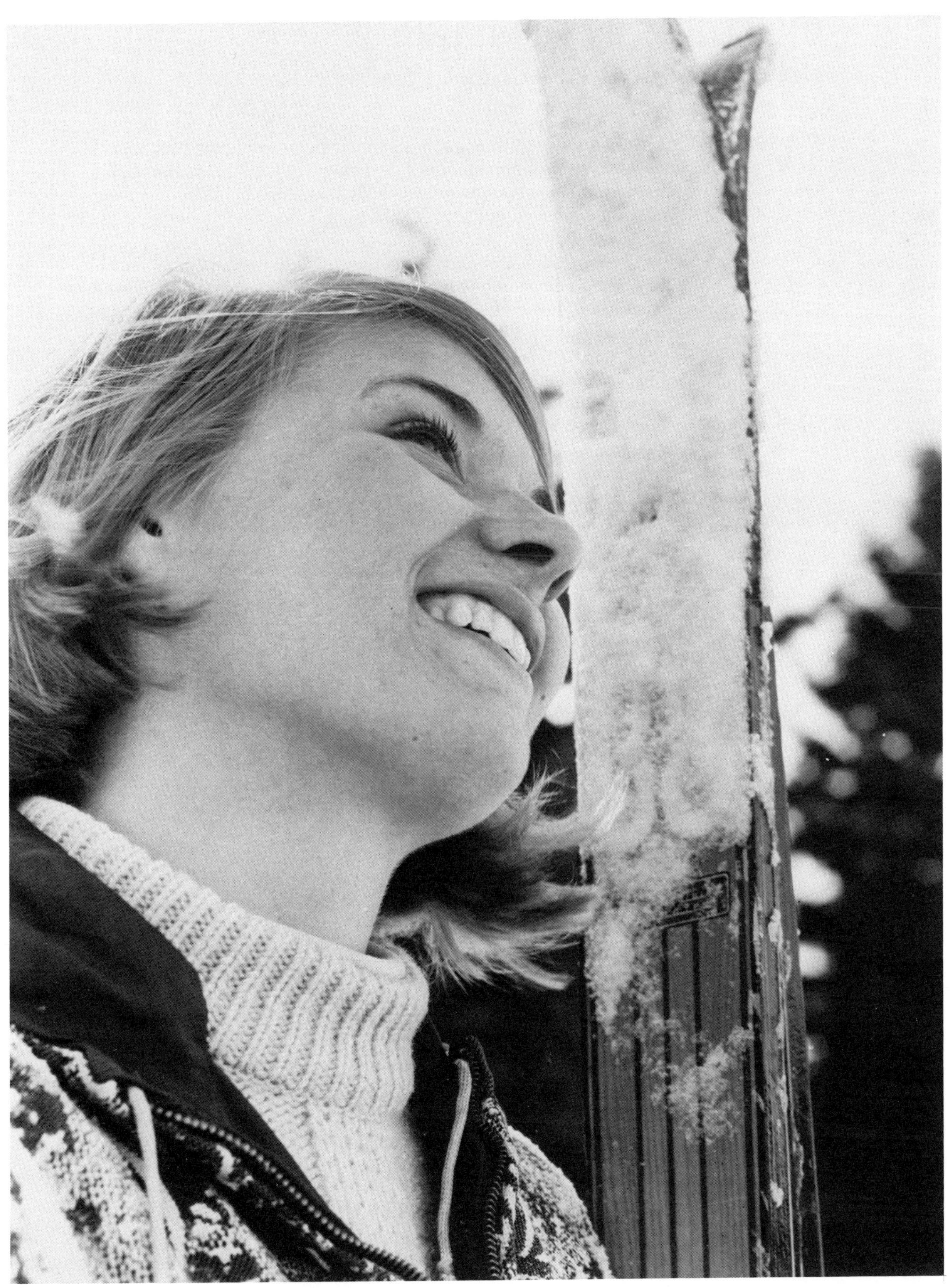

When photographing someone in snow, you will have to calculate the correct exposure. One way to do this is to take a light reading off the snow and then a reading off of the person. Then set your lens opening somewhere between the two extremes.

PICTURES IN SUMMER: PROBLEMS WITH EXPOSURE

When you take your camera to the beach in summer you run up against many of the same exposure problems you had to deal with last winter. Sand and water, like snow, are highly reflective, and there's always more light around than you're conscious of. It pays to take extra precautions in calculating your seaside exposures.

If your camera isn't equipped with a light meter and if you don't carry a hand-held meter, your best bet is to read, very carefully, the exposure instructions packed with your film. There's an awful lot of light rattling around out there on the shore, even in the open shade, and it's too easy to overexpose if you go by sheer guesswork.

Load your camera with a slow or medium-fast daylight film: something with an ASA rating of, say, 64 or 100. Color films are available in these speeds from a number of manufacturers for both slides and negatives. And there's an advantage: the slower films are finer grained than the fast ones, and they enlarge beautifully to 8″ x 10″ or larger.

If your camera is equipped with a meter, it will average out the lights and darks confronting it and give you an exposure somewhere in the middle. It's no problem when there's no great range of contrast before you. The difficulty is, of course, that there's likely to be a great deal of light and much less dark. Yet it may be the dark object—a person, a sailboat—that you want to come out clearly.

But your meter can be overwhelmed by all that light, and the end result can be a photograph in which waves and water are clearly defined, but your main subject is a mere silhouette with no visible detail. What you need to do in such cases is to decide what's most important in your picture, and expose for that.

If you can approach your primary subject, do it, and use your meter to read the light reflected from it only, excluding the brightly lighted background. If you can't get near it, find something nearby that will serve as a satisfactory substitute—something that is lighted by the same light that strikes your subject, and which is of about the same shade and tone. Take your light reading off the substitute, and use that reading in making your picture.

It's less of a problem if you're photographing one or a few persons from relatively short range. You can walk up to them, calculate your exposure from the light reflected from them, back off, focus, and shoot.

But if people are your subject, watch what the sun is doing to them. Are they squinting? Are there dark, contrasty shadows falling across their faces and obscuring details? Are you, in short, being unkinder to them than they deserve?

If you are, simply move them into the open shade where the light is softer, more diffused, and a lot more flattering. They will appreciate it, and you may be mentioned in their wills.

This is the sort of into-the-light picture that forces the photographer to make an either/or decision. If he bases his exposure on the highlights in the scene the water in the background will come up in satisfactory detail but the bikinied model will become a semi-silhouette. If he bases it on the shadows, the background will do what it does here: practically disappear. An attempt to average out the difference would produce a picture with insufficient detail in both foreground and background. Since it is the model who's important here, the photographer opted for the shadows and let the background overexpose. The model is Loren Daniels.

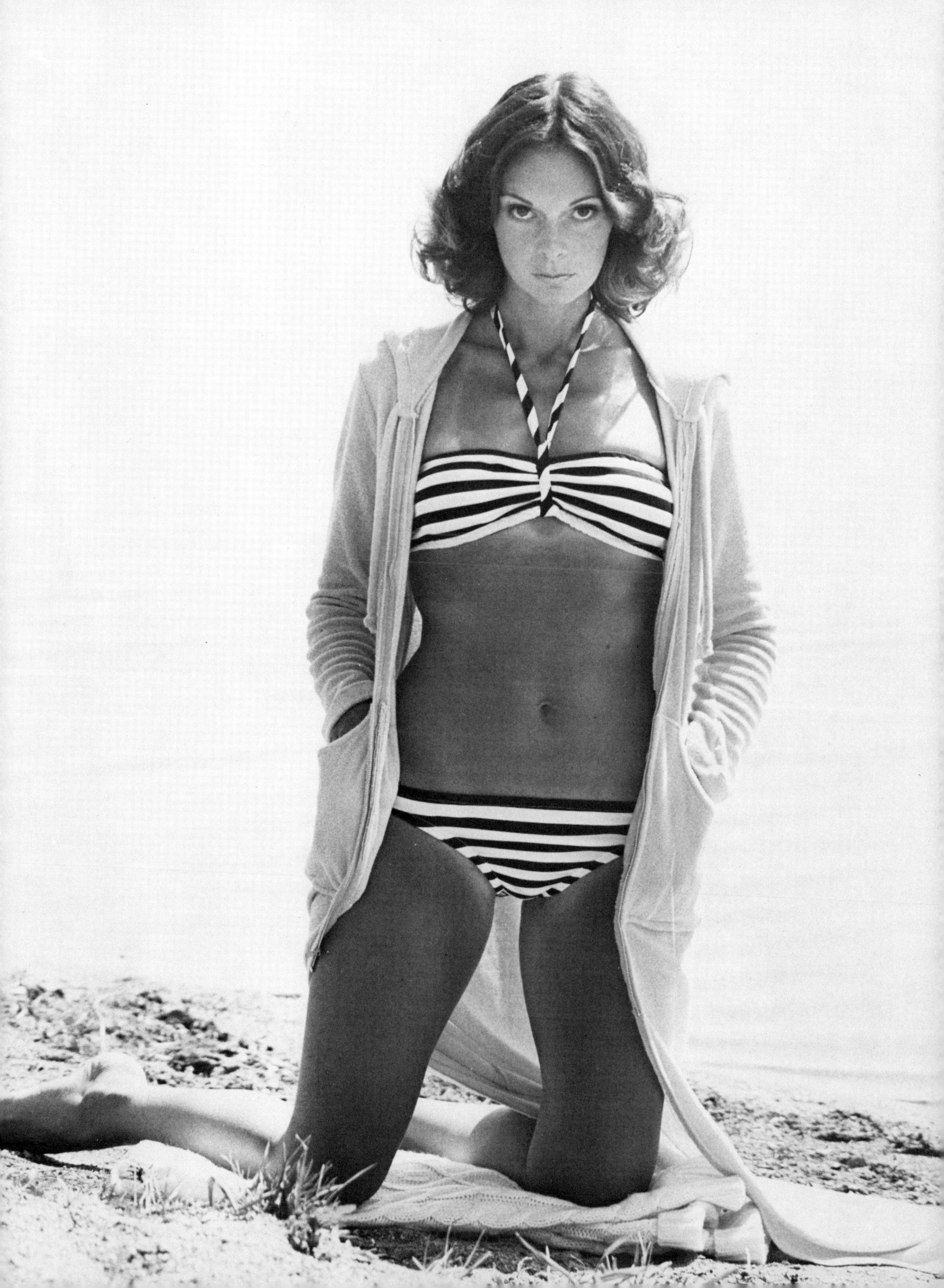

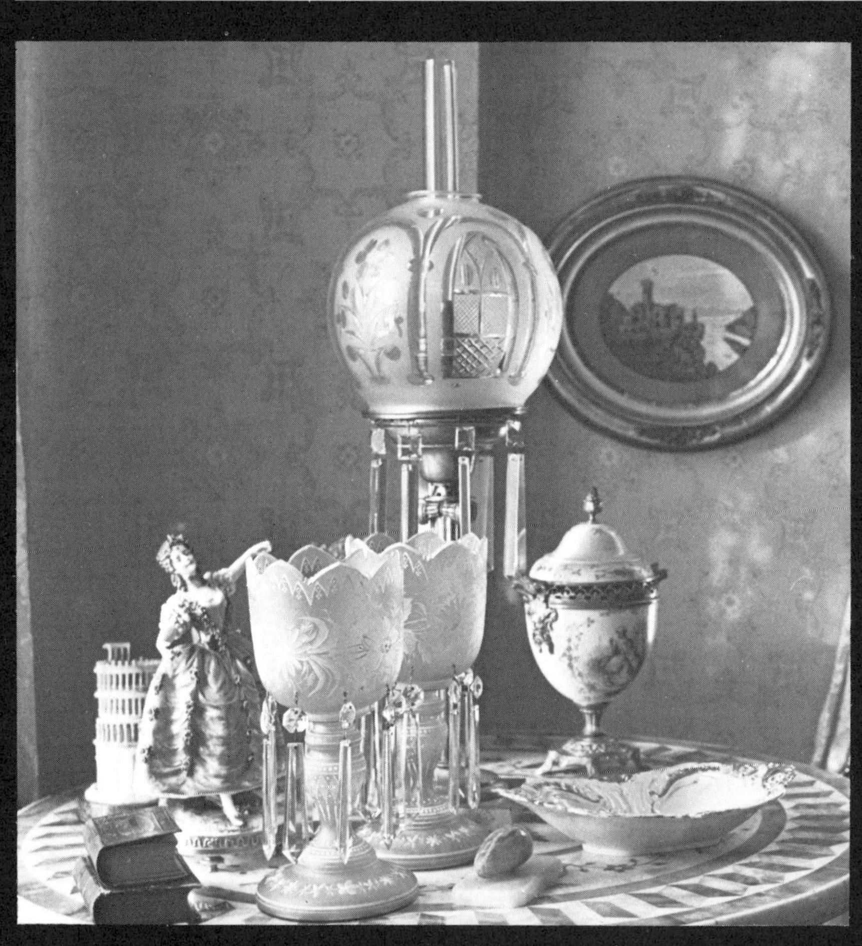

Chapter 4

PICTURE-TAKING ON SPECIAL OCCASIONS

There are, of course, special occasions to which you bring your camera, and that is the subject matter of the following chapter. It deals with taking pictures at the theater, at formal and pop concerts, museums and art institutes, fairs, carnivals, weddings, and commencements.

Each section discusses the particular nature of the event, what to bring with you in the way of photographic gear, and what to expect when you get there. There are hints about what kind of film will work best under the lighting conditions you're likely to find, along with some suggestions about when and how to make exposures, what lenses might prove useful and, occasionally, how to find the best vantage point for the picture you want.

All of this is prefaced by a short, rather stern lecture on good manners. It is a topic that, somehow, usually gets overlooked by camera fans when they're comparing lens openings and shutter speeds and how to get the best camera angle.

But it's an important subject, especially when you're away from home with your camera.

AMATEURS WITH CAMERAS: GOOD MANNERS, AND HOW TO AVOID BEING A PAIN IN THE NECK

Once upon a time there was a young man who began a career as a photographer, but for several years he made no progress. His name remained unknown, and no one bought his work.

Then a kindly and wealthy woman took an interest in his career. She commissioned several portraits, recommended him to her friends, and introduced him to editors, art directors, and other people in a position to help him.

He lost touch with her as his career gained momentum. Thirty years later he had become a successful and internationally known photographer. Then, one day as he walked through a park near his studio, he met a poor, bent, gray-haired old lady dressed in rags. It was the woman who had helped him in his youth. She had lost her fortune and her health, while he had prospered.

The next day he told a friend the whole story. "How fortunate that you should have an opportunity to repay her," said the friend. "What did you give her?"

"I gave her," said the photographer, "1/125 sec. at f/16."

And what may we learn from this cautionary tale? Well, for one thing, it is important to remember that carrying a camera does not exempt you from good manners.

Technical improvements in equipment have combined with an increased interest in photography as a hobby to produce a world in which, with a little planning, any beginner who wants to photograph anything anywhere can do it. But this does not mean *carte blanche*: tradition, protocol, and just plain politeness should always govern your behavior at both public and private events.

No one wants some thick-skinned snapshooter pushing through the crowds, ordering people around, and firing off his flash at solemn and inappropriate moments.

But somehow there always seems to be one of them at every wedding, every play, and every concert. And they usually turn out to be amateurs. Professional photographers know better.

There are two fundamental steps you can take to avoid turning into one of these flatfooted and insensitive camera boors. Before leaving home, you can prepare yourself to be as silent and unobtrusive as possible, and you can determine in advance the ground rules that cover photography at the particular event you plan to attend by calling the minister, rabbi, or priest before the ceremony. Ask him when photographing is allowed.

Being unobtrusive means equipping yourself with a fast film, so that you'll rarely need to use your flash attachment. A film with an ASA rating of 400, for example, will let you make exposures under extremely marginal lighting. For color prints, try Kodacolor 400 or Fujicolor 400. For slides, Kodak's Ektachrome 400 gives excellent results and, with special processing, can even be exposed at ASA 800.

It also helps to use a quiet camera, especially if you plan to make exposures during hushed, critical moments. The big offenders in this respect are the 35mm and 2¼" x 2¼" single-lens-reflex cameras. It's not their shutters that make the racket—it's the sound of the mirror moving out of the way while the exposure is made and then returning to position.

The rangefinder cameras—those with one lens to view through and another to take the picture through—have no moving mirrors and are the cameras of choice when soundless photography is critical. If you must use a single-lens reflex, fit a telephoto to it, so that you can remain a discreet distance from your subject and, with luck, call less attention to yourself.

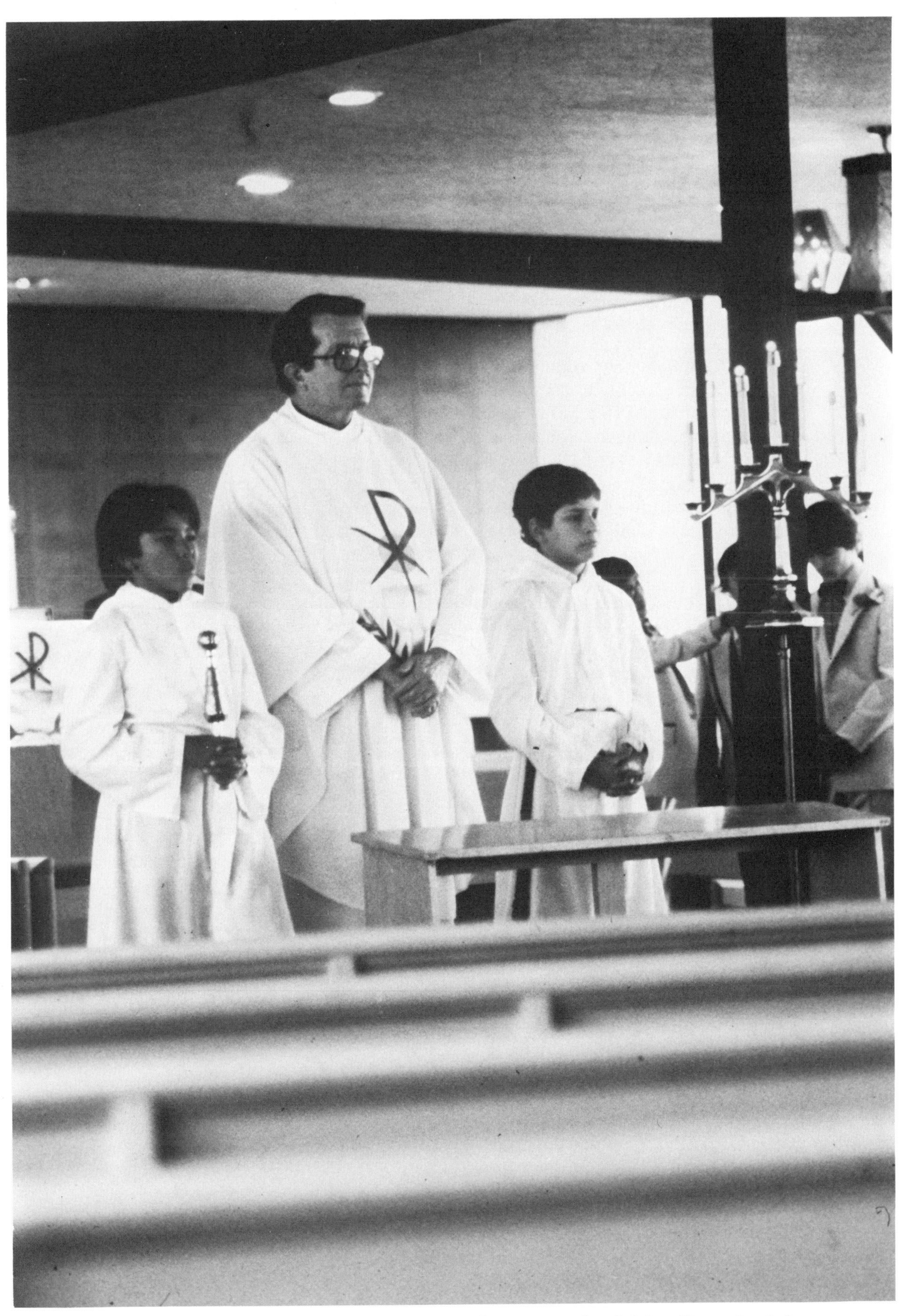

When photographing public and private events, keep tradition, protocol, and plain politeness in mind.

PHOTOGRAPHY AT THE THEATER

Theater managers tend to get pretty testy about cameras in the audience, and with the best of reasons. They're as annoying as a crying baby: they interrupt the performers, distract the audience, and destroy a carefully built mood. At professional performances it simply isn't done.

Even during amateur productions, where the audience is full of enthusiastic relatives and where the atmosphere is likely to be less formal, there's no real excuse for it. If you want pictures of your Pride and Joy as he or she carries a spear in the high school production, get them during play rehearsals or backstage after the performance.

Never during the performance itself—at least, not without the foreknowledge and approval of the play's director. And, even with approval, it's necessary to be discreet. No flash, and only cameras with quiet shutters.

A far better idea is to secure management's okay to take your pictures during dress rehearsals. Instead of resistance, you're likely to get cooperation. Especially if you're smart enough to offer to let the play's director see the results of your work and offer him prints of anything he likes.

Most directors schedule what's called a "photo call" at some point late in the play's preparation. It's a time during which production and publicity pictures are taken by the official photographer. The odds are that then is when you'll be most welcome.

During dress rehearsals you'll have a chance to select those points in the performance during which you'll want to make your exposures—the high points of dramatic action. And at the same time you can note the location of the actors on the stage in order to get some idea of the lighting available to you.

Few theatrical productions are evenly lighted. They're lighted for dramatic effect, not for your convenience, and you'll have to go with what you find.

What you'll find is likely to be patchy: light here and dark over there, with the performers constantly moving in and out of puddles of light. As a rule, it's best to expose for the puddles, where you'll have lots of light and can shoot at smaller lens openings and faster shutter speeds.

You'll want the faster shutter speeds because the actors may be moving and because you'll be hand-holding your camera. A shutter speed of 1/125 or 1/250 sec. will reduce camera shake and increase your chances of getting a crisp, blur-free picture.

This is even truer of telephoto lenses: the slightest shake will be magnified and transmitted to the film. Therefore, make it a rule to give fast shutter speeds first priority, even if you have to open up your lens to its widest aperture to compensate.

Anything you can do to steady the lens will help. Rest it on the back of the seat in front of you, or brace yourself firmly against your own seat, using your arms to form a sort of bipod to support the camera.

Theatrical lighting often includes spotlights or floods of varying colors, and this can be a bit of a problem. The easiest solution: Kodak's Kodacolor 400 negative film. It's fast, which means you'll be able to shoot at reasonably brief shutter speeds, and it'll give you pleasantly warm, accurate colors without the need for tinkering with color-compensating filters.

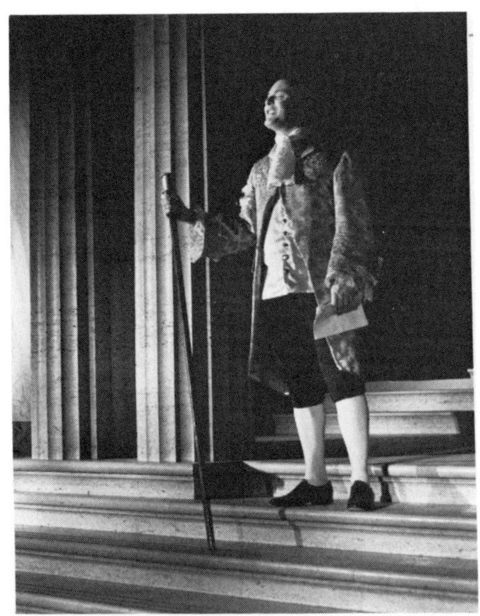

The contrasty lighting typical of most stage productions is apparent here. You will do best if you make your exposures while the actors are in the more brightly-lit areas.

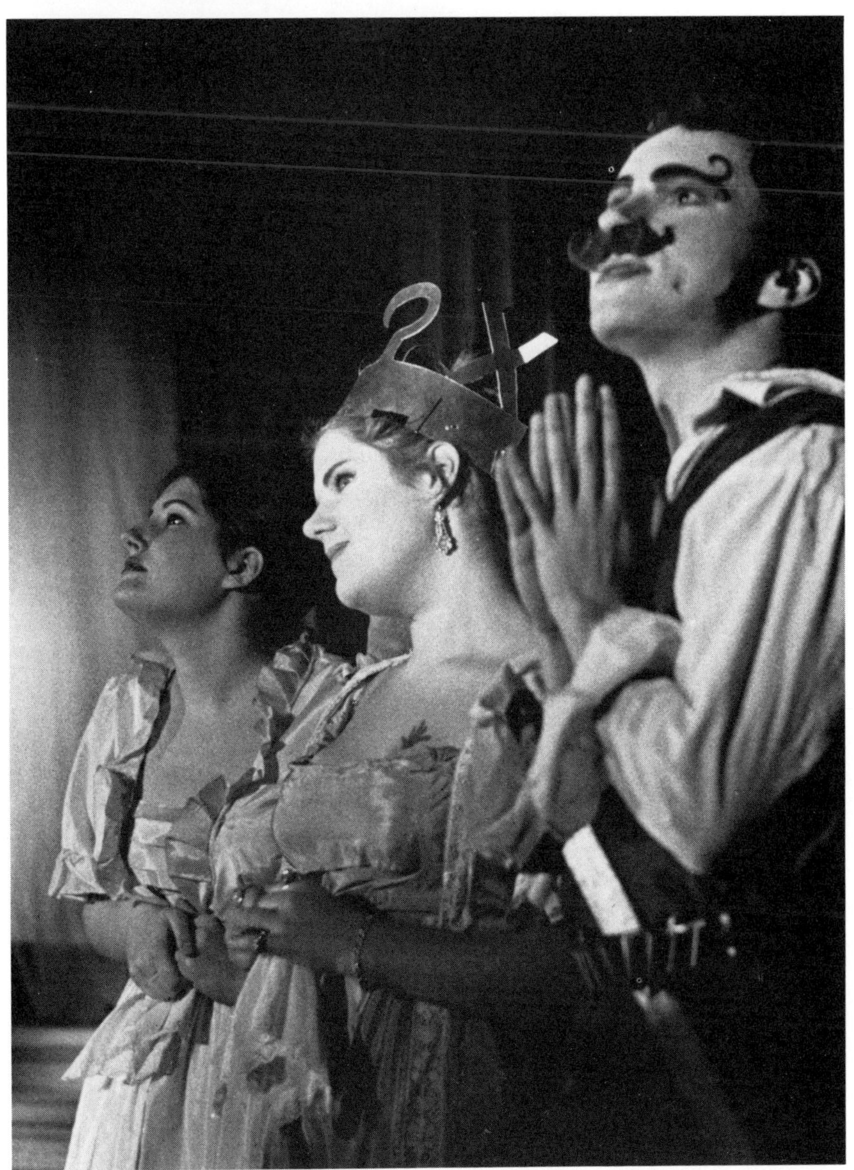

FORMAL AND POP CONCERTS

Much of what has been said about photographing dramatic productions can be said about concerts.

For symphonies and similar formal gatherings, the basic rule is the same: always ask for management's permission before taking pictures during performances. The reason for the rule is the same, too—flashing bulbs and clicking shutters are distracting. If you can't take your pictures without attracting attention, you won't be welcome.

Assuming you can be unobtrusive, and assuming you have management's sanction, you'll find symphonies easier to photograph than dramatic productions. For one thing, the lighting will probably be more evenly spread. You're not likely to run into the extremes of contrast typical of the theater.

For another thing, there are usually frequent points during a concert when the performers are onstage but not performing. You can get excellent candids during these between-number intervals.

It used to be that you could bring along a camera to a rock concert without worrying much about whether anyone would disapprove. Indeed, a few years ago cameras were very much a part of the atmosphere, and there were often as many of them in the crowd as there were open-toed sandals.

But times have changed and today's rock stars can be as touchy as any virtuoso about snapshooters in the audience. Increasingly, performers are stipulating that *no* pictures be taken without permission.

It's not only that photography during a performance can be distracting. Sometimes there are less obvious reasons. Entertainers, like actors, work very hard for recognition—to reach a point where their talent and their faces are marketable. They don't want their pictures taken unless they know what is going to become of those pictures.

Your motives may not be commercial, but they can't be sure of that. Therefore, back to Rule One, Ask.

Sometimes you'll get approval to take pictures, provided you don't use flash. Sometimes they'll let you take them at certain points during the concert but not at others. Sometimes one of the performers will okay your taking his picture, while another won't. And sometimes there are no holds barred.

And there is no reason to believe that country and western, jazz, or folk-music performers are any different in their opinions on the subject.

Take lots of rolls of film with you because you'll find likely subjects in the crowd as well as onstage. A telephoto lens of moderate length is a good thing to bring along, too, since you can't always be as close to your subject as you'd like. If you're using a 35mm single-lens reflex, a 105mm or 135mm lens will be very useful in pulling your subject up close.

If you're outdoors and it's daylight, you'll have your choice of a wide range of color films, both slide and negative. Just be sure that what you use is balanced for daylight. If you're indoors, and the light is a little iffy, you'd be best advised to stick with the faster (ASA 400) black-and-white or color films.

Constantly changing colored lights, typical of many pop music concerts, can create special problems of exposure. The faster films work best in such situations and, when many colors are present, the daylight-balanced films generally provide the best color renditions.

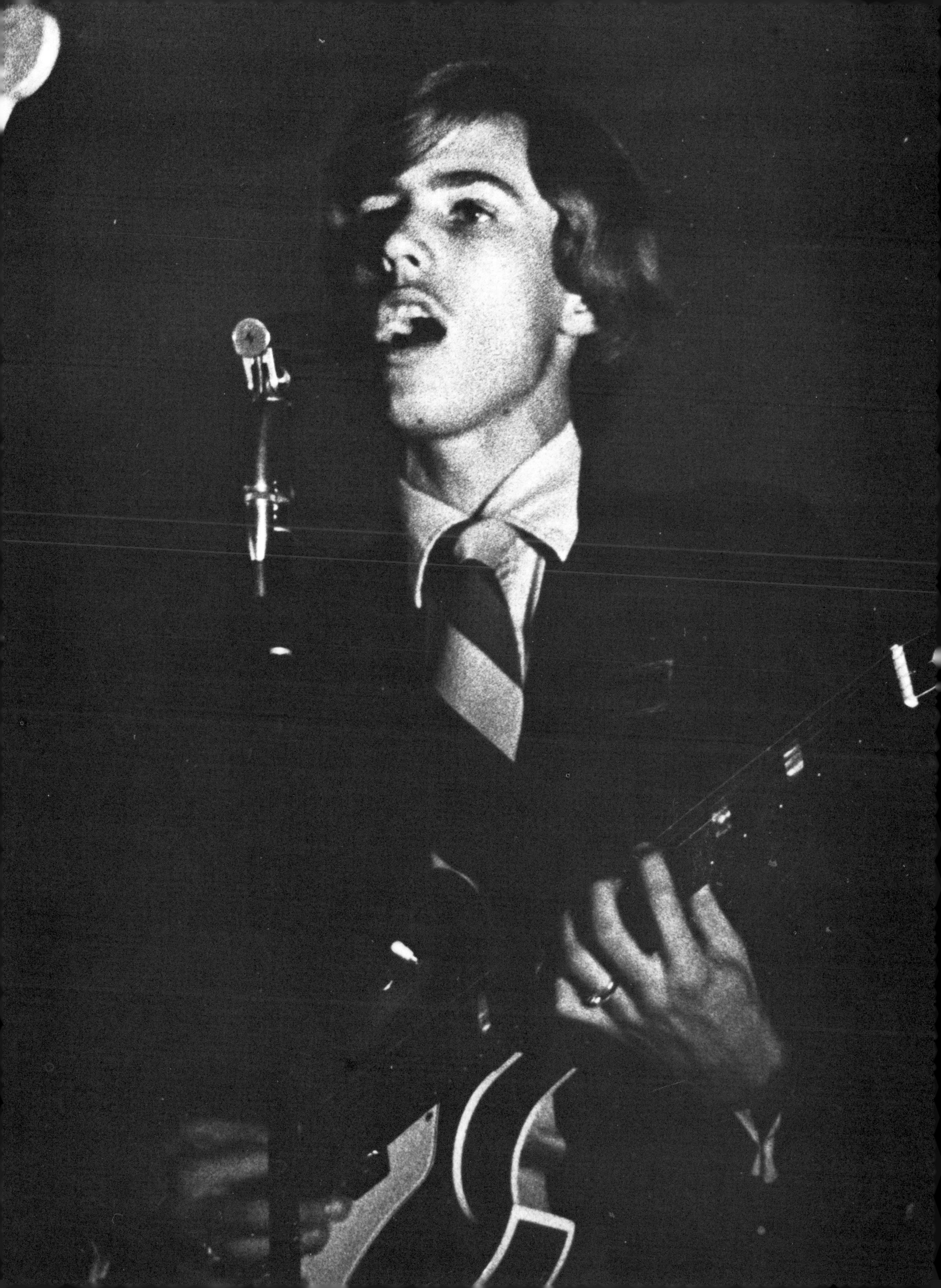

MUSEUMS AND ART INSTITUTES

You probably won't encounter restrictions on photography at trade or consumer shows, art fairs, handicraft exhibits, or similar one-time functions. But established museum and art institutes, public or private, large or small, are likely to have some sort of policy about cameras on the premises.

Those policies will vary from institution to institution. A few may impose an absolute prohibition on photography, requiring that you deposit your camera at the front desk as you enter. Others are more relaxed about it, specifying only that you do not photograph certain exhibits.

Few museums or galleries will allow you to photograph a traveling exhibit—one which does not belong to the institution, but is there only on temporary loan. It is a matter of extending extra security to property that is not theirs, and the institution makes the rule for the protection of the visitor as well as of the exhibit.

The Detroit Institute of Arts has a very simple camera policy, and one that is typical of most large museums: you are free to photograph pretty much as you please, with the single exception of traveling shows, and with the provision that you stop at the desk first and get a permit to take pictures.

The Toledo Museum of Art doesn't issue a permit, but they make similar requirements. Anyone with a camera is welcome, provided they don't photograph exhibits there on loan. They also ask that you do not photograph exhibitions of contemporary art because there are often copyright restrictions involved.

New York's Museum of Modern Art is the same: you may photograph anything except traveling exhibits.

All galleries make one important stipulation: do not bring a tripod with you. They're dangerous. It's too easy to puncture a painting or shatter a fragile vase with an out-of-control tripod leg. And tripods tend to block lanes and passageways, making it difficult for tour guides to shepherd their groups past them. Some institutions extend this restriction to include *any* pointed objects, incidentally. Don't be surprised if you're asked to check your cane or your umbrella along with your tripod.

Flash attachments are okay, provided you don't attempt to use old-style flashbulbs. They sometimes explode, and flying glass can damage both photographer and subject. Bulbs must be covered with a protective shield if they're used. An easy solution is to use electronic flash or flash cubes; an even easier solution is to use no flash at all.

If your motive in bringing a camera with you is to get a good picture of one of the exhibits, remember that most museums sell professionally made prints and slides of their paintings, sculptures and other displays, and these are likely to be better for the purpose than anything you'll get with your own camera. If your motive is to photograph people responding to art or to document your visit, here are some suggestions:

A wide-angle lens might prove more useful than your normal lens because it can reach out and encompass more detail in a confined space. If your 35mm camera permits you to remove one lens and replace it with another, bring along a 28mm or a 35mm lens.

In a reasonably well-lighted gallery you won't need flash if you use a fast (ASA 400) film. When the lighting is marginal, flash is one answer, but be careful of highlights bouncing off metal or glass, or off the varnished surface of a painting.

Often you can get what you want without flash, even in dim light, by combining fast film with a slow shutter speed. And this is where you'll wish you had your tripod with you.

But you won't. So the best bet is to borrow some support. If there's a convenient table or shelf on which you can rest your camera, try that. Leaning back against a

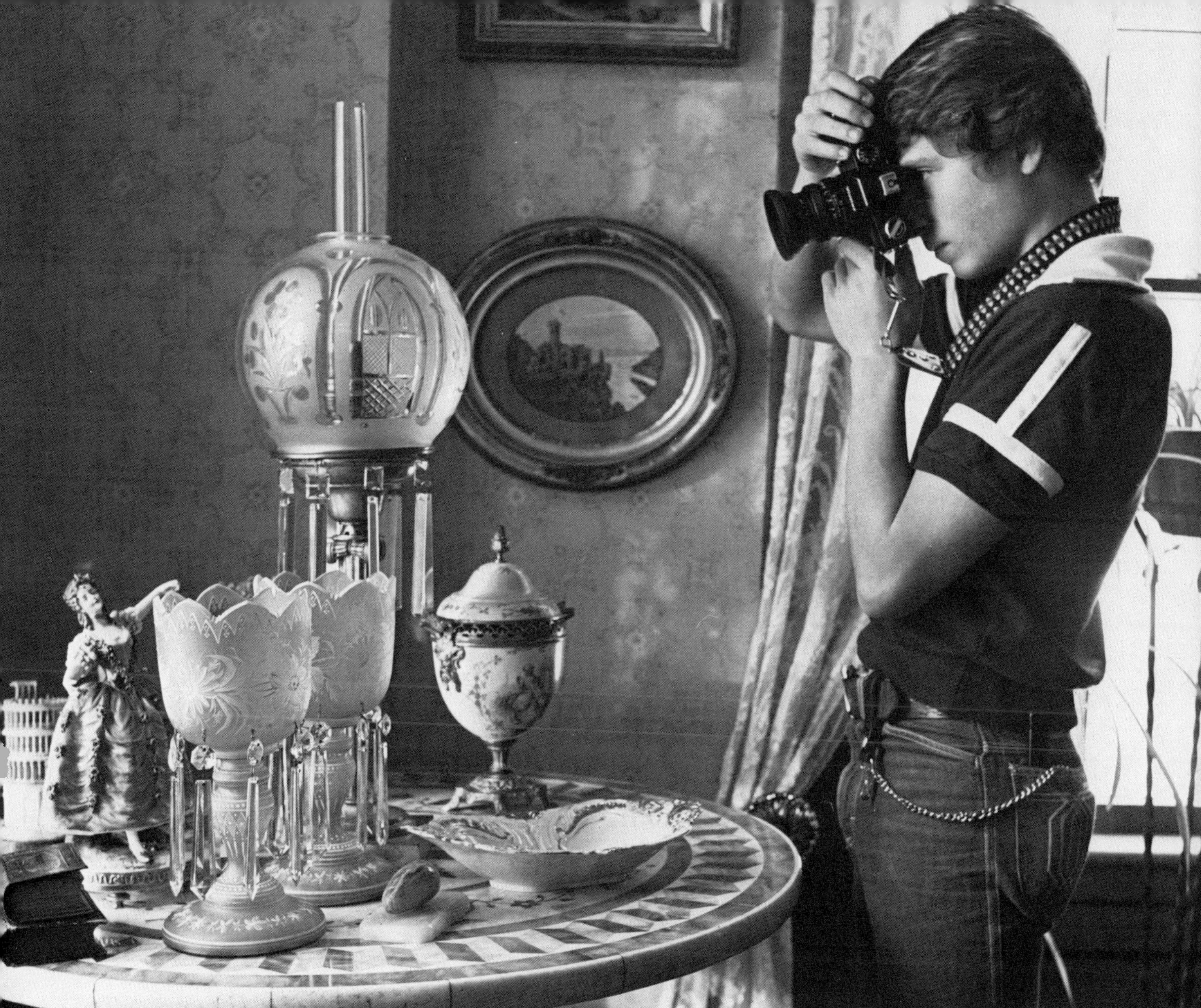

A display of fragile 19th Century domestic artifacts poses a special problem for a young museum visitor. Luckily, the glass and ceramic objects are lighted by daylight from two nearby windows. Direct flash would tend to wash out their delicate coloring, produce undesirable reflections, and build up dark shadows behind them. To get the picture the photographer will need a fast film, a shutter speed of about 1/60 sec., and a very steady hand.

wall will help, or bracing yourself against a door or a pillar . . . anything that will impart a little rigidity to your arms and body. As a general rule, this kind of borrowed support is essential whenever you have to make exposures at 1/60 sec. or slower.

The color print film of choice for amateurs in such situations is rapidly becoming Kodak's Kodacolor 400 film. It's balanced for daylight, blue bulbs, and electronic flash, but it produces a pleasant, warm image even in the presence of tungsten or fluorescent-light sources. For slides, use daylight-balanced film if you're using your flash attachment or if your subject is lit by daylight.

If you want slides, and if your subject is lit primarily by tungsten or fluorescent light, consult the film manufacturer's instructions to see whether you'll need a corrective color filter or if you should be using a tungsten-balanced film.

FAIRS AND CARNIVALS

Few events are more public than a fair or a carnival, but there's nowhere else you can feel freer to take pictures without worrying about other people's sensibilities. For sheer excitement, color, and variety of subject matter, it's hard to think of a better place to practice your photographic skills.

There are the people: in crowds, in small groups and singly, everyone's doing something, everyone's having a good time, and no one's likely to care much about what you and your camera are up to. It's the ideal opportunity for unposed, exuberant candids.

There are the sideshows, the rides, the penny-pitches and ball-tosses, the barkers, the pitchmen and the vendors, JoJo the Dog-Faced Boy, the Giant Rat of Sumatra, and all the other gaudy midway attractions.

At county and state fairs there are also less flamboyant but no less attractive subjects for your lens: animals, agricultural exhibits, hobbies and crafts, grandstand features, and competitions of all sorts. And don't let sunset stop you. You can get dramatic, exhibition-quality pictures at night without even changing the film in your camera.

All you'll need is plenty of rolls of daylight film, either slide or negative. For all-around convenience you might prefer the faster films, rated at ASA 400, because they'll let you use faster shutter speeds for stopping action. Even after dark the daylight-balanced films will give very satisfactory colors, despite the fact that you'll be shooting pictures by some wildly mixed light sources.

If you have the kind of camera that will let you interchange lenses, and if you have a wide-angle and a telephoto lens, you might find it useful to bring both, along with your normal lens. The wide-angle will let you get crowd shots along the midway, for example, with a great deal of depth of focus. The telephoto will permit you to isolate individuals or small groups from a discreet distance. And the normal lens will deal with everything in between. A moderate zoom lens—say a 35mm-70mm or a 35mm-85mm—will, of course, let you cover it all.

After dark at a fair or carnival is magic time: bright, colorful lights moving and standing still against a black blanket; patches of lights and darks; floodlights picking out people and objects; ordinary objects acquiring a brief and spurious glamour. There's a tinselly, temporary look to the whole thing, and it demands to be photographed before it all disappears.

You'll need a tripod, because you'll be shooting at extremely slow shutter speeds: a half-second or longer, depending on the speed of the film you're using and the effect you want. If you're using a high-speed color film, like Ektachrome 400 for slides or Kodacolor 400 for prints, try setting your lens opening at f/5.6 and your shutter speed at a half-second. Then try it again at the same lens opening but at a full second. Then try two seconds, then three, and so on, up to five or six seconds.

With slower films you'll need to extend your exposure times even more. But don't hesitate to experiment. There are many variables in night photography and little predictability: the trick is to make several exposures, so that you'll have a choice among them. One or another of your shots is bound to stand out like a wedding cake at a pauper's funeral.

For panorama shots of, say, the midway, you'll need some elevation. Getting up high will keep people from wandering in and out of your shot and blocking your view. But there's almost always a ramp or a platform handy from which you can make your picture, if you're willing to look for one.

And that's an important point. Toting a tripod, fussing with long exposures, and looking for effective camera angles may strike you as more trouble than you're used to taking. And it may be. But it's how better pictures are made.

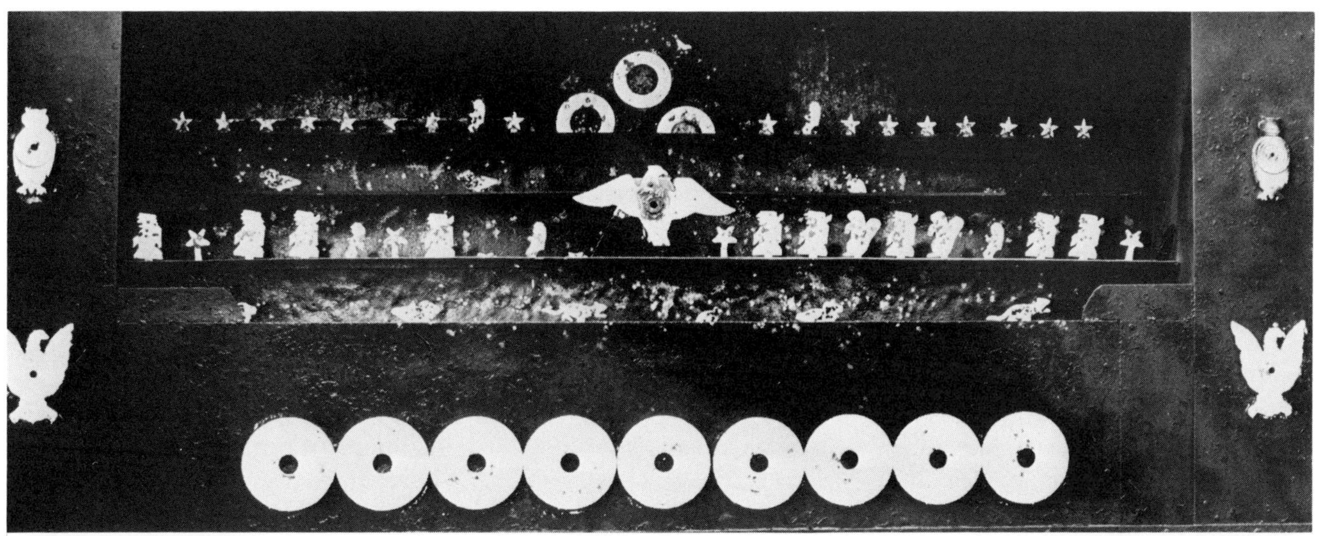

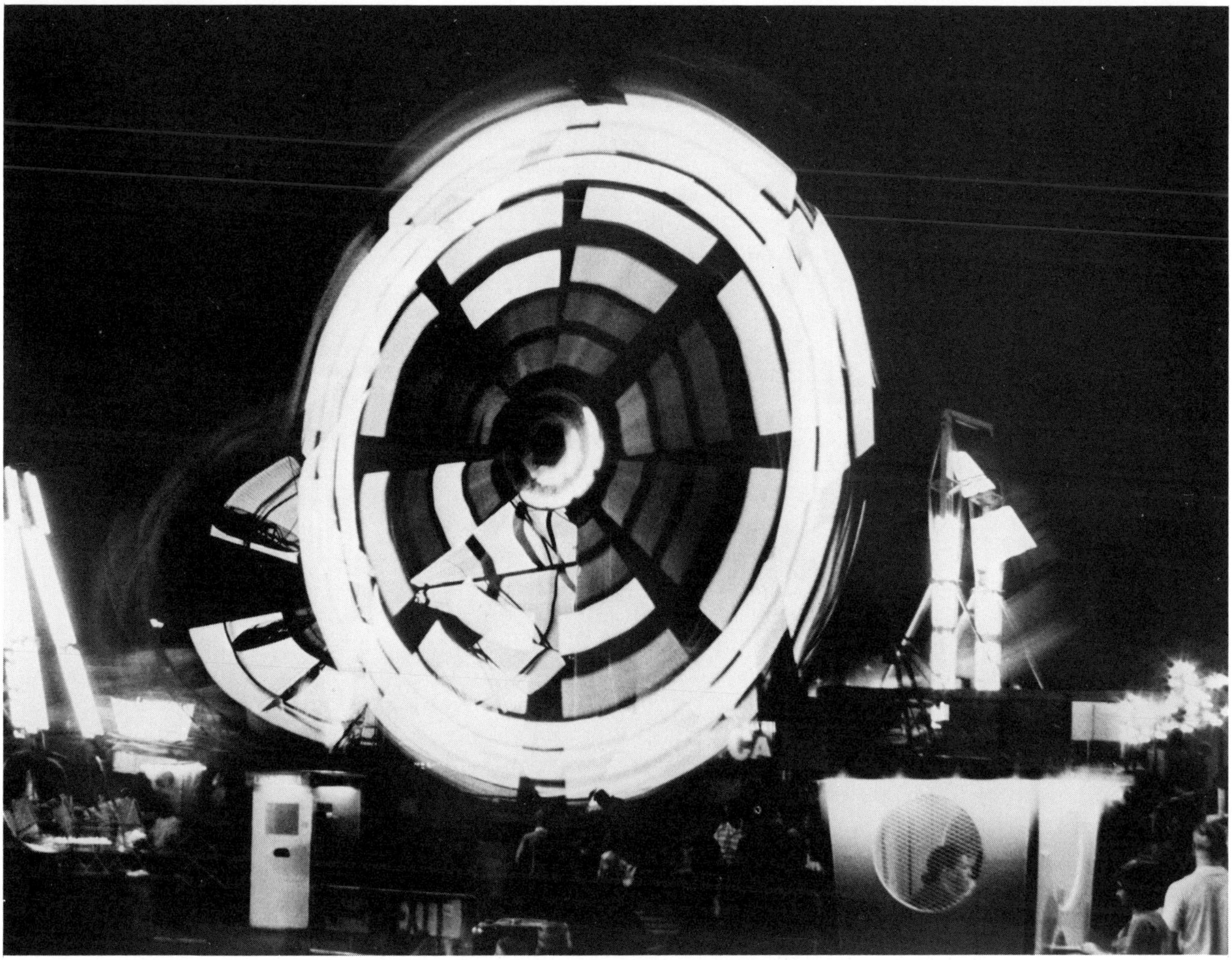

Top: The photographer has emphasized the geometrical quality of the design by cropping out every thing that does not reinforce that feeling. By printing it on an extremely contrasty paper, he has eliminated most of the middle tones, turning a very familiar carnival sight into an abstraction by controlling every step in the making of the picture. *Above*: Fast color or black and white films make it easy to get vivid, dramatic pictures along a carnival midway after dark. But use a tripod for steadiness whenever you can and, for pictures like this one, try to get some elevation above the crowd. This picture was made from the top of the entrance ramp of one of the rides.

WEDDINGS AND COMMENCEMENTS

Weddings and commencements have something in common: both of them are very "family" events. You're not likely to be at one of them unless someone in your family or someone very close to it is a principal participant. Which, of course, is exactly what makes either occasion one you'll want to photograph for your personal album.

But they also have something else in common. They're both very solemn and very important events to the participants. And this imposes a particular obligation on you as an onlooker to mind your photographic manners. Neither event should be turned into a picture-taking free-for-all.

There are intervals during both ceremonies when courtesy demands that no pictures be taken: during speeches, sermons, prayers or invocations, for example, or during any part of the formal, liturgical segment of the ceremony. As a general rule, you're free to take pictures before and after, but not during.

Few people object to flashbulbs and noisy shutters during the academic procession preceding commencement ceremonies, during the handing-out of diplomas, or during the graduates' exit after the formalities. And certainly not during the reception held afterwards.

At weddings you're on touchier ground. Generally, you're free to photograph the preparations, provided you can manage to avoid impeding them, and it's usually allowable to photograph the bridal procession on its way to the altar. But after that, put away your camera until the ceremony is completed and the bride and groom leave the altar.

It is worth noting here, incidentally, that an increasing number of clergymen are turning thumbs down on *any* use of flash or strobe lights, by guests, in the church or temple.

You must remember that every clergyman has his own rules about cameras at weddings and that, if you'll call him a day or two in advance, he'll let you know what they are. It may keep you from making a pain in the neck of yourself.

Remember, too, that there will be a designated professional photographer at the wedding with a specific job to do, and that he or she has been granted license to go places and do things that has not been extended to you. It is absolutely mandatory that you stay out of the official photographer's way. He is part of the ceremony. You are an onlooker.

There are important intervals during the festivities when the professional photographer will be setting up shots requested by the bride: the wedding party group pictures, for example. It will not help if you interrupt, or rearrange people, or fire off a flash during one of his exposures. Let him do his job.

Which doesn't mean you can't get the pictures you want. Most clergymen are very cooperative about re-enacting key points of the ceremony for the benefit of camera-carrying guests. So you needn't worry about missing a critical shot at the church. Later, at the reception, you'll be free to wander around and shoot anything you care to.

And by the way—you may have achieved something of a reputation in the family as a photographer, but please think twice about accepting any invitation to be the official photographer yourself. You know how it goes: "Let's ask Uncle Sidney to take the pictures! He's got a camera, and it'll save us the cost of hiring a professional!" Any event as important as a wedding ought to be covered by a professional who knows exactly what he's doing, and who has both the equipment and the expertise to do it. And if you louse up the job, you'll never be forgiven.

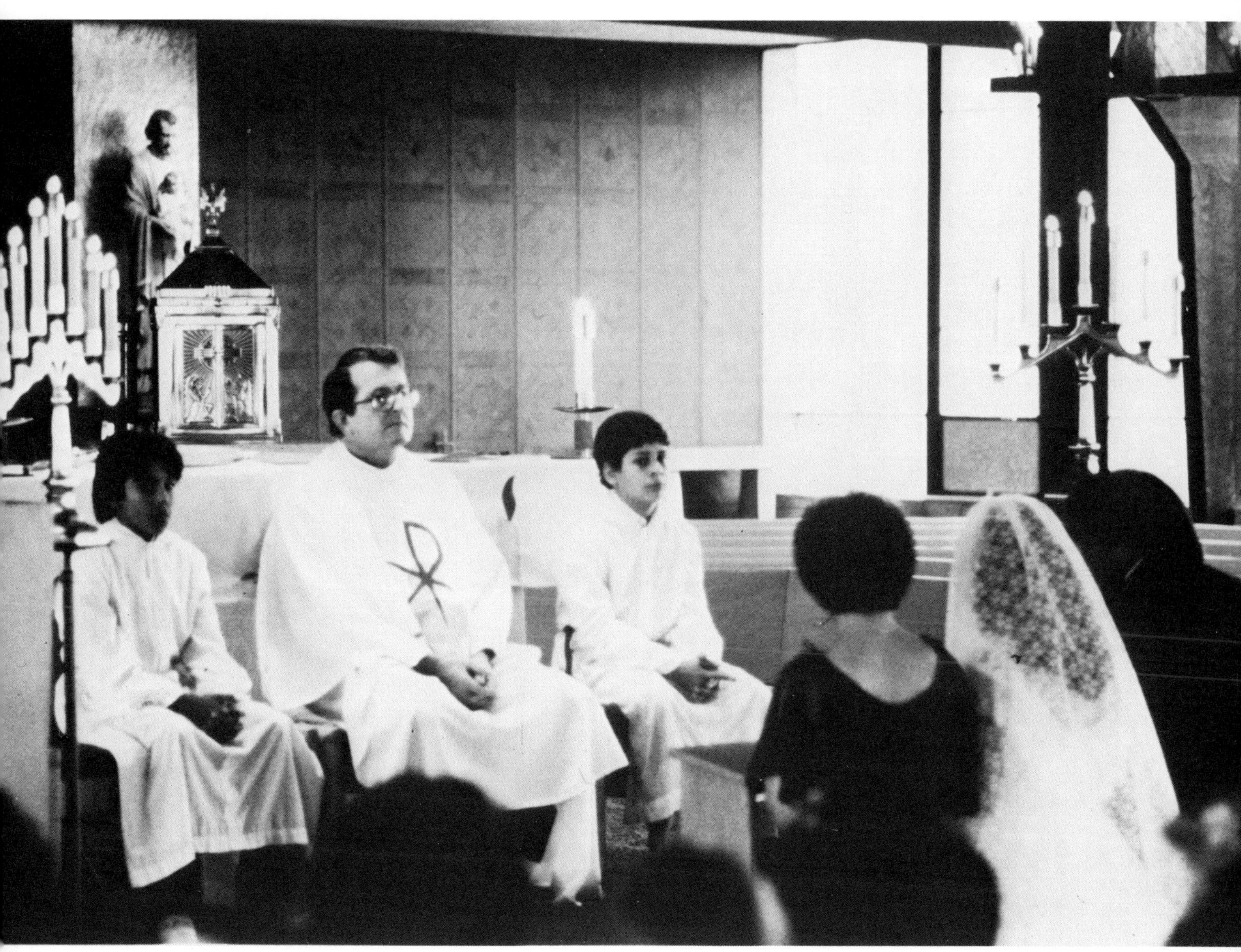

Religious services, weddings, commencements, and other formal ceremonies should never be photographed without the foreknowledge and permission of those in charge of the occasion. Flash light and noisy shutters should be avoided.

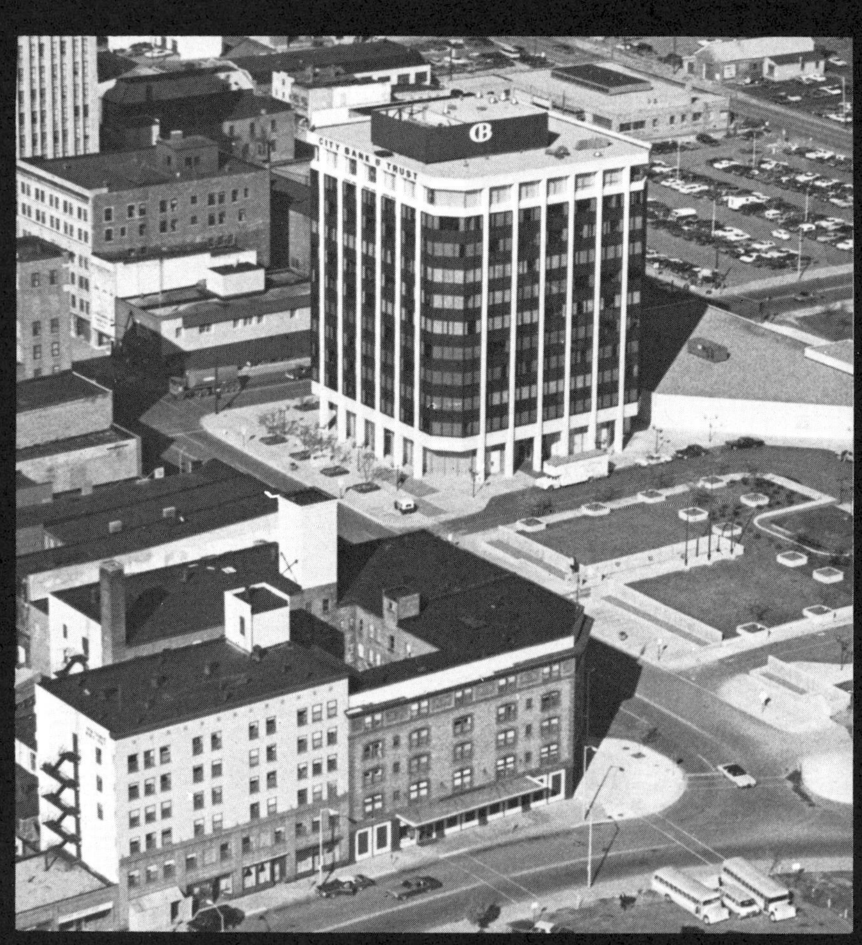
CITY BANK & TRUST

Chapter 5

MORE ADVANCED TECHNIQUES

Here is a chapter for the amateur who, having mastered some of the more obvious elements of good photography, would like to experiment a little with some slightly more advanced techniques.

The chapter includes some suggestions for the scale model enthusiast who might like to combine his hobby with photography. For beginners who have access to a darkroom, there are some ideas for altering or combining routine photographs to produce dramatic solarizations or composites, and for making photographic abstractions using nothing much more than printing paper and light.

Also included is a section on how you can use special-purpose films in your camera and, finally, some suggestions for taking photographs from the air.

SPECIAL EFFECTS: SCALE MODELS AND MINIATURES

The use of image-altering lens attachments is probably the easiest device available to the amateur for producing trick effects. But there's another method worth investigating which involves the manipulation of the subject itself. It's a little more difficult, but it can produce some extremely impressive results.

It involves the deliberate distortion of props or backgrounds; the substitution of miniatures for the real thing; back-projection; or the combining of life-sized objects with models, scale drawings, or photographs. Done carefully and with imagination, the end result can be photographic trickery of a very high order, imperceptible to any but the most experienced eye.

Movie-makers have carried this sort of thing to very sophisticated extremes, of course. Science-fiction, space films, and disaster pictures, in particular, depend heavily upon the talents of art directors and cinematographers who are adept at combining these techniques.

Basic to most trick photography is the "model shot": photographing miniatures against a scaled-down background to produce a convincing full-sized effect. It's an exacting, fussy art, requiring much attention to detail in setting up the picture, lighting it, and making the exposure.

The model should be set in a scene typical of its normal environment. This background is called a "diorama," and it should be constructed a little larger than what your viewfinder will show. If it's an outdoor scene, hang a sky-blue backdrop behind the diorama to provide a natural skylight effect. This is especially important if you're shooting color.

A low camera angle will help to accentuate the size of the model and give it a massive, solid look.

You will need a camera that will let you focus closely on the subject. A single-lens-reflex is indispensable because its viewfinder will show precisely what you'll be getting, and because it will provide a choice of lenses. You can use a macro lens (which will let you focus from infinity to a 1:1 reproduction ratio). Or, if you use your normal lens, you can add clear close-up lens attachments if they're needed.

Close-up photography always raises the problem of depth-of-field—the area within which objects before your lens will be in sharp focus. Generally, the closer the object you're photographing, the narrower will be the depth of field.

You can minimize this problem by closing your lens aperture down to its smallest opening. Most adjustable lenses can be closed down to f/16, f/22, or even f/32. Remember: the larger the f-number, the smaller the lens opening, and the smaller the opening, the greater the depth of field in your picture will be.

Realistic lighting is essential in achieving a convincing illusion. If the scene is an outdoor one, the lights must be arranged to duplicate the natural effect of sunshine—two or more photoflood lamps, grouped closely together and angled to produce authentic-looking shadows. If the lamps are too far apart, each will produce a separate shadow, making it look as if there are two suns. And there goes your illusion.

Standard tungsten photoflood lamps may be used if you're shooting black-and-white film. If you want to project your pictures on a screen, use color-slide film with lights recommended by the manufacturer. Blue photofloods or electronic flash will require film balanced for daylight.

If color prints are what you have in mind, try a color negative film. Be careful to read the film manufacturer's instructions, with particular attention to what they have to say about proper light sources and/or filters. Accurate rendition of color is an important element in model photography.

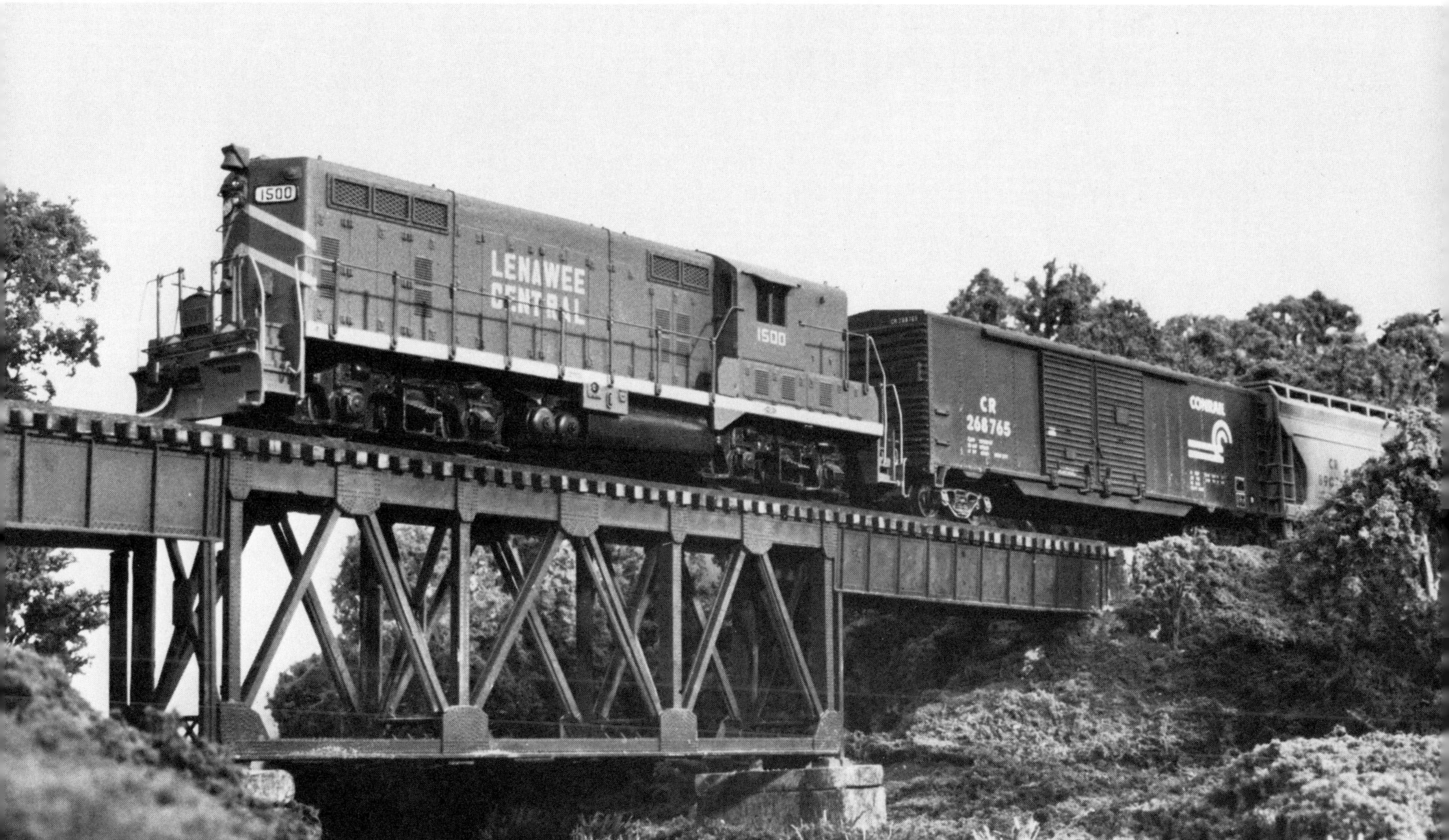

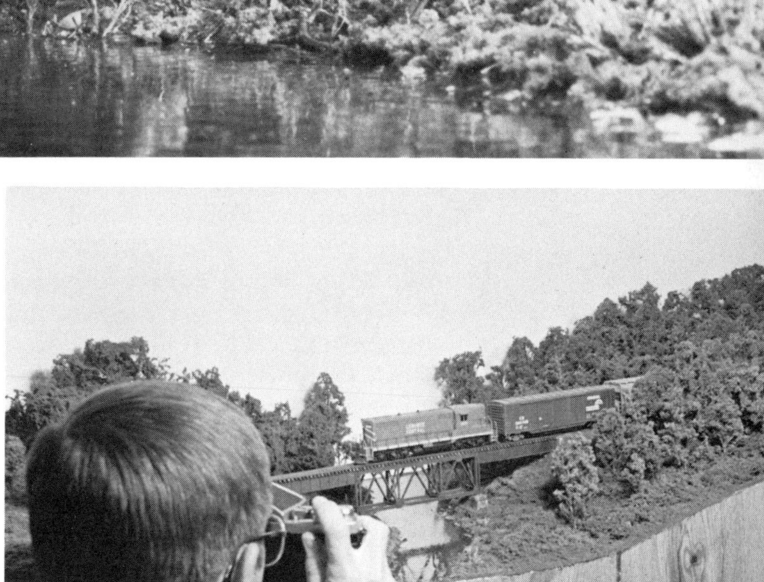

Above: Looking very much like the real thing is this model shot by hobbyist/photographer Doulas Leffler, of Jackson, Michigan.

Right: Model-maker Douglas Leffler is shown here setting up his picture. The locomotive is six inches long, the river is clear plastic, and the diorama is less than three feet deep. All of them were built by Leffler, who is a frequent contributor to railroad hobbyist publications.

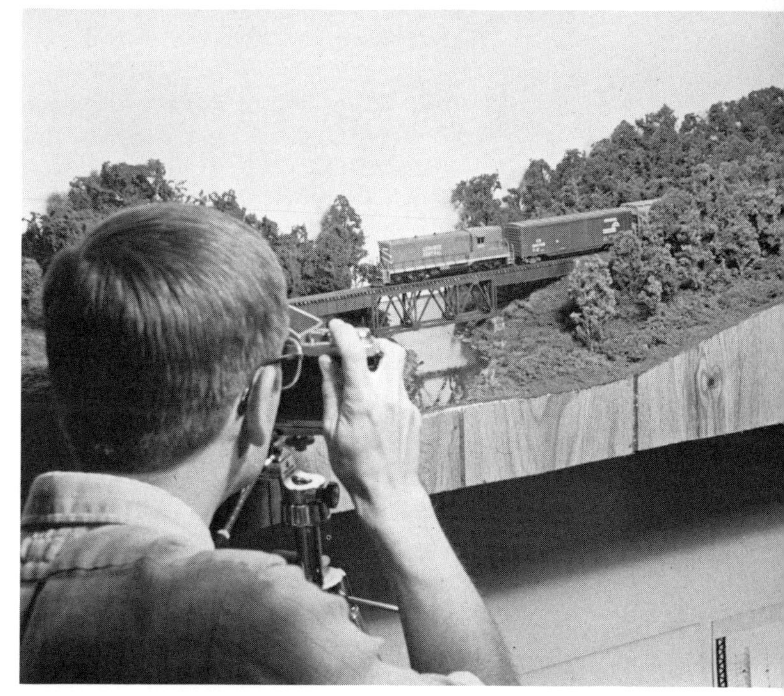

SPECIAL EFFECTS: SOME EASY DARKROOM TRICKS

If you have a darkroom, or access to one, there are some simple things you can do to alter or modify your black-and-white pictures to produce some impressive special effects.

One of the most dramatic of these techniques is solarization: turning the picture into part negative, part positive by deliberately exposing the print to light during the developing process. Rather routine photographs can be given a mysterious, unearthly quality by this procedure.

Besides your regular darkroom equipment, all you need is an ordinary light bulb hanging about three feet directly over the developing tray. You expose the print in the enlarger in the usual way, transferring it to the developer and proceeding as though you were making a regular print, with this difference: about midway through the developing process, switch the light bulb on and off as fast as you can. Then continue developing the print.

The brief flash of light will produce peculiar effects: the dark areas of your print remain pretty much unchanged, the lighter areas turn varying shades of gray, and hard black lines will appear where light and dark areas meet. There are all sorts of complicated chemical reasons for these changes, but we can afford to ignore them. It's aesthetic results we're interested in, not technical explanations.

Pictures with lots of lights and darks work best when you're tinkering with solarization. For this reason choose a contrasty negative. If you prefer a negative of normal contrast, make your print on a high-contrast paper or, if you're using multicontrast paper, use a high contrast filter.

There are a lot of variables in the solarizing process: how bright is the bulb, how far is it from the developing tray, at what point in the process do you flash the paper, and how fast can you turn a light on and off? Because of them, you'll find that no two prints solarized from the same negative will be alike. You'll need to experiment a bit.

The finished print can be modified even further by a little localized bleaching to lighten certain areas. Use a dilute solution of liquid laundry bleach or try Farmer's Reducer, available at photo stores. Apply the solution to the wet print with a small brush or cotton swab. Watch the areas being bleached very carefully and, just before it reaches the shade of lightness you want, dunk it in the fixing solution to stop the bleaching action. Refix, then wash and dry the print as you normally would.

You can do your solarizing on newly exposed black-and-white film, too. The method is the same: about midway through the developing process remove the film from the developer, hang it up in the darkroom where it can be briefly and evenly flashed, flash it, and then return it to the developer and complete its development normally.

You might also like to try making photograms in your darkroom. For this you merely spread one or more small objects across the surface of your printing paper, expose the paper evenly to light from your enlarger or some other source, and then develop the print.

Solid objects like paper clips or clothespins will produce instantly recognizable silhouettes. Transparent objects, like bottles, will refract and bend the light rays into surprising three-dimensional shapes. Twine or thread can be looped in and around the other objects to provide sinuous connecting lines. As with solarizing, the trick is to combine experimentation with imagination. The possibilities can be limitless.

A third and equally easy method of producing trick effects in the darkroom involves sandwiching two or more negatives in your enlarger and printing them both together, thus producing a multiple print. Don't pick the negatives at random:

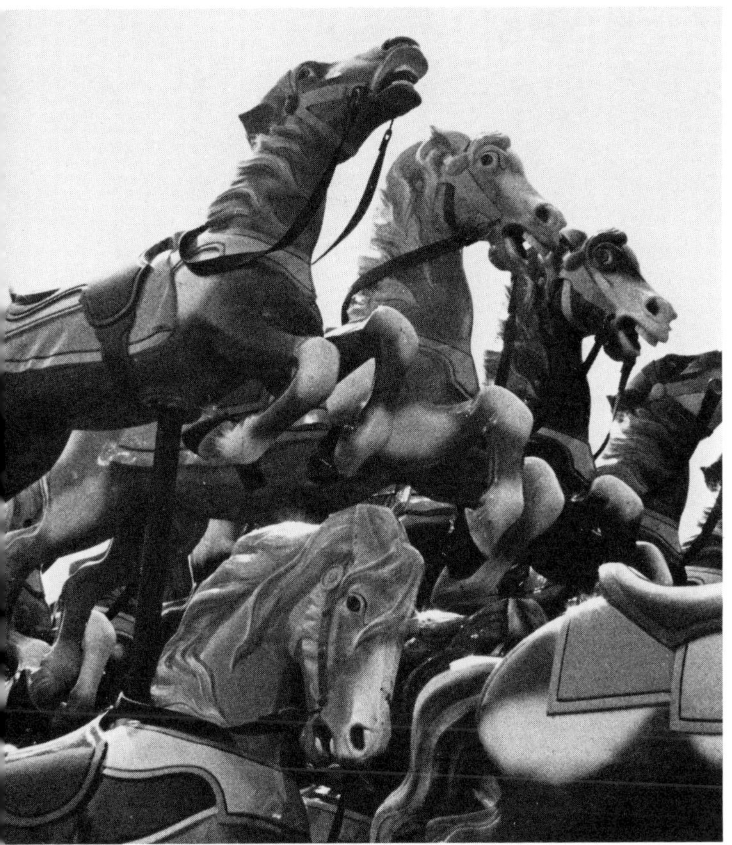

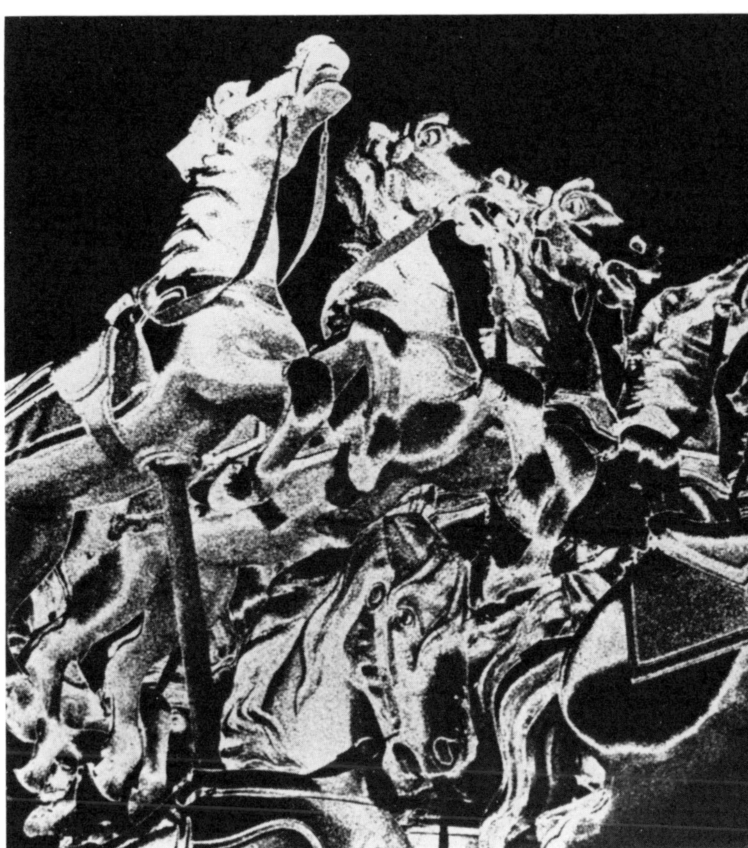

Above left: Before solarization, this picture was a straightforward shot of some carousel horses loaded on the back of a truck. *Above right*: After solarizing, the photograph takes on an entirely different feeling. A grade four paper was used to heighten contrast, and the solarized print was bleached briefly to bring up the whites even further.

choose them because they complement each other, or because together they add up to something new.

It will help if one of the negatives has a large, uncluttered area in it. A lot of sky, for example. Then arrange the two in your negative carrier so that the important part of the second negative overlays the clear area of the first. This will ensure that the final print is something more than just a mishmash of overlapping images.

There's a variation on this method that gives you a little more control over the print, let's say you want to print two negatives on one sheet. First, compose the first picture and print it. Don't develop it—just put it away, out of the light, while you compose the second on your printing easel. Adjust the second picture so that its image will fall in an uncluttered area of the first picture. It will help if you make a pencil outline to give yourself an idea of where the two images will combine in the final print.

Then you turn off the darkroom light, replace the original paper in the easel, and make the second print. Then develop normally.

A number of negatives can be printed on a single sheet of paper in this manner. The only requirement is that you anticipate the final effect by mapping out where the successive images are to fall on the print.

These are only three of many darkroom tricks that can be used to produce pictures the camera never saw. As with all such techniques, the more you experiment with them, the more control you acquire over them, and the more effective your finished picture will be.

SPECIAL EFFECTS: INFRARED AND HIGH-CONTRAST COPY FILMS

There is a third way of producing special effects in your pictures: by the use of films not really intended for normal photography. For the beginner, two of the most interesting films in this category are infrared film and high-contrast copy film.

Infrared film is simply film that is sensitive to light waves existing at the far end of the color spectrum—light waves longer than the red ones normally visible to the human eye. They can be recorded on film, however, even if you can't see them, and they produce effects especially intriguing to the amateur interested in experimenting.

High-contrast copy film is a film intended for copying line art, printed matter, halftoned photographs, or anything else that has first been reduced to black-and-white, with no continuous gray tones.

Both films are available on 35mm spools and can therefore be used in any 35mm camera. In addition, infrared film is also available in color. Both the black-and-white and the color infrared films, when used in daylight, require inexpensive screw-on color filters for proper results.

The results are always dramatic and often bizarre. Don't look for accurate, realistic color rendition: used with a deep yellow filter, color infrared produces reddish foliage and green skies. Black-and-white infrared film is used with a deep red filter. It turns the sky dark and the leaves and grass white.

Using infrared film requires that you understand a couple of simple principles. First, infrared light rays have a longer wavelength than visible light. This means that thay do not focus on the film plane at exactly the same point as do normal light rays. You have to compensate a bit for this when focusing. Fortunately, most modern lenses have a helpful red mark on their focusing rings for this purpose and you focus by that instead of by the usual eyeball method.

Second: in shooting outdoor scenes on infrared film you should always expose your picture at the smallest lens opening available. This will insure the sharpest definition possible with your particular lens. Use a tripod for steady support.

Infrared film has all kinds of valuable practical applications in such fields as aerial photography, criminal investigation, the study of heat distribution, the validating of documents or works of art, and in many technical and industrial areas. But for the beginner looking for dramatic pictorial effects its greatest value is in landscape and architectural photography.

High-contrast copy film can be used to greatest effect when you want a strong black-and-white image with no middle tones, much like a line drawing. It does not seem to work well in portraiture, where gray tones are practically mandatory, but it works effectively in photographs of buildings, streets, and anything with a strong, recognizable pattern. It can also be used to reduce objects to near-abstractions.

Infrared color film can be processed routinely by the film's manufacturer or by independent color labs. But if you're experimenting with either black-and-white infrared or high-contrast copy, you would do well to ask your photo dealer about custom black-and-white processing. Both films require more attention than a drugstore or variety-store processing service can give it.

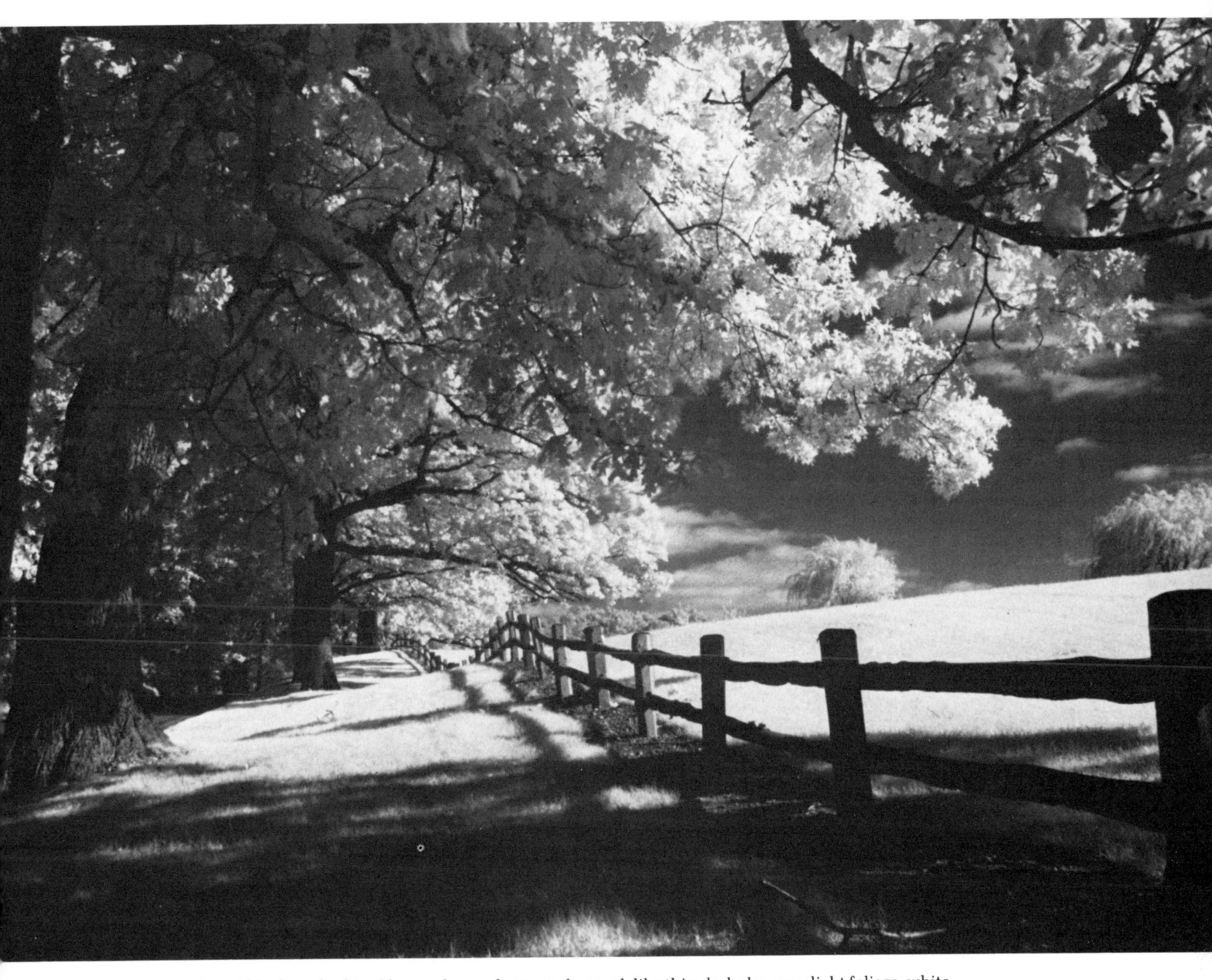

Infrared black-and-white film produces photographs much like this: dark sky, very light foliage, white grass—an almost moonlight effect. Yet this picture was made in midsummer on a sunny afternoon.

TAKING PICTURES FROM A PLANE

The next time you have occasion to fly somewhere—on vacation, on a visit, on business, or for pleasure—don't pack the camera with the luggage. Keep it with you, grab a seat by the window, and try your luck at aerial photography.

There's less to it than meets the eye. Especially if you keep some simple suggestions in mind.

Whether you're traveling in a small private plane or in a big commercial airliner, you must shoot your pictures at a very fast shutter speed: 1/500 or 1/1,000 sec. Because of this, it's a good idea to load your camera with one of the fast films . . . something with an ASA rating around 400. This will let you shoot at faster speeds, using filters over your lens if you wish, and still get a good exposure.

In shooting pictures from a plane, hang loose. I mean that literally. Keep your body away from seat backs and your elbows off windowsills. Touch the plane at as few points as possible. The idea is to prevent the aircraft from transmitting its vibrations through you to the camera. The lens should be kept close to the window glass to prevent it from picking up reflections, but it must not touch the glass.

There will almost always be some atmospheric haze between you and distant objects, and you can reduce the haze by using filters over your lens. If your camera is loaded with black-and-white film, a yellow filter will cut through the haze markedly. If the problem's really bad you can use a No. 25 red filter, which absorbs ultraviolet light, minimizes haze, and turns grass and trees very dark. In any case, remember that when you use a color filter you cut down on the light reaching the film, and, since you don't want to change your shutter speed, you must compensate by opening up your lens to a larger f-stop.

Find the "filter factor" for your particular filter. Multiply the exposure recommended by your light meter or by the instructions packed with your film by the filter factor to get the corrected exposure. If the filter factor is two, for example, you would open up your lens one full stop, thus doubling the amount of light reaching the film.

The larger passenger planes have plastic windows through which you must shoot. Don't try a polarizing filter, since the plastic is already polarized. You can, if you have color-slide film in the camera, use a skylight filter, which will reduce some of the blue in the atmosphere and for which you do not have to make compensations in lens openings. The skylight filter won't help if you're shooting color negative film, but any excess blue in your picture can be removed when the picture is printed.

Things are a little different in small, private planes. You can often lower a window or shoot through one of those little air intakes, in which case you can try a polarizing filter. High-winged planes are convenient because you don't have the problem of wings sticking into your picture, but if you're in a low-winged plane, you might talk the pilot into banking a little to drop the wing out of the frame.

In all cases, use the lens that is normal for your camera. Telephoto lenses don't work very well because they pick up vibrations from the aircraft, magnify them enormously, and transmit them to the film. The result is blur. Your lens setting will, in almost all aerial photography, be at infinity.

If you're a pilot yourself, don't try to fly *and* photograph, lest you get preoccupied with one thing and forget the other. Changing film in mid-flight is difficult enough, especially since the faster films have to be carefully loaded in the shade, and shade is hard to find while you're trying to control a small plane.

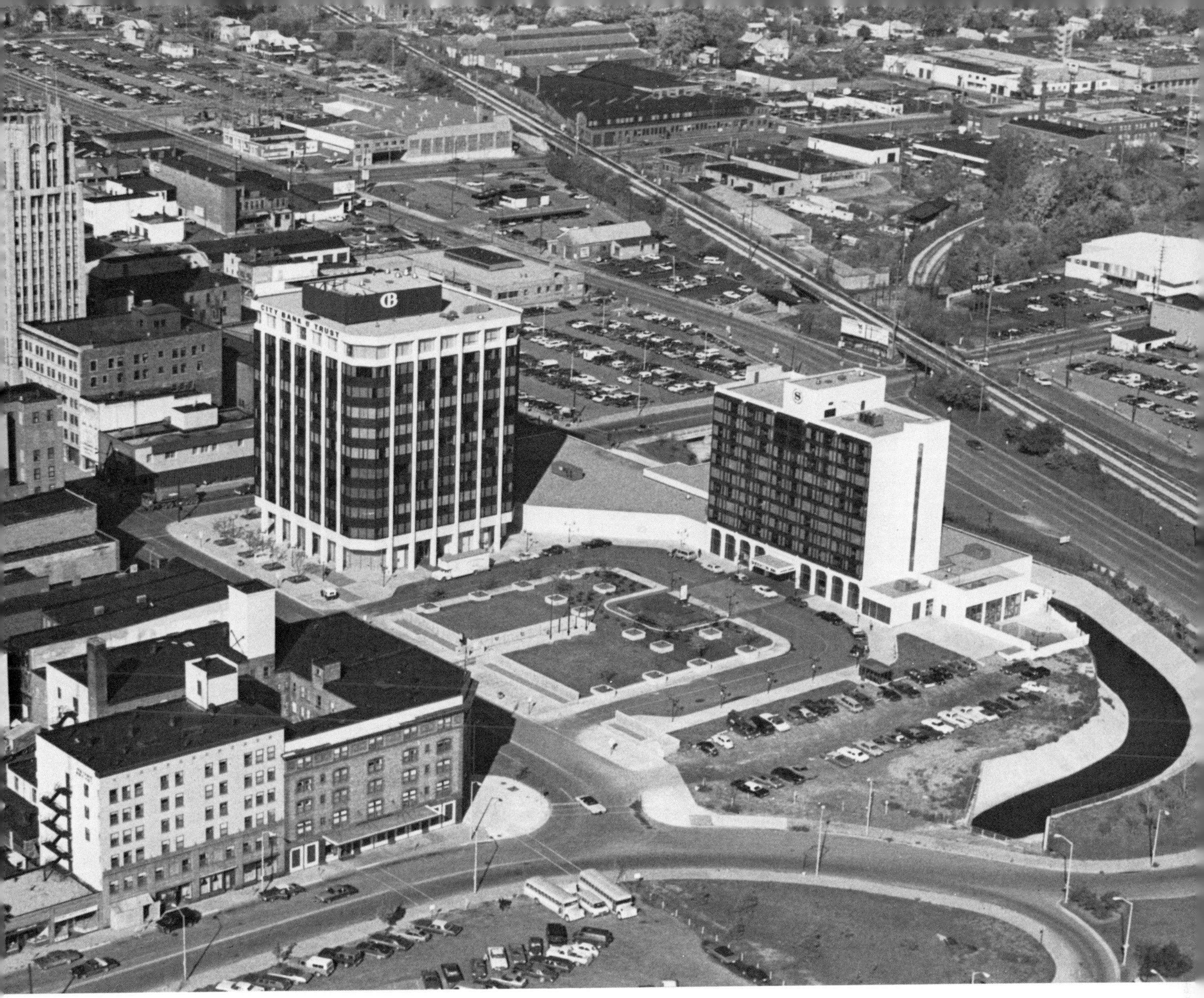

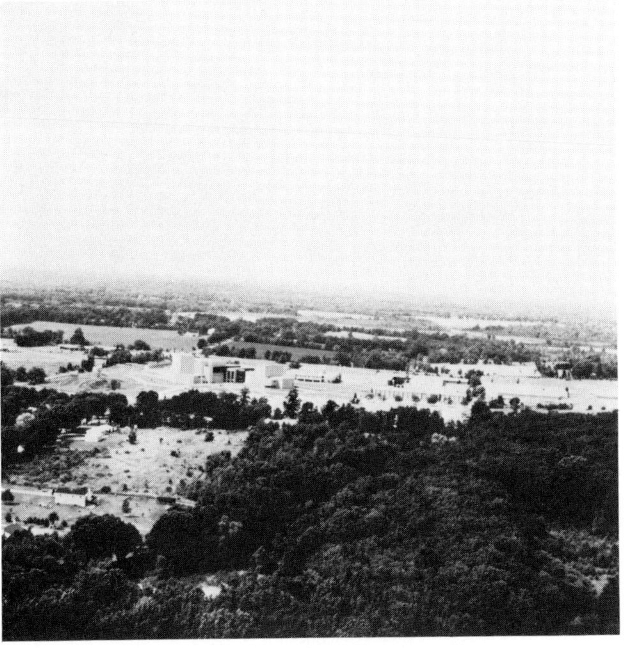

Above: This aerial photograph was made on a mid-October morning at about ten a.m. from a small private plane. The time was chosen carefully, so that the faces of the buildings would be well lighted. A yellow-green filter was used with black-and-white film to minimize ground haze.

Left: Shooting pictures from the air requires a very fast shutter speed to minimize the effect of vibrations produced by the aircraft. With color slide film, a skylight filter will help reduce ground haze.

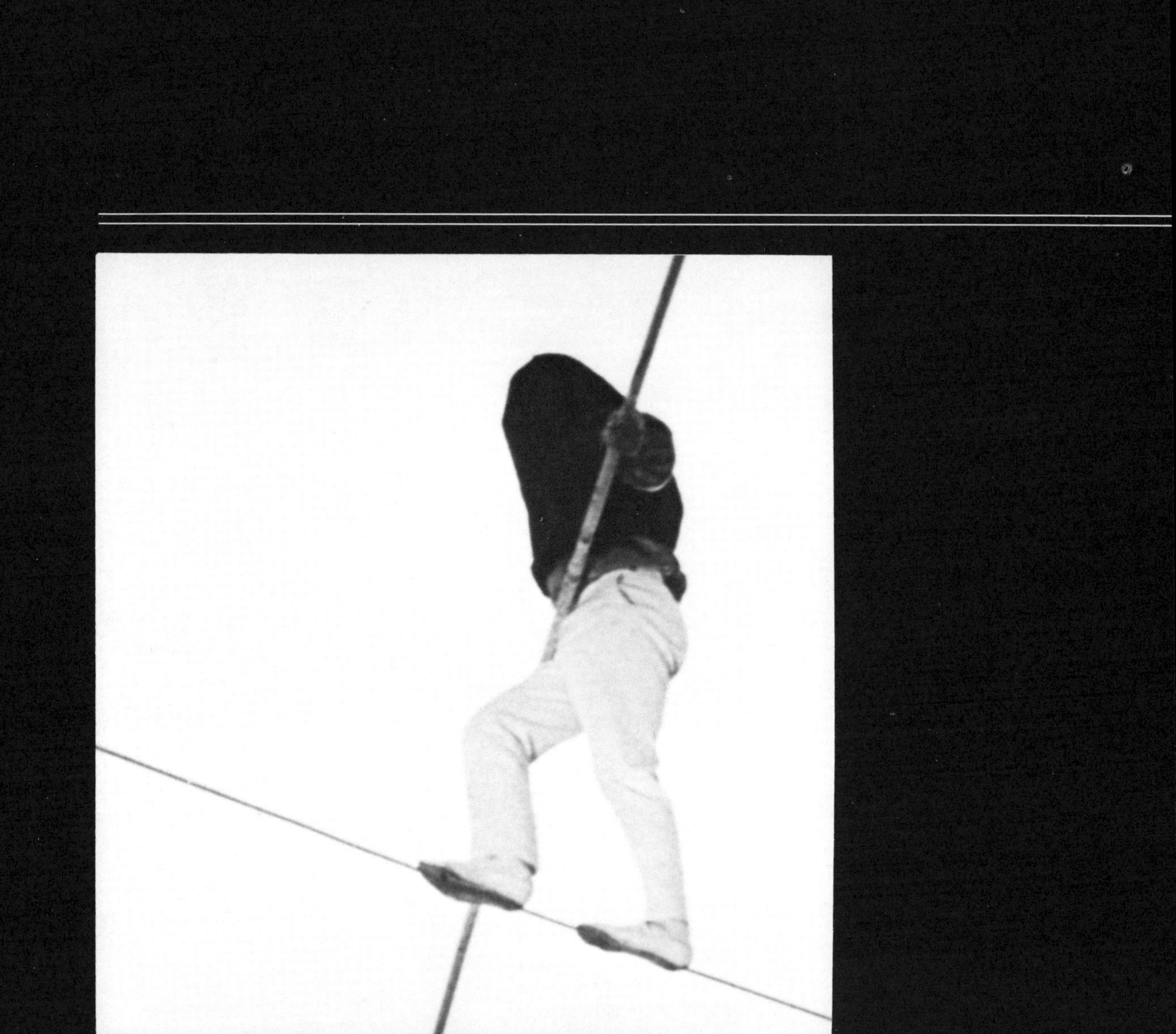

Chapter 6

ENTERING YOUR BEST PICTURES IN CONTESTS

You might not think of yourself as a competitor—at least where photography is concerned—and it may not have occurred to you that some of your pictures may be potential prizewinners.

Your first hint usually occurs when a friend picks up one of your photographs and says "Now, this is a *good* picture! You ought to enter it in a contest!." And, if it happens two or three times, maybe you ought to.

There's no shortage of opportunities for submitting your work to the impartial scrutiny of qualified judges. Most county and state fairs include a photography contest. Many newspapers sponsor them, as do photography magazines and hobby publications. So do chambers of commerce, tourist councils, private corporations, civic organizations, and manufacturers of photographic equipment.

If you have a picture you're particularly proud of, keep your eyes open for a contest in which you might enter it, and read the chapter that follows, which analyzes photographic competitions how to enter them, and what kind of pictures usually win them.

WINNING PHOTO CONTESTS

No one knows the exact number, but there must be thousands of photo competitions, large and small, going on at any given moment. They range in size from large international contests like the annual Kodak-sponsored Newspaper Snapshot Contest to small, local ones intended to promote tourism or to generate publicity for one project or another.

Awards are usually offered in such contests, and they vary widely from a ten-dollar first prize to a trip around the world. It all depends on the motives and the bankroll of the organization sponsoring the competition.

Some contests are restricted to amateur photographers, some to professionals, and others are open to all comers. Some provide rigid specifications as to what the photographs can be about; others accept pictures on just about any subject.

But despite the enormous numbers of photographs and photographers involved, there seems to be a relatively limited number of competitors who are consistent winners. These people are doing something right, and maybe we can learn something from them. Here are some suggestions, therefore, for those of you who contemplate submitting some of your favorite pictures to contests.

The first and most obvious recommendation is this: know the boundaries of the competition and stay strictly within them. All contest rules place limitations on subject matter, number of entries, size of prints, the acceptability of slides, and that sort of thing. They are also very clear about mailing deadlines. In a word: read the contest rules carefully.

Another important recommendation: if the contest is one that has been run before, take a look at previous winners. Evaluation of them can give you useful insight into what the judges are after.

Equally important is a third consideration: submit the best possible print of your picture, and submit the largest size allowed by the rules. Theoretically, size may not be important, but in practice it usually turns out that a large, well-made print will get the most attention.

Finally, get your entry in early, especially if the contest is a large one and will involve the evaluation of hundreds of pictures. In such a competition, judging is usually done over a period of time, not all at once. Inevitably, the pictures first received get closer and more leisurely attention than do the ones that show up at the last minute.

And here are a couple of footnotes useful to would-be competitors. First: think black-and-white. Most competitions divide entries into two divisions: color and black-and-white. Yet fully ninety percent of the entries will probably be in color. It follows that competition will be nowhere near as strenuous in the black-and-white division.

Second: be a little distrustful of contests whose rules say something like, "All entries become the property of . . ." This can be interpreted to mean that, even if you don't win, the sponsors of the contest have the right to use your picture for whatever purpose they care to put it. By entering the contest you are giving tacit approval to this idea.

Most well-planned and well-run contests provide for the return of your entry if you enclose a stamped, self-addressed envelope. If the print or slide you're entering is the only one you have, and you want it back, be sure to do this. Or, better yet, have duplicates made before you enter and keep a set for safety's sake.

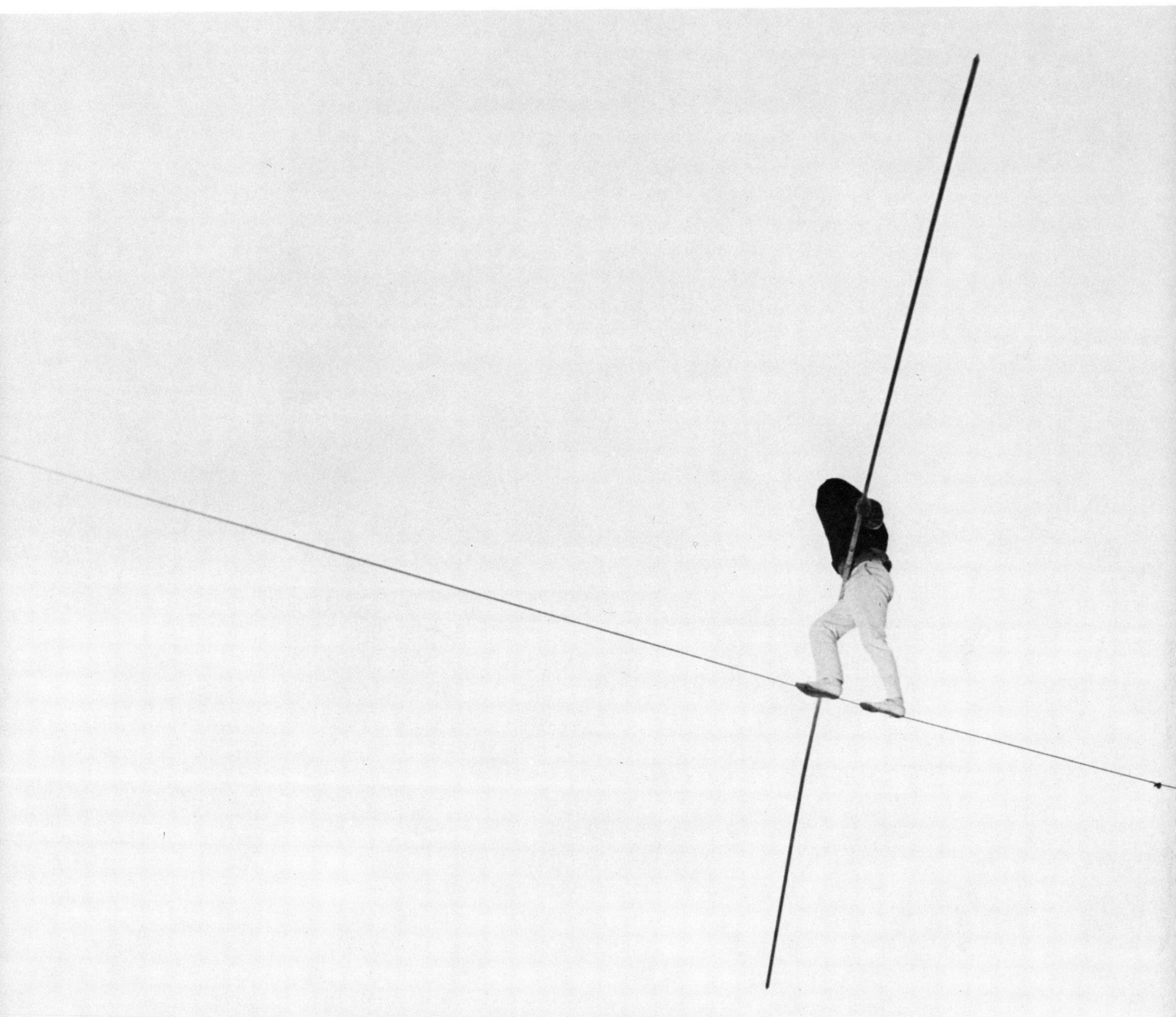

This picture of a hooded wire walker at a fair illustrates the kind of visual simplicity that most judges look for in photo competitions. The viewer's eye goes right to the subject. There are strong compositional elements: the wire and balancing pole form an X with the subject at its center, and there is nothing in the background to distract.

WHAT KIND OF PICTURES WIN PHOTO CONTESTS?

Call it schmaltz if you will, but pictures of puppies, adorable children, sunsets over Grand Canyon, and similar wholesome subjects are, and always have been, the big winners in photo contests. Pictures, in short, that reinforce the popular concept of America as a nation of small towns, friendly neighbors, helpful policemen and a cheerful citizenry.

It's not surprising. Most of the big photo competitions are sponsored by organizations looking for pictures that can be used for publicity. And the best publicity pictures are ones that are not upsetting.

There are exceptions, of course. Once in a while there will be a competition for pictures that illustrate urban or ecological problems, for example. But certainly the larger contests, and the ones offering the most impressive prizes, are seeking pictures that reassure rather than upset us about the state of the world.

All of which leaves the would-be competitor with a problem: how can you treat these familiar, well-worn topics with a fresh outlook? How can you introduce novelty into a badly stereotyped subject?

You can begin by knowing a photographic cliché when you see one, and by steadfastly avoiding it. We have all seen one too many pictures of a sun-bleached steer's skull lying half-buried in the desert sand. Or ocean waves breaking on a stern and rock-bound coast. Or a closeup of gnarled old hands holding a crucifix. Or a loving couple holding hands as they walk along the shoreline while the sun sets behind them.

So have the photo-contest judges. These are people who deal in photographs, and if you can find a new way to say the old things, they'll appreciate it, and they'll notice your work.

You can do it by thinking long and hard about your subject: by circling around and around it, looking for a new way in. Perhaps the whole story can be capsulized by concentrating on a single element: maybe the sideshow barker with his megaphone and his straw hat says more about the carnival than does a long shot of the whole midway.

Your picture will also get attention if it has a strong, simple visual impact. You can do this by rigorously eliminating everything that does not belong. This can be aided by careful composition—by arranging the elements in your picture so that the eye is inevitably led to the picture's core.

One judge involved regularly with a major national weekly photo competition reports that, during their contest, they often receive more than a thousand entries in a single week. And he adds that ninety percent of these are eliminated immediately because the pictures do not have this quality of instant impact.

None of this is easy to do, especially when you can't reach out and rearrange things to your taste. Move around, always looking for the most visually satisfying point of view.

Most judges of photo contests are not impressed by evidences of artificiality or of too much manipulation by the photographer. If people are included in your picture they ought to be moving spontaneously, and not behaving stiffly according to directions. And signs of tinkering in the darkroom do not usually go over too well, either. Judges usually look for strong, straightforward, natural-looking pictures.

Finally: if you read about a contest, and if you think you have a picture that would compete effectively, SUBMIT IT! The photo will do you no good in a desk drawer. Make sure you understand the rules, fill out the entry blank, package up the picture securely with cardboard stiffeners to protect it in the mails, and mail it. You might surprise yourself.

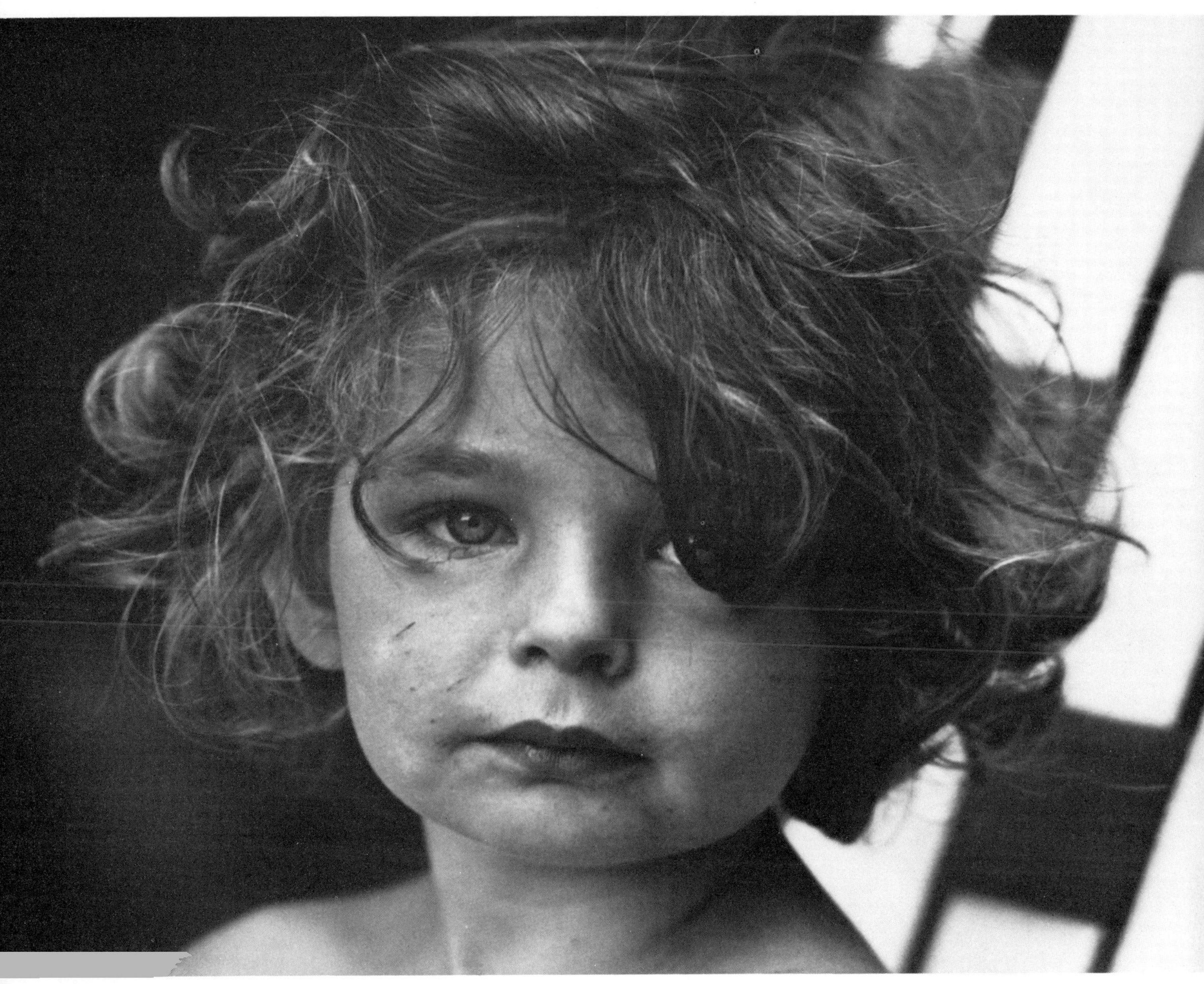

This picture, a winner in the annual Kodak-sponsored Newspaper National Snapshot contest, has the sort of simple, direct appeal that usually attracts the attention of photo contest judges. Shot on black-and-white film, this was the most successful of twelve exposures made in rapid succession. (Courtesy of Eastman Kodak Company).

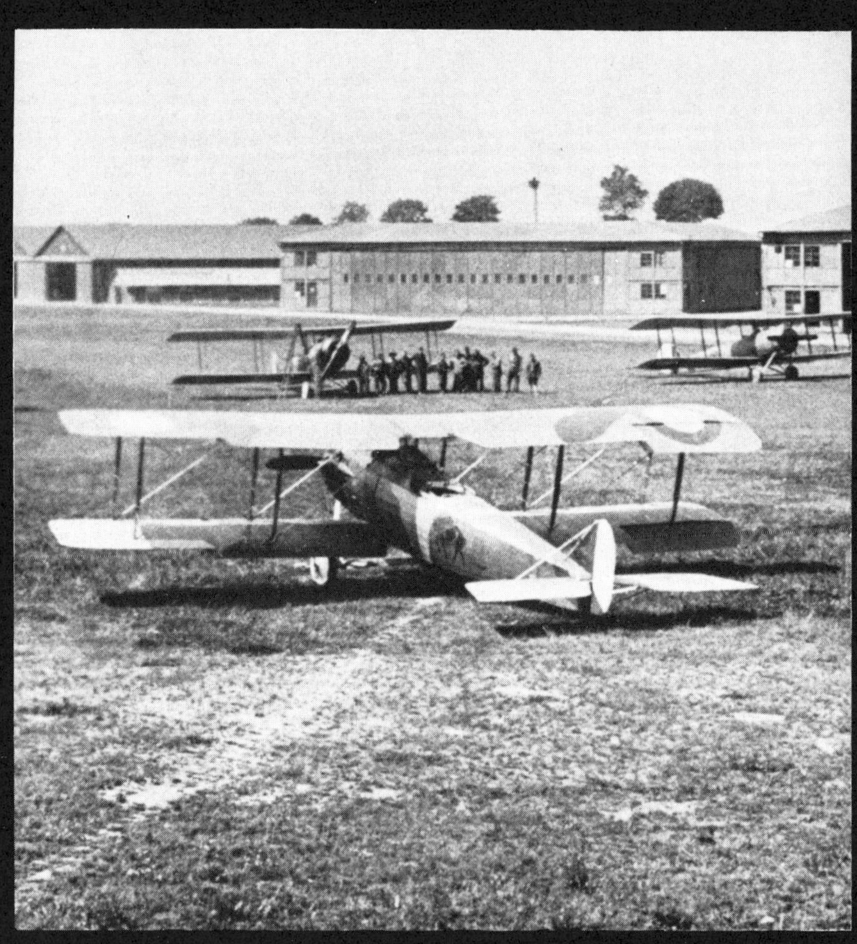

Chapter 7

PUTTING YOUR CAMERA TO PRACTICAL USE

Your truly dyed-in-the-wool amateur tends to buy a camera in order to record family occasions, like birthdays and vacations, and special events, like weddings and bar mitzvahs. Then he forgets it in the intervals between such occasions, and the camera sits on the closet shelf, ignored and unused.

It seems a shame, since the camera and its accessories represent a sizeable investment, and since there are other, practical uses to which it can be put.

The following chapter discusses some of those practical uses—some of the things you can do to extract a little more mileage from your investment.

There is a detailed discussion of techniques for copying old and fading family pictures, so that they won't be lost to posterity. And there is a section on using your camera to supplement your insurance records.

PRESERVING OLD FAMILY PICTURES: WHAT YOU'LL NEED

Back in the Age of Aquarius it wasn't fashionable to be seriously interested in the past. But the seventies brought us "Roots" and family geneologies and a growing interest in our own origins. Every family produced its own self-appointed historian, and people began to get out the old family albums for another look—only to find, in many cases, that the old snapshots had cracked or darkened with age or had become faded and mildewed.

These are decaying processes, and they must be reversed promptly before the pictures are irrecoverably lost, and with them the glimpse of the past they represent.

Fortunately, much can be done, even by amateurs with minimal equipment, to rescue aging photographs. In some cases, merely a careful cleaning and re-fixing of the picture will be enough. In other cases, where fading, darkening or spotting have gone too far, it will be necessary to copy the original. For this you will need a 35mm single-lens-reflex camera, an inexpensive (or homemade) copy stand, a light meter, floodlights, some filters and, if the picture you are copying is small, some close-up lens attachments. These will enable you to get in more closely to your subject, filling up the frame, and producing a copy negative of maximum size.

You may own an extension tube which fits between the camera and its lens. These are excellent for close-up work, but they're more expensive and they introduce complications in calculating exposures. For inexperienced amateurs the clear-glass close-up lens is simpler.

If a copy stand is not available, satisfactory negatives may be made by simply centering the picture to be copied on a large black card and hanging the card on a wall. The black card will reduce the amount of unwanted light bouncing back into your lens. Your camera should be mounted on a sturdy support and, whether you're copying vertically or horizontally, great care must be taken to ensure that the image is centered accurately in your viewfinder. If the film plane and the picture being copied are not parallel, distortion will result.

For illumination, two ordinary lamps in reflectors are sufficient, Photofloods work well, too, especially the type with their own built-in reflectors. These should be located on either side of the subject at equal distances (two or three feet), illuminating it at a forty-five degree angle. The point here is to make sure that the light striking the subject is evenly distributed across it and that there are no patches of light here and there. It is a good idea, too, to make sure that no unwanted extraneous light is hitting the copyboard from nearby windows or floor lamps: these can produce unexpected highlights on your copy negative and will appear on the finished picture.

While you're focusing and framing the picture to be copied, be on the lookout for reflections coming off the picture's surface. Readjusting the lights carefully will eliminate them. If the reflections come from a crimped or buckled photograph, try laying a clean sheet of non-glare glass over it. This will keep the photograph flat, and it will help in eliminating or diffusing reflections.

Since most photographs old enough to acquire historical interest are in black-and-white, you'll probably be doing your copying in black-and-white. The choice of film is wide: my own preference is for panchromatic films of slow or medium speed, like Ilford FP-4, Kodak Pan-X, Ilford Pan-F, or Kodak Plus-X Pan. Kodak's Technical Pan film 2415 is excellent for copying, but it requires special development for best results. If your photograph has faded evenly to a pale yellow-brown, try one of these slower films. They are finer-grained, and inherently contrastier than the faster films, so they can help bring back lost contrast.

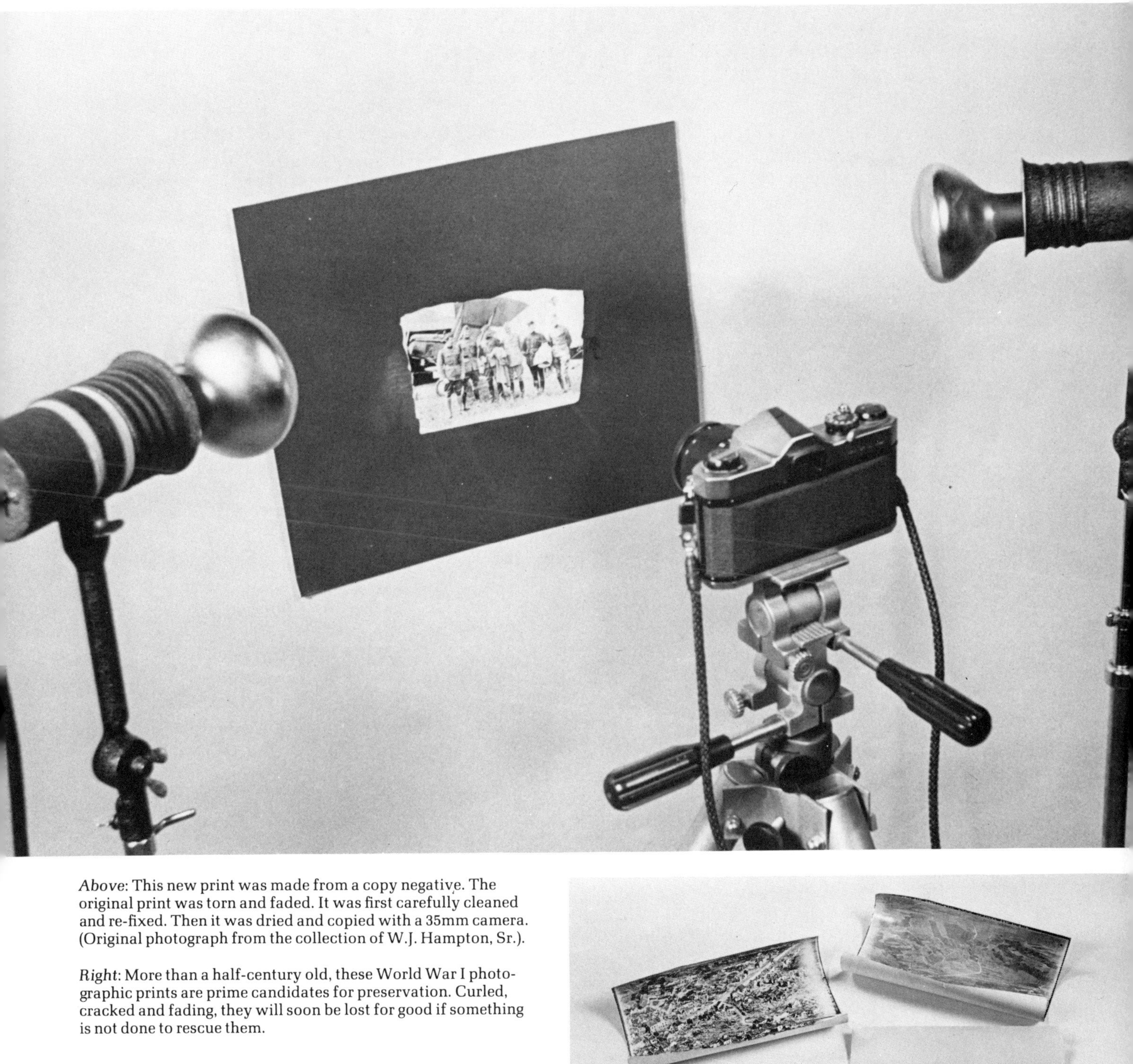

Above: This new print was made from a copy negative. The original print was torn and faded. It was first carefully cleaned and re-fixed. Then it was dried and copied with a 35mm camera. (Original photograph from the collection of W.J. Hampton, Sr.).

Right: More than a half-century old, these World War I photographic prints are prime candidates for preservation. Curled, cracked and fading, they will soon be lost for good if something is not done to rescue them.

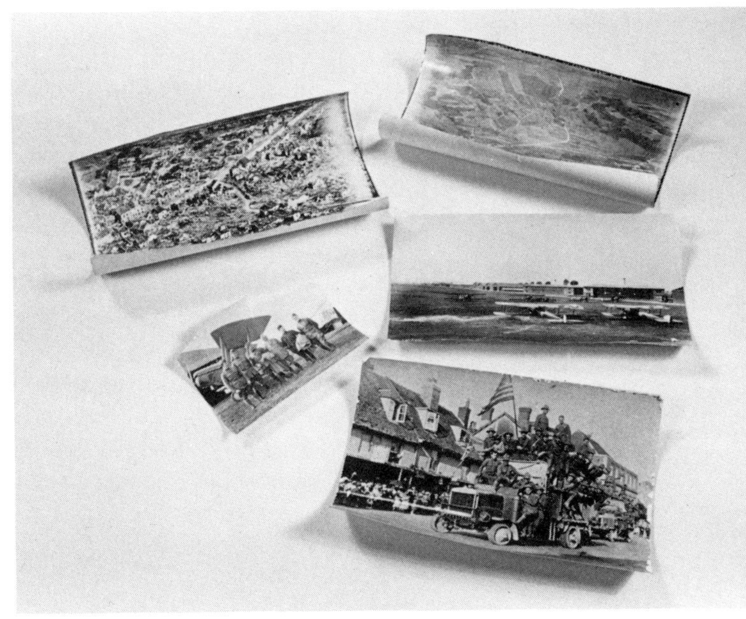

PRESERVING OLD FAMILY PICTURES: PREPARING FOR COPYING

Once you've prepared your setup and are ready to make the copy there is a very important step to take. Make a preliminary warts-and-all copy. This is a safety precaution just in case something goes wrong in preparing the original for re-photographing. Merely copy the original picture, as it is, before attempting to clean it, flatten it, or eliminate wrinkles or cracks. Only after this is done should you take further steps.

If the old picture you're copying dates from about the middle of the last century and is printed on metal, it is probably a daguerreotype or a tintype. It can be copied as it is, but any attempt to clean it should be left to an experienced professional. This is also true of photographs on glass. Most of these date from the turn of the century and are very fragile. Don't try to wash or retouch them.

In most cases, however, the picture to be copied will be on paper and of more recent origin. Gentle re-washing will do a lot to restore it. Soak the print in a tray of room-temperature water for a half hour or longer. When the paper is saturated, gently clean the surface of the print with your fingertips or with a soft cloth to loosen any embedded dirt. Be extremely careful not to scratch or abrade the softened surface of the picture or to tear the paper. The addition of a drop or two of a wetting agent will aid this process and will promote spot-free drying. Longer soaking might prove necessary if the photograph's emulsion has become hard and brittle and resists softening.

After washing, sandwich the damp print between two sheets of photographic blotting paper to remove excess moisture. If the print has a cracked or shiny surface, you may want to try copying it while it is still damp: it will lie flat easily, it will be less reflective, and the cracks in its surface will not show as readily.

When you're ready for photography, mount the picture on your copyboard, framing it carefully in the camera's viewfinder. Fill the viewfinder with the picture: you want the largest negative you can get. Take care that it is centered, and that the film plane (the camera back) and the copyboard are parallel.

Here you may very well encounter a problem in focusing. The normal lens on 35mm single-lens-reflex cameras will let you maintain focus to about two-and-a-half feet from your subject, and this may not be close enough to give you a full-frame negative. It all depends on the size of the picture you're copying.

To get in closer you can use a clear close-up lens. These screw into your regular lens, and are available in different optical strengths, depending upon the focusing range you want. Camera stores carry them and they cost, currently, about six or seven dollars.

At this point there are some further things you can do to eliminate fading or staining in black-and-white pictures. Faded yellow patches in dark areas of the picture can be photographed through a blue filter, which will turn them dark like the area surrounding them. Yellow stains appearing in light areas call for a yellow filter. Dark, colored stains can be eliminated by photographing them through a filter of the same color as the stain. Colored filters are obtainable at camera stores for about five or six dollars.

If you're copying in color the basic technique is the same, but you must remember to use lights balanced for the film you are using. You must also remember that color filters intended for black-and-white film can't be used with color film.

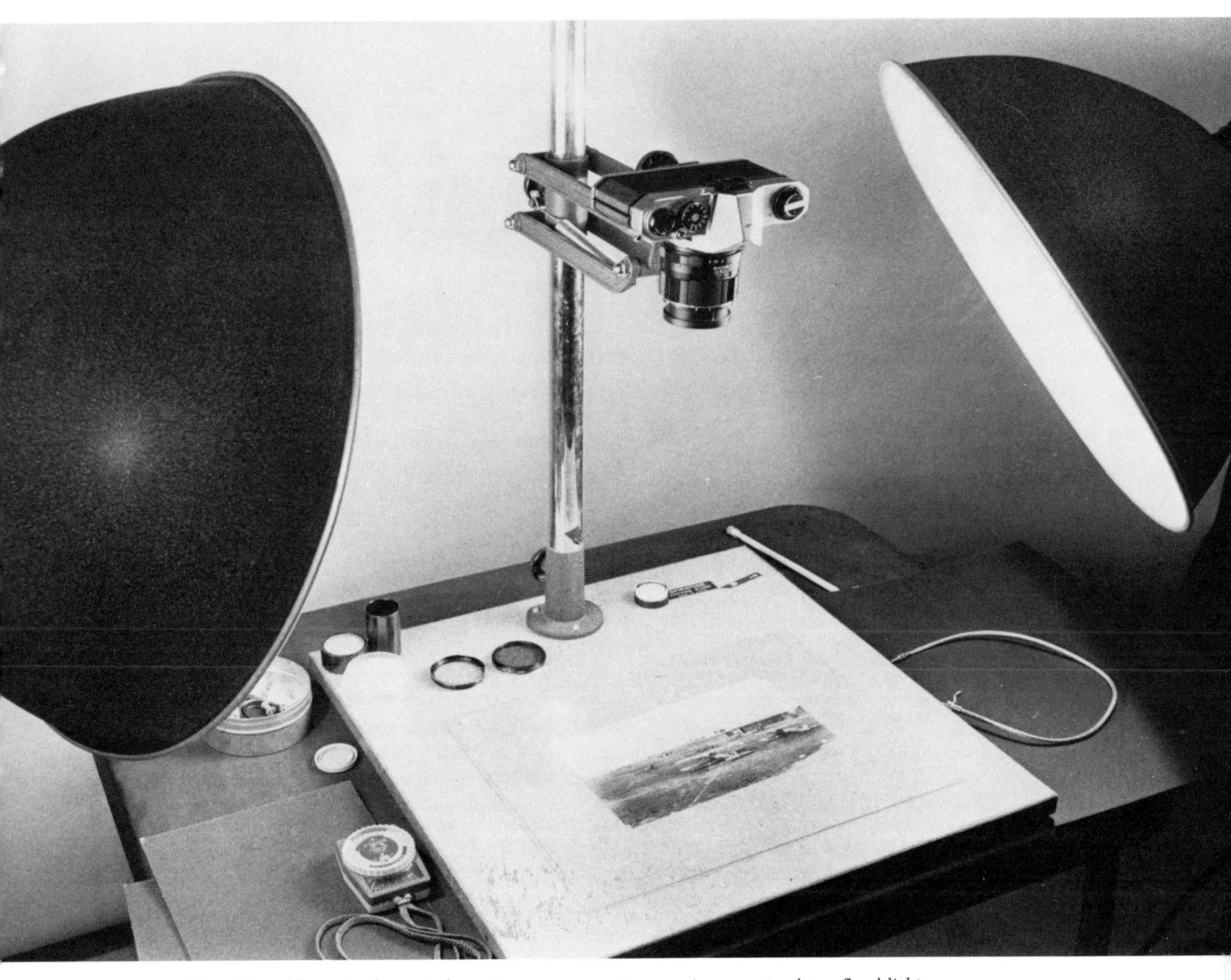

All you'll need for a simple vertical-copying setup are an inexpensive copy stand, two flood-lights, closeup attachments, and a 35mm SLR. The picture to be copied is held flat under nonreflective glass, and a light meter is available to determine exposure.

PRESERVING OLD FAMILY PICTURES: EXPOSING AND PROCESSING

If a supplementary close-up lens is needed to get a full frame, select the lens or combination of lenses that will give you the image you want. Focus carefully, meter the light reflected from your subject, set your lens opening and shutter speed, and make the exposure.

Calculating the correct exposure can be helped by the use of a neutral test card. These are gray cards having a reflectance of 18 percent, and all photo shops carry them. Simply lay the card across the picture to be copied and take your light reading off the light reflected from the card. If you're using a camera with a through-the-lens metering system, it will compensate automatically for any color filters you are using. With a hand-held meter, remember to correct for the loss of light subtracted by the filter.

Each colored filter has a "filter factor," and you multiply the exposure indicated by your meter by the filter factor to get the adjusted exposure. If the filter factor is two, for example, you would either double your exposure time or open up the lens one full stop. If you are using bellows or tubes you will need to correct further for light loss produced by the lens extension.

When you make your exposure, don't be stingy about using up your film. Make a number of exposures at varying shutter speeds or lens apertures. The cost of the film and its processing is probably the least expensive item in rescuing old photographs from oblivion, and the importance of what you're doing far outweighs the few dollars that film and processing will cost you. Go for the best negative you can get.

If you have your own darkroom, or have access to one, you have probably already found your own favorite film developer and have worked out your own techniques for increasing or minimizing contrast in your negatives. If you don't plan to process your own film, have it custom-developed and printed, rather than machine-processed.

Most camera stores can deal with requests for custom processing. Drugstores, variety stores, or overnight processing services can't. In most towns of any size there is likely to be a custom lab or commercial studio that can hand-process and print your picture. A good lab will understand what you are doing and will cooperate to give you the best print possible from your negative.

There are some things you mustn't expect from copying. Restoring old pictures cannot put into them what was never there in the first place. If the original is out of focus or lacks detail because the camera that took it had a poor lens, copying won't clear it up. Some cracks may prove so bad that nothing short of retouching will eliminate them, and some stains may refuse to yield to anything but the airbrush. Even so, you'll find that merely cleaning and copying will give you a vastly improved image.

Indeed, the results are likely to surprise you. Old, faded pictures come to life again. Details you never really noticed become apparent. And, best of all, you've given an old piece of family history a new lease on life.

Top: For horizontal copying the original picture is mounted in the center of a black card to reduce reflected light. Two floodlamps are mounted in screw-in holders. The lights are arranged to illuminate the copyboard evenly. *Bottom*: This new print was made from a copy negative. Copying has restored lost contrast, minimized stains and cracks, and given the picture a new life expectancy. (Original photograph from the collection of W.J. Hampton, Sr.).

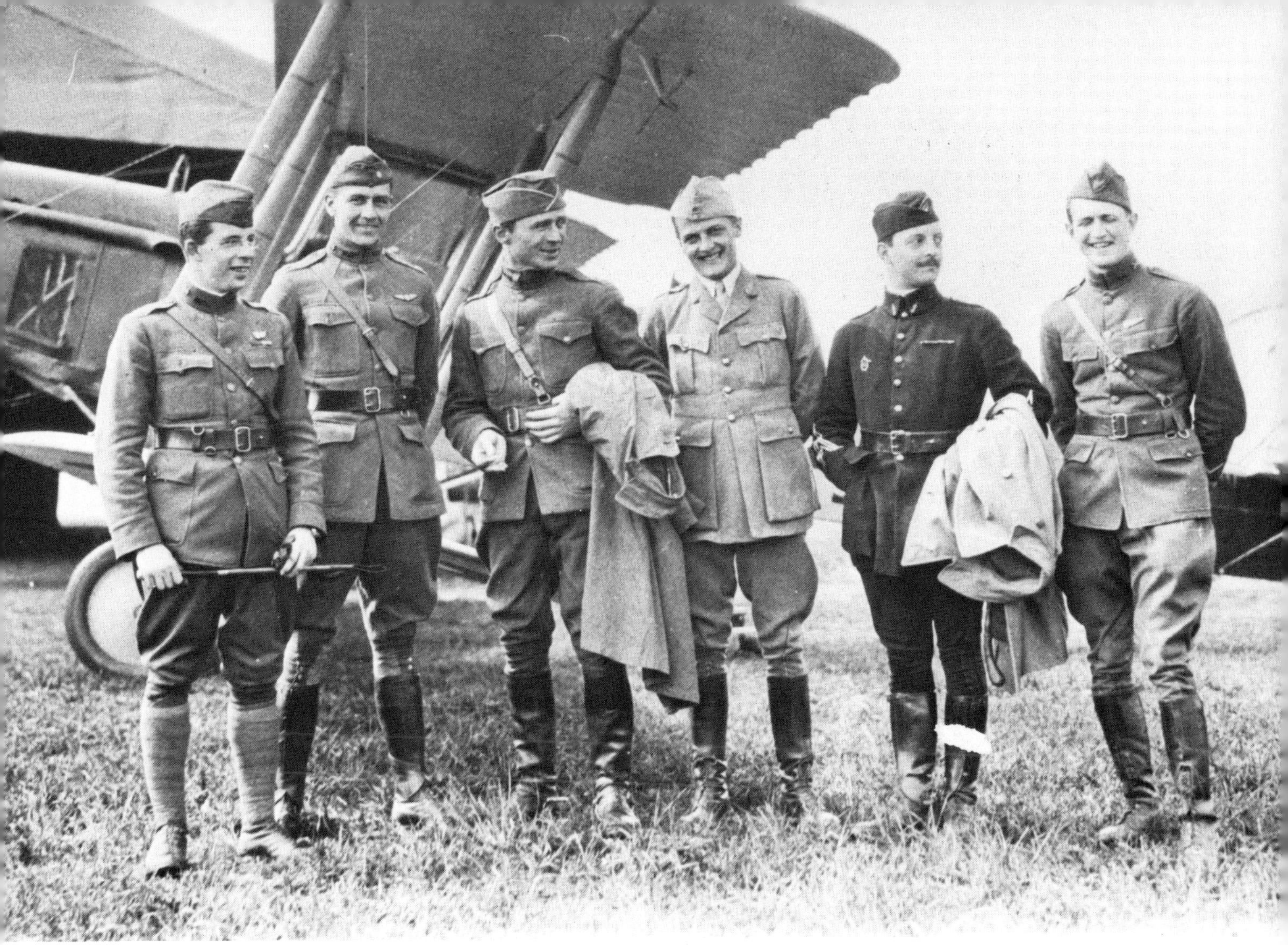

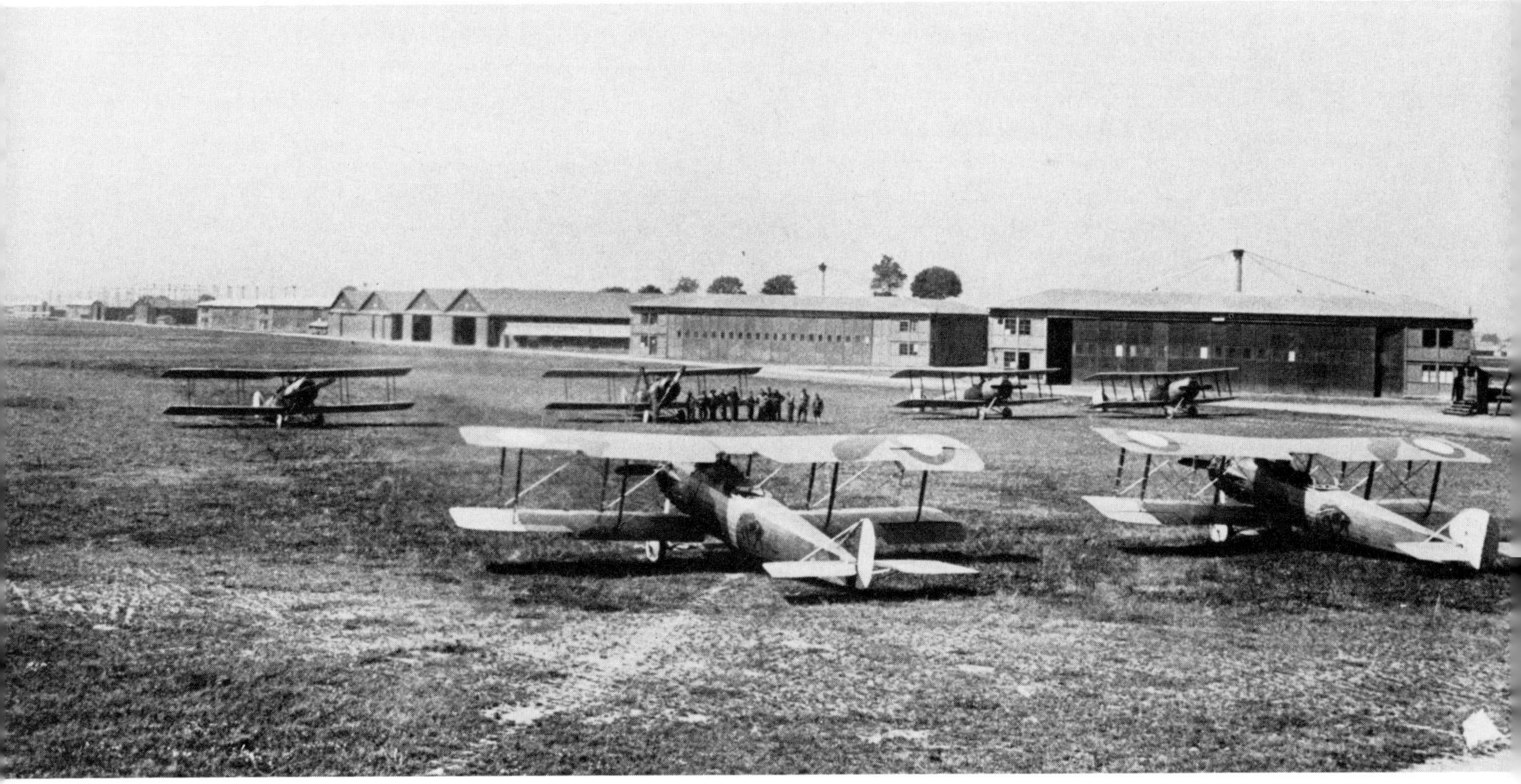

USING YOUR CAMERA TO SUPPLEMENT INSURANCE RECORDS

This business of leaving a half-finished roll of film in your camera for several weeks or months until the next picture-taking opportunity is a very bad idea. The latent image, especially if it's in color, will begin to deteriorate quickly, and if you wait too long to have your film processed you can wind up with some sadly off-color pictures.

It's a far better idea, always, to shoot straight through a roll of film and send it off to the lab promptly. And if you have trouble thinking of something to shoot to finish off a roll, here's a useful idea: use the leftover film to supplement your insurance records.

In the past few years the price of almost everyone's house has ballooned beyond anything that might have been expected a decade or two ago. And the value of the contents of the home has gone up with it, making it extremely important to maintain an updated inventory of everything you own of value.

If there is fire, theft or wind damage, filing an insurance claim is made much easier if there's an up-to-date written inventory available, supported by photographs of the contents of the damaged rooms.

Compiling such an inventory needn't be the tedious task most people fear it is. You merely take a tape recorder and a camera with you as you go from room to room describing the items in those rooms and photographing them. Most people can do it in less than an hour.

Each room should be photographed from at least two angles to make sure that everything in it is covered. The contents of closets and drawers, if they can't be photographed, can be itemized on tape. Especially valuable items like jewelry and furs should be laid out on a table and photographed. You should also take care that such expensive items as stereos and television sets are included in your pictures, and that their serial numbers are recorded on tape.

Experienced insurance-claims people also suggest that photographs of especially costly items should include a member of the family whenever possible because it adds credibility to the claim of ownership.

And, while you're at it, don't forget to include the contents of the garage or any outbuilding that might contain important possessions.

Photographs are an invaluable memory aid when you're filing an insurance claim. People are usually under considerable strain after they've suffered, say, a loss by fire, and the pictures will help them remember items they might otherwise easily forget.

The photographs and tape recordings should be kept, along with a written inventory, in a safe place outside the home. Put them in a safety deposit box or leave them with a friend.

Photographic expertise is not a factor. An Instamatic will do as well as a Hasselblad, and drugstore processing will serve as effectively as custom printing. The point of the whole thing is to provide yourself with a useful memory-jogger, so that if you have to recall what was in a room you can do it.

If you have a 35mm camera with removable lens you might find it easier to use a wide-angle lens in shooting your pictures because it will cover more area in a single shot than will the normal lens. What you can't get in one shot, however, you can get in two or three.

And you will have put those leftover unexposed frames to immediate and practical use.

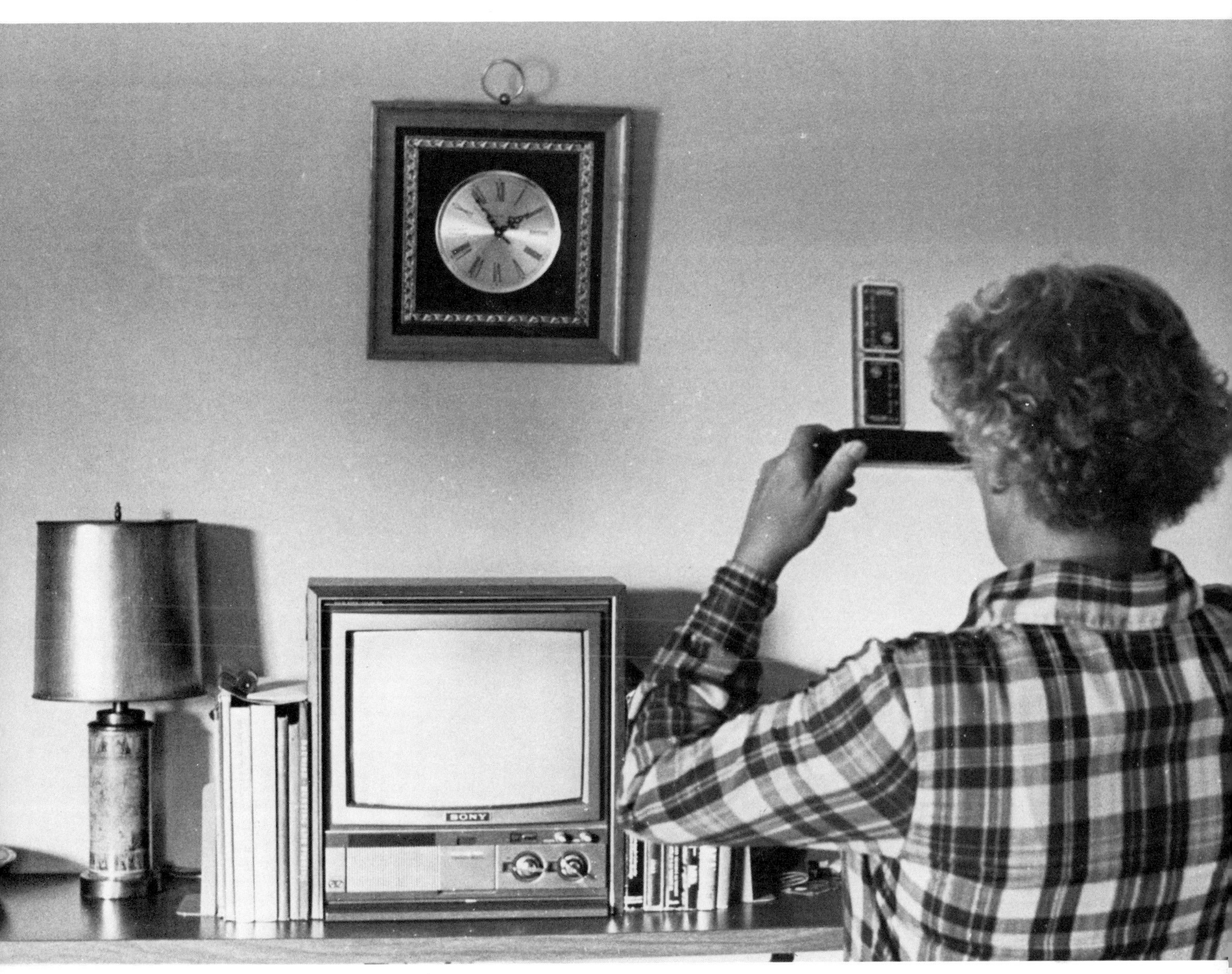

Expensive items in a room, such as stereo and television sets, should get special photographic attention.

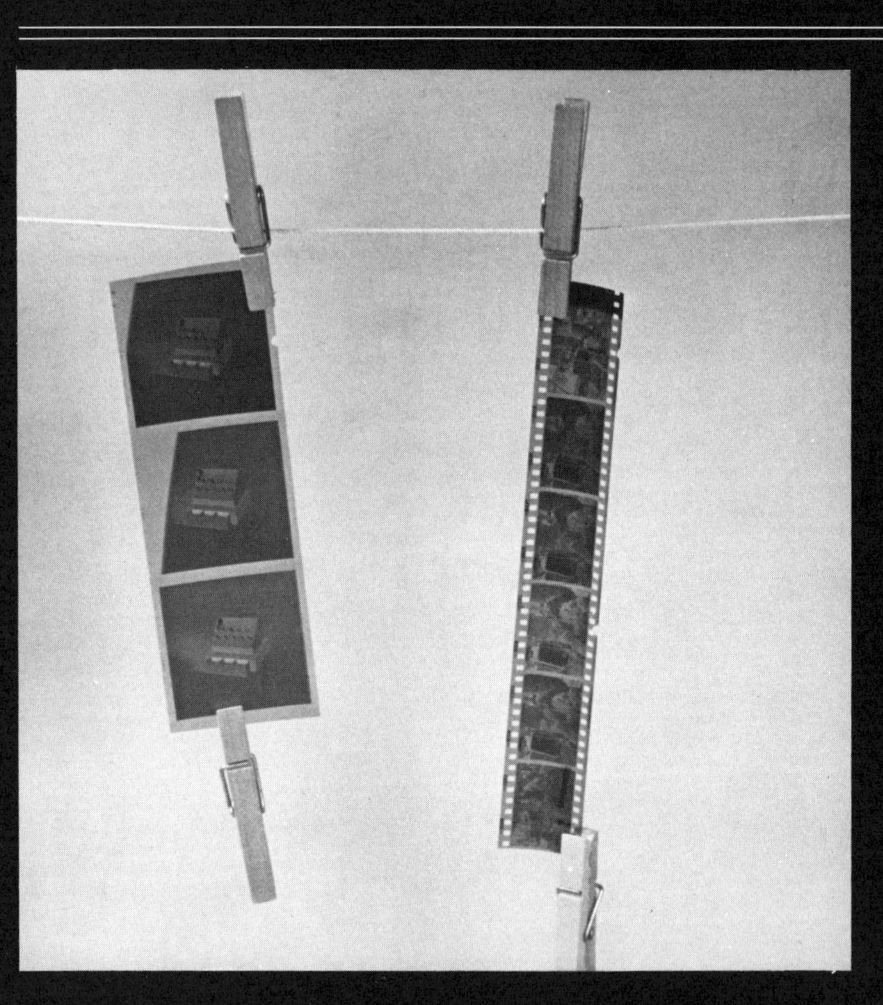

Chapter 8

CARING FOR YOUR NEGATIVES

This final chapter may be last, but it is by no means the least important one in this book. It's about something so obvious and so fundamental to photographers, both amateurs and professional, that it hardly ever gets mentioned.

It has to do with the care of your negatives.

It's the finished print that gets all of the attention when your pictures come back from the photo finisher. But it's the negative that you must go to if you want additional copies or enlargements, or if the print gets lost or becomes hopelessly faded. If the negative has been treated as they usually are treated, you may have a problem.

So this chapter describes the best way for preserving your negatives and, for those that have become damaged through neglect, it outlines a simple procedure for cleaning and restoring them.

PROTECTING YOUR NEGATIVES

If the only pictures you ever take are on slide film or on "peel-apart" instant film, you may be only distantly interested in what follows. But you would also be among a very small minority. Today the great majority of amateur photographers expose negative film in their cameras and have positive prints made from the negatives.

And then, once the prints arrive, they pretty much forget the negatives; which then get lost, neglected, or thrown away. It's a fate they do not deserve, because they are your best recourse when you want additional prints or enlargements, or if the original print becomes faded or damaged. They should be given the same careful attention you'd give a quality print.

A word, therefore, on the care and protection of your negatives. In the early days negatives were a piece of glass coated on one side with a light-sensitive emulsion. You put it in your camera, exposed it, and then processed it to bring out the image and to make it permanent: the "development" stage. Then you used the negative to produce a positive image on a piece of paper similarly coated and similarly processed: the "printing" step.

It hasn't changed. Today's emulsions are coated on a flexible base, so that you can pass a whole roll of film through your camera and get a number of negatives on a single strip of film. We've got better lenses and more sophisticated emulsions. But the old one-two processing sequence remains. First the negative, then the print.

From which this follows: damaged negative, unsatisfactory print.

If you examine a negative at an angle to the light you'll see that one side is not as shiny as the other. That's the emulsion side, where the image is chemically stored. Most negatives have a tendency to curl inward toward that side. And it's the emulsion side that's most vulnerable to scratching, fingerprints, and other kinds of injury. Film manufacturers add a scratch-resistant coating over the emulsion, which helps, but it doesn't relieve you of your obligation to treat the negative carefully.

Your instinct should be to protect your negatives, particularly the important ones. Don't leave them rattling around loose in the envelope they're returned in. Instead, store them immediately in inexpensive sleeves which you can get from any camera shop.

First, mark the sleeve with a note identifying the subject of the negative, then insert the negative. If you try to write on the sleeve after the negative is inside it, you run the risk, if you apply pressure, of damaging the film.

Then put the negatives away in a special envelope or box, marked "negatives," and store them where they won't be subject to extremes of heat or humidity.

Some processing labs still return negatives in uncut rolls. It's a bad habit, because a single piece of grit trapped between the layers can do considerable damage, especially if you try to cinch the roll up into a smaller circumference. It's best, as soon as you receive the film, to cut it into segments of five or six negatives and store the individual strips in sleeves.

Cut carefully along the unexposed area between picture frames to avoid slicing into the picture area. And never cut negatives into single frames: always leave them in strips of five or six. It makes it easier for you to handle them and for the lab to make reprints from them.

In handling negatives, incidentally, hold them by the outer edges only, taking care that your fingers don't touch the picture area. There's always a minute amount of perspiration on your fingertips which can leave an acid deposit on the film and which, in time, can become a permanent part of the negative.

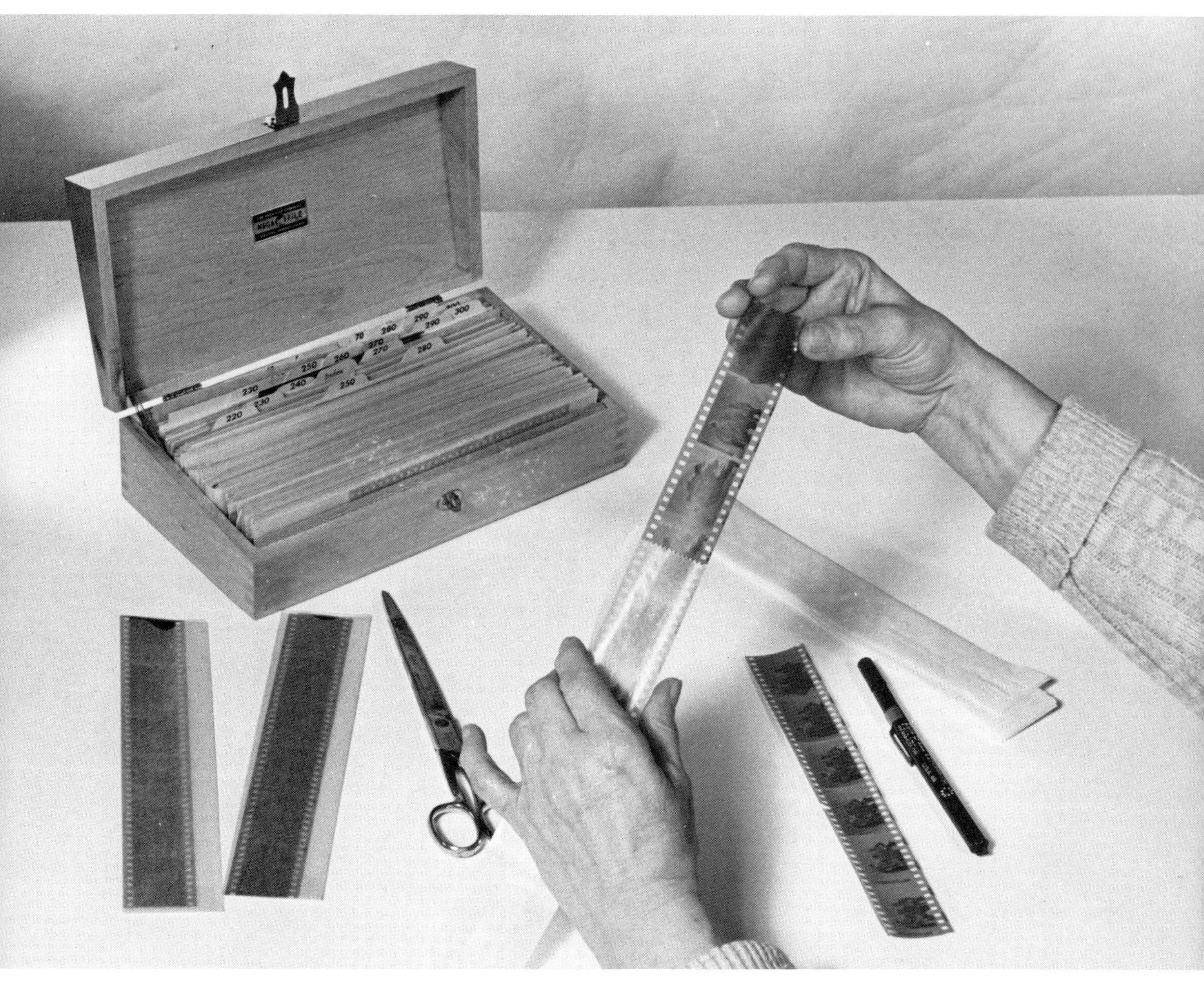

The best protection for important negatives is to cut them into strips and store each strip in a ready-made envelope, or sleeve, as shown here. Identify the subject of the negatives on the outside of the sleeve and store them in a cool, dry place.

CLEANING AND RESTORING OLD AND DAMAGED NEGATIVES

Time and the environment are hard on negatives, even as they are on you and me. A negative's most obvious enemies are dirt and scratches, but they're also susceptible to drying, which makes them curl and crack, and to fading and staining, which are usually the result of imperfect processing.

You can do something about the dirt and scratches yourself. Sometimes you can even reduce the effects of drying and curling. But for faded and stained negatives you may have to send for help. Black-and-white negatives fade or stain over a period of years because of careless darkroom technique. Residual silver compounds are left by incomplete fixing, and cause the negative to darken. Or incomplete washing leaves a trace of fixer behind in the emulsion which eventually produces fading or staining. These are conditions that can be corrected within limits, but if the negative in question is important, the job should be left to an expert.

Color negatives are particularly vulnerable to fading because they're made up of several layers of dyes which are much less stable than the silver used in black-and-white films. Faded color negatives can only be restored by an experienced darkroom technician.

Just plain dirt, on the other hand, is the most common problem, and it's something you can treat yourself. You won't need a darkroom, but you will need a shallow tray or bowl and a small amount of a wetting agent (such as Kodak's Photo-Flo). Then you'll need some coil-spring clothespins and a short, temporary line to hang the drying negatives on.

Soak the negatives for an hour or longer in a bowl of room-temperature water in which you've mixed a drop or two of the wetting agent. Allow plenty of time for the negative's emulsion to become thoroughly soaked: in the case of old negatives which have become very hard and brittle, overnight soaking may be necessary.

Then alternately soak and swab both sides of the negative with a very soft cloth, taking care not to scratch the surface. This should remove any dirt that has not already floated free. Rinse the negative in a fresh bowl of water and wetting agent. Then hang it up to dry, using one or two clothespins to hold it on the line and another to weight it at the bottom. Take care to attach the clothespins to the extreme outside edge of the negative, outside the picture area.

You can gently squeegee the hanging negative with a very soft, very clean damp sponge to remove excess moisture if you want to, but if you've used a wetting agent it really shouldn't be necessary. Air drying alone should leave it without spots or streaks.

This treatment sometimes produces an unexpected but desirable by-product. It may eliminate or reduce small scratches because the emulsion swells and expands as it absorbs water. When it dries you may find some of the smaller holes filled in.

Negatives which have been left rolled up too long, and which have taken on a permanent curl, can sometimes be straightened by the same treatment: soak them, then hang and weight them, leaving them to dry overnight. Sometimes it works and sometimes it doesn't—much depends on how long they've stayed rolled up and how much flexibility they've lost.

Thus, with only a little effort, you can restore aging negatives to something like their original condition. But if you take care to store them carefully in the first place, you won't need to.

Old negatives which have become dirty or scratched with age can be given a new lease on life by careful washing and drying. You'll need only these few familiar household items plus a wetting agent.

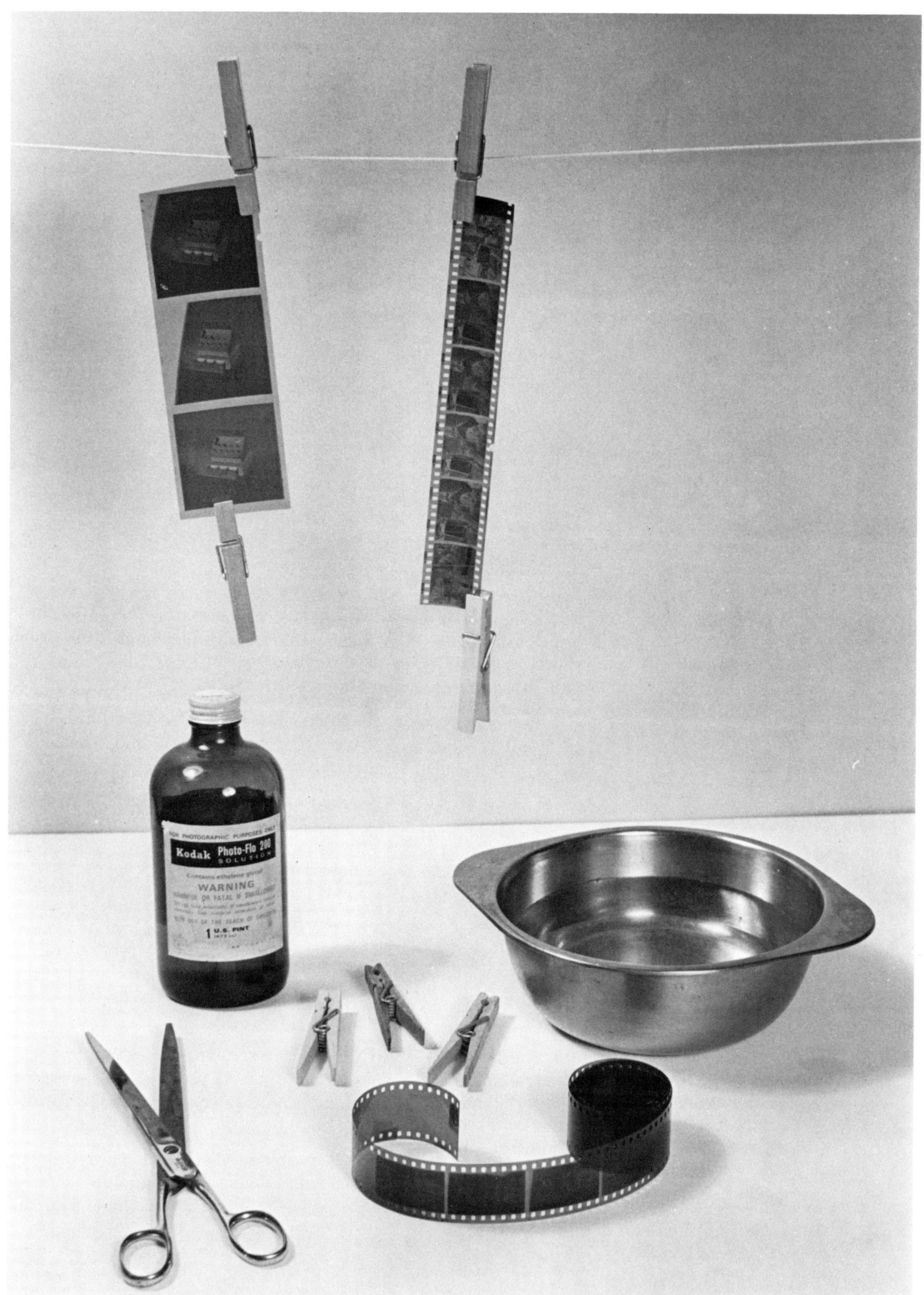
Kodak Photo-Flo 200
SOLUTION
WARNING
1 U.S. PINT

GLOSSARY

A GLOSSARY OF COMMON PHOTOGRAPHIC TERMS

In writing this book I've generally tried to sidestep technical terms or, when they couldn't be avoided, to define them on the spot. But there remains a handful of words which are essential for a basic understanding of photography. The most common of them are briefly defined below.

Aperture (See *f*-stop.)

ASA For *American Standards Association*. A system for classifying films according to their sensitivity to light. The higher the ASA number the "faster," or more light-sensitive, the film. (See DIN and ISO.)

"B" Setting For *Bulb*. A shutter setting that enables you to get exposures longer than a second. (See Chapter 3.)

Bounce Light Sometimes *bouncelight*. A technique, using electronic or bulb attachment, for distributing light over a broader area and for avoiding the flat, contrasty look often produced by head-on flash. (See Chapters 2 and 3.)

Bracketing A safety precaution used to increase the odds in favor of a good exposure. (See Chapters 3 and 7.)

Cable Release An inexpensive flexible extension which attaches to the shutter release and which permits you to trip the shutter at a distance, without touching the camera. Useful in avoiding camera shake during long exposures.

Chrome A suffix used by film manufacturers to indicate a film intended for slides or transparencies. Thus: Kodachrome, Ektachrome, Fujichrome, Agfachrome.

Color A suffix used by film manufacturers to indicate a film to be used as negative, and from which prints are made. Thus: Kodacolor, Ektacolor, Fujicolor, Agfacolor.

Contrast The degree of difference in a photograph between adjoining light and dark areas; the range of tones within a photograph. (See Chapter 1.)

Depth of Field Sometimes called *depth of focus*. The area in a photograph within which objects are in sharp focus. It is determined by the lens opening, or *f*-stop: the smaller the lens opening the greater the depth of field. (See Chapters 3 and 5.)

DIN For *Deutsche Industrie Norm*. Like ASA, a system for classifying a film's sensitivity to light. It is more commonly used by foreign film manufacturers. (See also ISO.)

Double Exposure Two exposures on a single frame of film. Sometimes accidental; sometimes done deliberately for special effects. (See Chapter 3.)

Electronic Flash Sometimes called *strobe*. Electronically regulated flash light of extremely short duration. Has largely superseded the flash bulb. (See Chapters 2, 3, and 4.)

Emulsion The suspension of silver salts, which are sensitive to light, in gelatin or collodion, and which is used to coat films. In color films, colored dyes are used. (See Chapter 8.)

F-Stop Also called *f-number, lens opening*, or *aperture*. On adjustable lenses, a series of lens openings which permit you to control the amount of light reaching the film. The openings are marked on the barrel of the lens. Each setting admits a measured amount of light. The larger the *f*-stop number the smaller the amount of light admitted.
Few lenses have all of them, but a full range of *f*-stops would include *f*/1.0, *f*/1.4, *f*/2, *f*/2.8, *f*/4, *f*/5.6, *f*/8, *f*/11, *f*/16, *f*/22, *f*/32, *f*/45, and *f*/64, with *f*/1.0 admitting the maximum and *f*/64 the minimum amount of light.
The smallest opening on a typical lens (say, *f*/16) admits half the amount of light as the next smallest, *f*/11, which in turn admits half as much as does *f*/8. And so on, by halves, down the scale until you get to the lens' largest opening.

Fast Film A film of extreme sensitivity to light. The degree of sensitivity is indicated by the film's ASA or DIN rating. ASA 400 is very fast; ASA 12 is very slow.

Fast Lens A lens capable of being opened to a relatively wide aperture: *f*/1.4 or *f*/2, for example. By comparison, an *f*/5.6 lens would be slow.

Filter You can modify your black-and-white and color pictures by the use of gelatin or glass filters in front of the lens.

Filter Factor In most cases, when you add a filter to your lens you reduce the amount of light getting through to the film, and you have to compensate by either opening up the lens to a wider *f*-stop or by slowing down your shutter speed. The amount of light lost is indicated by the filter factor, a number assigned to the filter by its manufacturer. You use the filter factor in calculating the corrected exposure. (See Chapters 5 and 7.)

Fixed Focus A lens, typical of simple cameras, which cannot be adjusted to focus on close-up or far-away objects.

Grain A speckled or granular texture apparent in a photographic image, especially when it is greatly enlarged. Generally, the fast films (ASA 400) are inherently grainier than the slow ones.

Hyperfocal Distance A lens setting which permits you to get the maximum depth of field at a given aperture. (See Chapter 3.)

ISO For *International Standards Organization*. The latest attempt to arrive at a simple international system for rating a film's sensitivity to light. It merely lists the two best-known systems, ASA and DIN, thus: ISO 400/27° means a film with an ASA rating of 400 or a DIN rating of 27°.

Latent Image The picture after the exposure has been made but before it has been processed. The undeveloped image.

Lens Opening (See *f*-stop.)

Normal Lens The lens that ordinarily comes with your camera and which gives you pretty much the view of your subject your eyes would naturally see.

Red Eye The red circle of light that sometimes appears in your subject's eyes when you use flash. (See Chapter 3.)

Reflex A viewing system which employs mirrors to conduct the image to the camera's viewfinder and then to your eye.

Shutter A device for regulating the amount of light reaching the film. On simple cameras these are set at a fixed speed. On more complex cameras they can be adjusted to move at a variety of speeds. By combining shutter speed with lens opening you can control precisely the light reaching the film.

Slide Often called *transparencies* by professional photographers. A positive picture on transparent film, visible when light shines through it, and which can be projected on a screen. Paper prints can be made from slides.

Strobe (See *electronic flash*.)

"T" Setting For *time*. A shutter setting that enables you to get exposures of longer than normal duration. Most lenses do not have this setting. (For the difference between "B" and "T" settings, see Chapter 3.)

Telephoto Sometimes called *long lenses*. A lens which produces a larger image of a distant object than would a normal lens.

Wide Angle Lens Sometimes called "short lenses." The opposite of telephoto lenses, they produce a viewing angle wider than would a normal lens.

INDEX

Edited by Michael O'Connor and Lynn Burrasca
Designed by Jim LaTuga
Production by Hector Campbell
Set in 8 pt. Melior